D0850625

Enterprise Integration and Modeling:
The Metadatabase Approach

ENTERPRISE INTEGRATION AND MODELING: THE METADATABASE APPROACH

by

CHENG HSU
Department of Decision Sciences and Engineering Systems
Rensselaer Polytechnic Institute
Troy, NY 12180-3590

Kluwer Academic Publishers
Boston/Dordrecht/London

Distributors for North America:
Kluwer Academic Publishers
101 Philip Drive
Assinippi Park
Norwell, Massachusetts 02061 USA

Distributors for all other countries:
Kluwer Academic Publishers Group
Distribution Centre
Post Office Box 322
3300 AH Dordrecht, THE NETHERLANDS

Library of Congress Cataloging-in-Publication Data

A C.I.P. Catalogue record for this book is available from the Library of Congress.

Printed on acid-free paper.

Printed in the United States of America

In the Memory of My Parents
who did their best for their child

CONTENTS

PREFACE

From as long ago as we humans can remember, an organization is always striving to work like one person; that is, breaking down the barriers of division within the organization and integrate them like an one person enterprise. However, history-proven formula for achieving this integration of many persons into one enterprise is, precisely, the creation of divisions (of labor) to divide and conquer the job. This ironical cycle is rooted simply in the means that enterprises use to communicate and coordinate - the traditional means for organizing resources are inherently rigid to be changed frequently, therefore the facilitator becomes the prohibitor of integration when the (original) premises of organization change. This cycle can be broken only when new means are invented, employed and deployed. The new means today is the enterprise level information technology. It is invented; but has only now started to be employed and deployed to bring about the new age of integrated enterprises that promises new levels of value, service, and productivity. Recent models such as Agile Manufacturing, Networked Corporation, and Enterprise Re-Engineering can all be understood from this perspective. More efforts on all fronts, including managerial and technical, are needed before the new information technology can really work for the enterprises and the society. We present a particular such effort in this book.

The Metadatabase model of enterprise information integration (for multiple systems) is developed at Rensselaer Polytechnic Institute under the sponsorships of Alcoa, Digital, GE, GM, and IBM (from 1986 to 1995 through the Computer-Integrated Manufacturing and the Adaptive Integrated Manufacturing Enterprises programs), the National Science Foundation (since 1991), Samsung (since 1995), and US. Army (since 1995). The technology is being developed into a product for Samsung and Army. This is the first exposition book on the topic.

There are two types of readers that I keep in mind when preparing the book: those who have an interest in the Metadatabase model as an integration technology, and those who also want a general discussion on information system analysis and design with applications in manufacturing. Therefore, a general conceptual framework of enterprise integration and modeling is provided in the first chapter, and is used to tie together all of the remaining chapters of the book. The next two chapters present some basics and examples of systems analysis and design for enterprise modeling; which serve the purposes of general discussion on the subject as well as illustrating the modeling methods particular to the Metadatabase approach. The particular methods are discussed fully in chapter 4. An overview of the Metadatabase Model is provided in chapter 5 and illustrated with a "paper demonstration" of a basic metadatabase prototype (for CIM) in chapter 6. The main technical elements of the model are presented in chapters 7, 8, and 9. The model is then applied to manufacturing in chapter 10, where a core information model for implementing the Metadatabase approach to integration is also included. Chapter 11 extends the Metadatabase technology into the realm of information visualization. The new user interface model developed can be applied to integrate the traditional enterprise information management with new cyberspace applications such as electronic commerce. This book provides a reference for Enterprise Integration and Modeling. It can also be used as a primary reading for an advanced topics course on Database, or as a supplemental text for Manufacturing Information Systems, Systems Analysis, and Database Design courses.

Many colleagues have contributed to the Metadatabase research over the past nine years or so. They are really the co-authors of this book. I would like to recognize especially the following friends who have developed or are in the process of developing a dissertation with me on the topic at Rensselaer:

Dr. Laurie Rattner Schatzburg, Assistant Professor, University of New Mexico
Dr. M'hamed Bouziane, R&O Software Technik, Gmbh
Dr. Waiman Cheung, Lecturer, Chinese University of Hong Kong
Dr. Gilbert Babin, Assistant Professor, Laval University
Dr. Lester Yee, Lecturer, Hong Kong University
Mr. Yicheng Tao, a doctoral student at Rensselaer Polytechnic Institute
Mr. Jangha Cho, a doctoral student at Rensselaer Polytechnic institute

Their particular contributions, along with those of others, are acknowledged at the end of individual chapters. Furthermore, Drs. Cheung, Babin, and Yee have co-authored with me for Chapters 8, 9, and 11, respectively. In addition, Mr. Otto Schaefer, Mr. Alvaro Perry, Mr. Javier Nogues, and Mr. Jingsong Mao have also written master-level theses that made significant contributions to the research.

I also owe many thanks to another able doctoral student at Rensselaer, Mr. Somendra Pant. Somendra's skills in word processing and care to details have made this book project possible. I'm deeply indebted to his tireless help. Although I have tried to recognize all colleagues participated , in the end-of-chapter acknowledgments, I cannot individually express my gratitude to everyone who deserve it dearly. I wish to extend my sincere appreciation to all of my friends and colleagues whose friendship, collaboration, and encouragement sustained me through these years.

Free CASE Tool

The Computer-Aided Software Engineering tool for the TSER method of the Metadatabase Model is provided free of cost. The CASE tool is an integrated modeling environment developed for systems analysis and design tasks, including (1) Data Flow Diagram and IDEF0 methods for information requirements analysis, (2) database schema generators for ORACLE, Rdb, Ingress, dBase V, and Access, and (3) the TSER proper, which supports semantic data modeling and data normalization (encompassing object-oriented modeling and entity-relationship modeling). The software can be downloaded from the following World Wide Web home page and public (anonymous) ftp site:

http://viu.eng.rpi.edu/

or

ftp.rpi.edu/pub/www/

by selecting theses files:

tser1.exe, tser2.exe(the software) and **ibmsv1_1.exe**(the manual)

More information about the CASE tool and the latest research on the Metadatabase technology are also available from the home page.

RELATED PUBLICATIONS

The following doctoral dissertations provide further details for the Metadatabase model. A copy can be obtained from the University Microfilm Services at Ann Arbor, Michigan.

1. Laurie Rattner, *Information Requirements for Integrated Manufacturing Planning and Control*, Decision Sciences and Engineering Systems, Rensselaer Polytechnic Institute, Troy, NY 12180-3590, 1990

2. M'hamed Bouziane, *Metadata Modeling and Management*, Computer Science, RPI, 1991

3. Waiman Cheung, *The Model-Assisted Global Query System*, DSES, RPI, 1991

4. Gilbert Babin, *Adaptiveness in Information Systems Integration*, DSES, RPI, 1993

5. Lester Yee, *Information Visualization Using a Paradigm of Dynamism*, DSES, RPI, 1994

Additionally, the following theses extend some of the results to include real time control and active databases development:

6. Otto Schaefer, *Metadatabase Integration in Shop Floor Real-Time Environment*, Diplomarbeit, Munich Technical University, Munich, Germany, 1994.

7. Jingsong Mao, *The Implementation of Rules in Two-Stage Entity-Relationship Model*, Master of Science Thesis, Computer Science, RPI, 1994.

1

INFORMATION-INTEGRATED ENTERPRISES

1.1 INFORMATION ENTERPRISES AND NEW ENTERPRISES

The Berlin Wall didn't fall as a direct result of information technology, but the fall of organizational walls certainly has. **Information Technologies** (IT) such as telecommunications, distributed computing, and databases have afforded people a phenomenal degree of freedom to form working relationships with others from anywhere in the world, and rearrange those working relationships with great alacrity as missions and conditions change, expand, or otherwise evolve. People and organizations have a growing potential to distribute throughout the world while remaining in dynamic alignment with other economic partners and valuable resources. IT has freed the enterprise from its history of geographical and physical constraints that allowed only for fixed and static alignment of resources, processes, and organizations with missions. As a result, the past decades have witnessed a parade of new business strategies focusing on the potential of the new enterprise. In the late 1970s and 1980s, we strove to create Computer-Integrated Manufacturing and Concurrent Engineering. Since then, we have seen a continuous stream of new visions each promoting a new enterprise model that claims to improve productivity, quality, and market timing. These models have included Agile Manufacturing, Virtual Corporation, Total Quality Management, Enterprise Re-engineering, Horizontal Corporation, Electronic Commerce, Global Information Enterprises, and many more models adopted within particular contexts, such as the Adaptive Integrated Manufacturing Enterprises developed at Rensselaer Polytechnic Institute.

All enterprise models have one thing in common: they build a vision of how IT will affect the future of dynamic alignment within an enterprise. Within this vision, each model predicts which new modes of production or products will enable an enterprise to pull ahead of its competitors. Defined as such, they are all examples of how the technological innovation called IT *extends new core competencies to a firm through dynamic alignments that create new competitive advantages.* Enterprise models also hold in common the fact that they are each but a transient model in the fast moving age of information. As long as IT continues to remove old constraints and open up new possibilities for innovative enterprises, one can count on the proliferation of new models that explore the theme of dynamic alignment and predict the fall of some physical or logical block to perfect dynamic alignment. To be sure, there are many walls that restrict free exchange among and across the customer, the producer, and the supplier.

We refer to the removal of walls as **enterprise integration** and the preparation for new alignments, **modeling**. There are ways to foresee to where this wave of integration is leading. We explore what knowledge and tools will be required to envision, develop, and realize the enterprise of the future. The vision elaborated within this book is predicated on five enablers of IT:

- Consideration Of The Extended Enterprise
- Integration Of Information, Integration Through Information
- Planning For Strategic Goals
- Implementing IT Using Organic Architecture
- Managing With Ubiquitous Enterprise Metadata

One can best forecast the future by understanding the limitations of the present. Any new vision for building and deploying IT structures needs to consider the five enablers presented here. For example, Enterprise Re-engineering is a celebrated case of dynamic alignment. Yet, it is constrained by not considering the extended enterprise nor information integration using organic architecture and ubiquitous metadata.

1.1.1 Consideration of the Extended Enterprise

No company is too small to conduct business at a global scale. Many family restaurants or small retailers order ethnic foods or deliver purchased clothes in small packages via international shipments. An enterprise is considered global when it considers its customers/prime contractors and suppliers/vendors, yet is never so large to be able to ignore its extended constituencies. By its very nature, an enterprise is extended beyond the boundaries of the immediate organizations involved; it is an endeavor spanning the customers (and to some extent the customers' customers), suppliers, vendors, dealers, distributors, creditors, shareholders, as well as the product producer and service provider of the enterprise. When modeling for integration, it is natural to consider all of these extended economic members of an enterprise. The sole reason for not considering the extended enterprise would be the difficulty of doing so. Due to the growth and development of more powerful IT, management has more options to develop creative solutions to integrating and modeling the extended enterprise than ever before. The examples of integration and modeling given below demonstrate recent capabilities, yet they are merely the prelude to mind-boggling new visions that will arise along with newer and more powerful IT. The examples below are success stories of firms that have applied the traditional notion of systems integration. Systems integration is concerned with automating the intra-organizational flow of information across functional systems to similar functional systems distributed inter-organizationally when all organizations belong to the same extended enterprise.

Electronic Data Interchange (EDI). EDI models automate routine order processing and billing functions of an extended enterprise. Rather than circulating papers, organizations send electronic files or forms through networks to other organizations. Applications of EDI typically include aligning the order-origination at the producer side with the order-entry at the supplier side, or similar alignments involving billing procedures between the producer and the customer. The mechanism EDI uses to align is an electronic linkage using protocols (that usually include bar coding systems and other standards of automation) and a dedicated application system that can be a third-party value-added network (VAN) that processes the orders. EDI has been employed for intra-organizational order processing such as work orders across shops. However, the inter-organizational order processing illustrates the power of the concept of an extended enterprise. The health care industry and other distributed systems overwhelmed with paperwork are emerging as the dominant domains of EDI applications.

Just-in-Time (JIT). The original concept of JIT was practiced in Japan to streamline production planning and control functions across the producer and the supplier of the extended enterprise. In essence, the supplier must deliver parts at the point in production when the producer needs them. Therefore, the supplier is in fact considered as another shop or factory in the producer's production planning and control, effectively eliminating "in-process" stock, that is, the producer's inventory. JIT is fundamentally an alignment of the extended enterprise's production resources. Transportation systems are used in addition to conveyor systems to move materials while global scheduling systems are developed to move information. The concept and technology of JIT are and have been scalable to intra- and inter-organizational applications. This scalability is a testimony to the "natural logic" of an extended enterprise.

Concurrent Engineering (CE). Promoted by the U.S. Department of Defense, the original concept of CE required that the voluminous design information such as engineering drawings and product design files be electronically sharable among all contractor and sub-contractor design engineers working on the same weapon system. Such a network of shared resources would most certainly represent an extended enterprise. However, we would better understand the past, present, and future of CE as the alignment of design resources within and across organizations within an extended enterprise. While JIT involves the flow of materials as well as information, CE and EDI are primarily information technologies that integrate the enterprise through the flow and management of information resources.

These three examples are all based on the logic of aligning producers with providers to achieve global savings and optimization of effort. Understanding the logic of aligning producers with providers, one can easily generalize the concept and apply it across the entire enterprise for inter-organizational integration and modeling. Practically, we must work out more logical than physical means when using IT to align such massive enterprises.

1.1.2 Integration of Information, Integration through Information

The examples of extended enterprises given above demonstrate a salient principle of **Information Integration**. CE and JIT have demonstrated that IT is the logical alignment of resources that hinge foremost on the integration of information resources and systems, such as illustrated by connecting the design databases or production planning with control information across organizations. In turn, this integration creates synergism with other resources that affect the physical production. In this sense, *enterprise integration is about using IT to achieve dynamic alignment of resources through information and information systems.* This focus is especially important when the physical scale of the enterprise is larger than what a typical local-area network (LAN) can sufficiently cover. For instance, in the case of EDI, there is no mechanism nor needs to place the order processing functions of different organizations under the perpetual control of a single fixed configuration that requires dedicated personnel organization, office, computer, and telecommunications structures. The relationships in an EDI enterprise change frequently from one contract to another; thus, the configurations must remain logical. Using a third-party VAN is one way to achieve a kind of logical integration for the enterprise. The VAN provides physical configurations such that the order processing functions of each (direct partner) organization can be logical and remain flexible, distributed, and autonomous. But the same function can also be achieved internally through proper use of information integration. In general, when it is feasible to integrate all resources into a single physical structure to achieve internal dynamic alignments, one would choose this simple design over the logical alternative. However, when it is not feasible to choose integration through a single physical structure, the case of all non-trivial enterprises, logical integration by virtue of information would be the only way to proceed. As IT has progressed technologically and enterprises have become global, information integration has flourished in virtually all of the visions mentioned above. Some recent achievements are discussed below from this perspective.

Computer-Integrated Manufacturing (CIM). The U.S. Air Force's Integrated Computer-Aided Manufacturing (ICAM) Program initiated the worldwide race to integrate manufacturing with computers in the late 1970s and early 1980s. In essence, the ICAM vision extended the previous efforts of CAD/CAM (Computer-Aided Design/Manufacturing), a physical integration approach, into an approach that focused on the logical synergism among CADs, CAMs and eventually all other major functions of integrated manufacturing. It became clear to all involved that there was no way and no need to unite CADs and CAMs in the same physical configuration with, for example, Manufacturing Resources Planning (MRP II) and administration systems. Thus, CIM established the principle since operative that information integration is the best means to achieve overall synergistic control of physical resources and operations in large-scale systems.

Agile Manufacturing (AM). Initiated by an effort at Lehigh University and supported by the Advanced Research Programs Agency (ARPA) of U.S. Department of Defense, Agile Manufacturing is concerned with adding flexibility to CIM to better respond to the market's changing demands (e.g., rapid new product development and flexible small batch production at mass production efficiency). In addition to IT, a new organizational mode—the team approach—is also featured in the definitive model of AM. Teams, however, are not to be confined to physical configurations. Virtual teams, whose members are not necessarily co-located in the same building or site but rather physically distributed and logically grouped through the use of IT, are the real backbone of AM in significant enterprises. These virtual teams and the processes that enable them to exist are all results of dynamic alignments through information integration.

Virtual Corporation (VC) and More. When the concept of virtual teams is generalized to encompass all aspects of a corporation, a VC results. Employees of a VC perform their assigned activities from anywhere, either within an independent consultant arrangement or under the virtual auspices of organizations that participate within the VC. As such, employees have a project-oriented association that precludes committing themselves to a fixed, traditional organization characterized by physical configurations. In fact, a VC is concerned primarily with forming external, flexible missions derived from multiple organizations.

When an organization forms flexible missions internally across its multiple divisions, the concept of a VC becomes that of **Enterprise Re-engineering (ERE)** and the **Horizontal Corporation (HC)**. ERE is focused on the internal business processes of an organization. Its goal is to promote optimal resource alignments that result in leaner running business processes that add net value to the enterprise. An HC features an organizational model centered around flexible internal processes that give rise to a lateral and flexible structure different from the traditional organizational hierarchy. Middle managers are either becoming entrepreneurs of such processes or eliminated altogether. The dynamic nature of alignments and processes revealed in these models illustrate once again the pivotal role of information integration.

The above visions employ information as the agent of integration and deploy IT to remove physical constraints within the enterprise. In a similar but more visible manner, other visions also exhibit a reliance on information integration. They include **Total Quality Management (TQM)** which uses the team approach to improve customer satisfaction by installing and managing quality and quality information processes throughout the enterprise; **Electronic Commerce** that renders the Internet and other emerging global networks a marketplace for conducting all aspects of commerce, ranging from transaction to production and organization; and **Global Information Enterprises** that combine information repositories and merge various information industries such as publications, news media, entertainment, education, software, and various information services into information conglomerates such as cyberspace. To the extent that IT has enabled these visions, information integration has been and will continue to be a strategic weapon for an enterprise to compete in the global marketplace.

1.1.3 Planning for Strategic Goals

The full promise of IT can only be revealed in strategic thinking and yet this level of thinking would not necessarily present itself without a proactive review of IT in light of *yet developing* competitive opportunities. Enterprise integration and modeling share many system development tasks with mundane operations of an organization; hence, they can often be cut to incremental projects that do not change the status-quo. However, the significance of enterprise integration lies precisely in its promise to effect new regimes and paradigms and to lift organizational performance beyond the status quo. In particular, IT's promise of dynamic alignment has served to remove organizational constraints and allow extended enterprises to develop, while information integration has suppressed physical barriers. Both have opened up new fundamental, strategic opportunities for enterprises. We derive several heuristics from past examples and theoretical analyses in order to facilitate new developments in IT planning and begin a concerted search for strategic IT opportunities.

Managing External Environments. The following heuristics focus on the direct, external application of IT on the market as a strategic weapon to gain competitive advantages. The principle is to manage uncertainty in the enterprise environment.

• *Provide Information Services to Customers.* The idea is to lure and lock customers in to the enterprise by investing in an IT that provides unique and crucial services to them. The added value is in external orientation. For example, an organization develops IT primarily for facilitating its customers' business rather than for its own internal use. Classical cases include the American Airline's Sabre system for travel agencies and Citibank's Automatic Teller Machine (ATM) for individual customers. Although both technologies have now become mundane operations holding little strategic value, initially they were conceived as strategic marketing weapons in order to leapfrog their competitors. They accomplished just that. There are numerous obvious opportunities for an organization to develop new generations of information services for customers and reap the same in strategic benefits, especially given extended enterprise and information integration. Generalizing the ATM to an on-line, free-of-charge banking and other services network for customers would be a natural potential. Healthcare Management Organizations have begun to explore the unlimited possibilities following along this line of thinking. Being the first innovator and possessing core IT competencies in terms of know-how, models, techniques, and systems are key factors for success.

• *Turning Information Services into Products.* We can extend the above notion of customer service to information products or information service profit centers. The Sabre system has become a major source of revenues for American Airlines since travel agencies pay significant fees for its extended services. As a matter of fact, the company later spun off the operation and expanded it into a significant travel information services company of its own. In a similar way, proprietary information technology and services that an enterprise develops can be turned into dedicated information service providers or spin-offs in the market. Electronic commerce and global information enterprises seem to be especially ripe for this type of opportunity.

• *Monitor the Market and Customer Behaviors.* Marketing databases have proven to be a potent weapon for gathering marketing intelligence and assisting in new product development. Their key is to exploit ubiquitous interfaces with customers (coupons, purchases, repairs, surveys, and the like) and turn them into intelligent information for strategic uses. Every organization by definition has numerous contacts with its customers throughout the life-cycle of a product. The question is only whether or not the contact is used to benefit the organization's marketing intelligence. Background data repositories such as the census database complement direct contact data. Between these two sources, organizations have unlimited possibilities for marketing research to create innovative strategies.

A broader implementation of managing external environments would include not only the customer but also the supplier and other constituencies of the extended enterprise including external users of the IT. Analyzing the information needs of these external users within the context of their respective enterprises and employing IT to satisfy their needs will work to the organization's benefit. Basic strategic gains result when an organization is able to do more in the way of extended contact and use the feedback gained to improve internal and external business processes.

Maximizing the Internal Networking of Processes and Resources. The second set of heuristics is oriented towards improving the production function of an enterprise, thereby enhancing its productivity (measured through cost and quality). Linkages will be created across an enterprise to connect all stages of cycles, including: differing levels of granularity (product, production, and part); flows (information vs. materials); and businesses (administration vs. production). By connecting all stages of the business cycle, maximum channels of communications can be created to minimize the internal uncertainties facing an enterprise, and resources can be pooled and utilized throughout the extended enterprise. Globally optimized performance can result.

• *Employ and Deploy IT to the Core Production Processes.* A production system that delivers higher quality at lower cost than competitors is the most fundamental strategic advantage for any enterprise. IT is proven to be a key element in achieving this goal within manufacturing enterprises and many other operations-oriented enterprises (e.g., the mail and parcel delivery industry). However, this previous utilization of IT is merely the tip of the iceberg. In manufacturing, the vast majority of robotics systems and workstations are "hard-coded" with control programs that cannot be easily changed. At this basic level of production, there is scarcely any use of rulebase and database technologies that can perform in real time. These technologies would allow a manufacturing plant to acquire a logical layer that can define the (re-)configuration of their systems in terms that would connect the part processing jobs directly to work order control, materials handling, in-process inspection, production scheduling, order entry, warehousing, processing planning, and product design. Even more promising is the direct application of IT to the very production systems that are not traditionally considered production tasks, such as the medical functions of a hospital (e.g., diagnosis, surgery, treatment, and pharmacy) and the educating function of a university (e.g., lectures, assignments, and laboratories). Although IT has been increasingly employed in these functions—with examples ranging from CATSCAN/MRI in medicine to studio style classrooms and World Wide Web-based virtual classes in education—the majority of them are still isolated within a traditional paradigm where IT is sequestered to administration jobs. Deepening the role of IT in manufacturing and broadening it to more traditional enterprises promises to provide new and endless strategic opportunities for IT use.

• *Create Forward and Feedback Linkages for All Cycles.* An enterprise has three basic cycles: part, production, and product. The product cycle includes everything from marketing and product planning to recycling used materials; the production cycle satisfies the customer's orders and demands; and the part cycle processes the individual elements involved in producing a product. Previous visions of integration tend to focus only on a single cycle apart and aside of the other two, primarily integrating the forward stages into a connected sequence in the cycle, but without closing the cycle through feedback. Forward linkage allows some jobs in the later stages to be performed simultaneously with earlier jobs; or, at least, the requirements of the later stages can be explicitly considered early in the product cycle. For example, Concurrent Engineering (CE) is primarily concerned with creating some forward linkage by overlapping the stages of new product development, product design, and process planning. The feedback aspects are largely overlooked. Thus, CE would incorporate a static set of assembly requirements into design (Design-for-Assembly), but not concern itself with on-line feedback of in-process inspection, nor shop floor control systems. Both forward and feedback linkages are needed to complete a cycle. Furthermore, all three cycles are interwoven in a truly agile enterprise. Therefore, new strategic opportunities for IT will arise from creating feedbacks to complete a cycle and from connecting all cycles through forward and feedback linkages. Both forward and feedback set the stage for dynamic alignment in its fullest potential.

• *Connecting Administration Systems with Production Systems.* IT has been historically applied to business administration functions of an enterprise first. Then, when it is also employed within production, the two sides are kept separate functions. Information Integration allows and asks that the walls separating administration from production come down, just as IT bridges information flow with material flow. An interesting example showing the significance of this connection is activity-based costing and management, in which the classical administrative function of accounting is conducted on the basis of monitoring the alignments of resources around activities. This monitoring certainly can be and should be made on-line and in real time. Total Quality Management (TQM) is also based on performance information cutting across administration and production. Calibrating and aligning administration with production on an on-line, real time basis produces the ultimate decision-making information within an agile, lean, and productive enterprise.

Transforming into a Three-Dimensional Enterprise. The following three sets of heuristics provide some proactive guidelines for high-level IT planning towards enterprise integration and modeling. They expand the scope of enterprise from the traditional view into both extended enterprises and information enterprises.

• *Think Extended Enterprise.* All the discussions pertaining to the internal production systems and administration of an enterprise are applicable to the virtual systems of an extended enterprise. As mentioned in Section 1.1.1, the strategic opportunities for streamlining operations across organizations to gain synergism and efficiency are practically unlimited. The fact that there are tremendous constraints and difficulties against fully applying IT to an extended enterprise is also the reason for its tremendous significance. The health care industry is arguably the most fertile ground for this concept. The opportunities implicit in connecting insurers, hospitals, physicians, patients, government agencies, and research institutes through information integration is mind boggling. Other industries have, of course, similar opportunities.

• *Establish/Expand to Information Enterprises.* Traditional business thinking focuses only on the material enterprises of products, resources, and the marketplace. Running parallel to the material enterprise is an equally large world of information enterprises in cyberspace that can utilize the same enterprise thinking. A virtual medical center could be constructed by using personal medical instruments located in patients' homes and linking them with doctors and researchers through multimedia telecommunication systems. A third-party information server/clearing house could provide pooled inventories and other resources to its client organizations through information integration in an extended enterprise manner. An Army/Defense logistics system could be integrated in cyberspace with visualization, simulation, and global information management capabilities. A studio-style virtual classroom could result from combining virtual laboratories, multimedia courseware, and the World Wide Web to enable distance learning. This kind of electronic commerce and global information enterprise opportunities are often hidden just under one's nose. When planning these new information enterprises, one could retain familiar paradigms by only transforming the perspective.

• *Evaluate IT on Micro-Economic Bases.* Mundane applications of IT are usually motivated by and justified on the basis of cost/expenditure savings. To move beyond this rationale looking for strategic opportunities, the valuation criteria must change. An enterprise can evaluate IT on three micro-economic criteria: transaction cost reduction, utility improvement (value/benefit added), and organizational design. In theory, the best representation of the role of IT is its impact on the basic production function of the enterprise. One could formulate information to be the fourth basic factor of production in addition to labor, land, and capital. In reality, however, such a function is impractical for any enterprise. Thus, these criteria become useful surrogates for the production function theory. They may not be specific enough to quantify the value of IT in operational terms, nonetheless; they are sufficiently substantive to shed light on qualitative investigations for IT planning.

All of the above ideas develop strategic opportunities for using IT and call for enterprises to build core competencies in IT concerning, in particular, dynamic alignment. Since the driving force of IT stems from its capacity to bring about dynamic alignment within and without an enterprise, the information architecture of the enterprise needs to be organic in order to allow it to fully exploit the potentials of IT.

1.1.4 Implementing IT using Organic Architecture

The strategic plans of IT must be mapped out to implement an enterprise information architecture for implementation. One thing is known about this architecture: there cannot be only one, single physical system that fits all requirements and yet supports dynamic alignment. Even for small enterprises that consider linking with external constituencies along with its own internal needs, there is no need nor way to satisfy all functions with the same uniform software and hardware environment. Multiple system environments all using different software (for example, Fox Pro, Lotus 1-2-3, Excel, Access, Oracle, Objectivity, C, C++, Pascal, FORTRAN, dedicated EDI systems, CAD/CAM systems, MRP II and other application systems) and hardware environments (e.g., IBM PC, Mac, Digital, VAX, IBM mainframes, and other computing and telecommunications systems) are bound to be the norm. Efforts to define standards that enable data exchange between diverse systems will not change the multiple-systems nature of enterprise integration. The reality of IT enterprise environments exhibit several characteristics that continue to make IT distributed, heterogeneous, and hard to control.

The Complexity of Reality. Consider a traditional organization. The introduction of information systems into such an enterprise is often ad hoc and "bottoms-up." This tendency to rely on customized and compartmentalized technology is due to technical necessity as well as the need of the organization to control. Technically, the most the most successful environments for automation are those in which well defined business requirements can be isolated and solutions customized to meet the specific user requirements. Such specialized systems are not designed to meet information access requirements from other enterprise users. Once specialized systems are in place; however, they must interact with other systems and software across local, wide, or even global area networks to support many different enterprise activities. In other words, an enterprise cyberspace environment must be created to accommodate interaction. It is difficult to implement information exchanges among independently designed systems in contexts that were not fully known or understood by their very designers. To enable the system access to multiple databases through decision support applications, procedural rules and data semantics that have been designed into the systems must be understood and often extended. Finally, systems must continually evolve if they are to respond to changes in technology and business requirements. Unfortunately, the need to understand complex integrated systems that serve many application systems and user communities in order to modify them often increases rather than reduces the expense and time required to adapt them to changing requirements. The integration of systems to meet enterprise needs rather than the requirements of their primary users can be perceived as an inhibitor to local autonomy, flexibility and performance. When finally this extended enterprise endeavors to integrate its processes, the complexity involved is clearly compounded many times over.

The Characteristics of Organism. The architecture that supports enterprise information integration must be able to grow, change, and adapt like an organic entity. The following working definitions list certain key requirements of such an architecture in multiple system environments distributed over wide-area or even global networks.

• *Scalability.* The total enterprise information integration environment must allow incremental development and expandability, such that the integration can start with a small part of the enterprise and gradually extend to the rest (even to other organizations) over time, without losing operational continuity and structural integrity.

• *Adaptability.* Systems that use either standard or non-standard technologies as well as new and legacy systems, can be incorporated into the integrated environment in a seamless way without causing any disruption to any existing systems.

• *Parallelism.* Multiple systems must be able to operate concurrently while achieving synergism for the enterprise and without imposing on any instance-level transaction a global serialization requirement or similar synchronization mechanism.

• *Autonomy.* Local systems need to have the flexibility to be designed, constructed, and administered independently by the local management, without having to conform, nor later convert, to a global schema.

• *Visualization.* The enterprise information should be represented and presented through intuitive visualization and virtual interface environments that avail the end users of an accessible cyberspace. This interface is essential in order for the system solution to be accepted and utilized by all employees.

An organic architecture clearly needs to be intelligent. Technically speaking, at the very least it needs to possess on-line knowledge enabling it to be dynamically (re-)configured to monitor the underlying processes and adjust itself to respond. With a system using internal knowledge, distributed and synergistic management of the enterprise information environments becomes feasible.

1.1.5 Managing with Ubiquitous Enterprise Metadata

Enterprise information architecture cannot rely on a global controller to manage the widely-distributed, multiple systems it supports. For performance reasons and many other practical as well as theoretical reasons, the architecture must have enough knowledge to sustain and manage itself, with only occasional instructions from distributed enterprise information managers who operate on a management-by-exception basis. The knowledge itself needs to be distributed wherever needed and embedded into the architecture without the users having to know nor to deal with them explicitly. Global information management, processes support, and a cyberspace user interface can utilize this ubiquitous knowledge. On-line knowledge is in essence to what we refer as *enterprise metadata.*

Categories of Enterprise Metadata. The traditional notion of metadata is simply "data about data," or a dictionary and summary for data. This notion is extended to include four categories of knowledge:

- Global Data Models,
- Contextual Knowledge and Processes Models,
- Software, Hardware, and Network Resources Models, and
- Information Users and Organizations Models.

The first two models, Global Data and Contextual Knowledge and Processes, represent the logical contents of enterprise information that characterize dynamic alignments. The last two models, Software, Hardware, and Network Resources and Information Users and Organizations, describe how to physically implement the first two models within an organization.

• *Global Data Models* provide an enterprise-wide, consolidated representation of information resources. They define the basic building blocks of the enterprise information which includes unit data items, the entities and relationships manifested by these data items, and application subjects that encompass these entities and relationships. Examples of Global Data within a factory environment would include part identification (an item), the part itself (an entity), and inventory control (a subject).

• *Contextual Knowledge and Processes Models* abstract the dynamism of alignments, such as work flows, process configurations, information management requirements, operating rules, and mission-critical events. The models also define the semantic and activity contexts of data, software, and users that are not sufficiently represented by the other three categories of models. For example, Contextual Knowledge and Processes within a manufacturing facility would provide an invaluable service: an alert would be triggered for shop floor operators if a part manufacture is at the point when the machining processes need to be changed, another alerts when the inventory of the part is depleted to a certain definable level, and yet another alert would re-route a part design file to design engineers in distant factories.

• *Software and Network Resources Models* define stand-alone and re-usable application programs such as formal conversion routines, applications management systems such as databases, and distributed computing and interface environments such as LANs and virtual reality systems.

• *Information, Users and Organizations Models* distribute enterprise information to its users, application systems, and throughout its organizational contexts. It includes user profiles, the clustering of enterprise information environments or managers, and boundary conditions for individual domains of the extended enterprise. This information architecture is able to support customized use, management and even appearance for differing constituencies and functions. For example, it allows users to tailor their information security, and even give access privileges to teams.

Unified Metadata Model. To support the ubiquitous applications envisioned above, enterprise metadata needs to be represented, processed, and managed in an integrated way. Metadata includes the following characteristics and requirements: (1) the representation method combines data and knowledge models, both of which are present in enterprise metadata; (2) the processing method, coupled with the representation of data, must allow enterprise information architecture to exhibit intelligence, such as that implicit within rule-based configurations and knowledge-based user interfaces; and (3) the management method should satisfy the organic requirements of the architecture (discussed in Section 1.1.4) by supporting, for example, the maintenance of a *logical enterprise layer* independent of its physical systems. This logical layer would span from the shop floor which uses real time control processes to high-level, executive support systems. The logical layer would be implemented and managed through the enterprise metadata.

Basic Applications. The enterprise metadata should be embedded into all key elements of the information architecture. It would be used within all key activities. A partial list of generic, basic applications for information architecture includes:

• *User Interface.* The enterprise metadata, specifically user profiles and contextual knowledge, is a potent source of on-line knowledge to support information visualization for the end users. Cyberspace cannot deliver on its full promise and be beneficial to enterprise users unless it possesses on-line knowledge used to interpret underlying systems and information for users dynamically.

• *Flows Configuration.* Paths and conditions for transferring files and charting work flow within an enterprise need to be "programmable," such as in a rule-based manner. Flow configuration would include a logical layer to network computing environments and application systems. Metadata would help to define the paths and conditions that constitute a logical layer.

• *Global Query.* Enterprise users need specific assistance from system intelligence to surf in cyberspace and retrieve or assemble information residing at single or multiple sources anywhere across the enterprise. Enterprise metadata needs to support the articulation, processing, and presentation of "location" queries for the system to be efficient, effective, and accurate for users.

• *Data Management.* Global data management traditionally required a global synchronizer that was fixed— hard-coded—into its control logic. This design is not amenable to the principle of organic architecture discussed in Section 1.1.4. In lieu of hard-coding a synchronizer, enterprise metadata should be used to provide flexible and distributed control logic.

• *Process Management.* The operating rules, events, and applications or users that define a process can themselves be defined in enterprise metadata terms. As such, it is possible to have a knowledge-based approach dynamically align and manage these management processes, including operation (real-time control) processes and higher level business processes. Data Management logic applies here as well.

• *Network Management.* Similar to Flows Configuration, a logical layer, parallel to the physically networked environments, will allow "virtual networks" to be developed using the same foundational facilities. Enterprise metadata define the logic and establish the parameters and scope of the virtual networks.

• *Global Transactions.* The functions of Global Query and Process Management also support Global Transactions. The same principles can also provide additional support to the complex problems facing global transactions, such as distributed control logic for coordination across multiple systems and recourse rules (back-up, roll-back, security, and the like) that occur under certain dynamic events.

• *System Development.* System planning, analysis, design, implementation, and control are traditionally conducted in a sequential manner and do not involve nor require enterprise information architecture. The development is typically based on information requirements that are determined at a fixed point in time with little regard to continuing evolution. In an information-integrated enterprise, however, distinct boundaries between these stages would no longer exist. The system development function would embody cycles that would require forward and feedback linkages across stages with shortened and overlapping cycle times. As such, the integrated system development functions need to be anchored on-line within enterprise information architecture. With sufficient metadata support, system development can actually be performed continuously in response to the changing requirements of dynamic alignments; thereby becoming a part of the business processes of the enterprise. The walls that divide the system and the process that the system supports are also dismantled.

1.2 ENTERPRISE INFORMATION MANAGEMENT

IT-based enterprises impose additional demands on information integration and management; therefore, all new visions for IT development must be based on the requirements of enterprise IT: organic architecture, multiple systems, and integration technology. The notion of an *enterprise information manager (EIM)* helps reveal the technical challenges. The EIM is a logical global structure that coordinates enterprise IT in order to provide the necessary information integration with which the enterprise achieves synergism. Its physical implementation can, however, be deployed in almost any conceivable way. The simple prototypical EIM sits on top of the enterprise information architecture and manages the multiple, heterogeneous, distributed, and autonomous information systems of the enterprise.

Since dynamic alignment requires dynamic exchange, sharing, and controlling of information stored in files and databases at these systems. The EIM needs to provide three levels of inter-operability among multiple systems: (1) file transfer (or work flow), (2) global query ad hoc inquiry and request, and (3) information (data, knowledge, and processes) management as summarized in Figure 1-1. File transfer is widely understood, and most large-scale integration technology commercially available today is devoted to it. Examples of file transfer would include users of office or personal information systems swapping files between Fox Pro and Lotus 1-2-3, customer order files from Oracle being submitted to Sybase for accounting, and design engineers exchanging CAD files in a concurrent engineering environment. Typically, file transfer is achieved through a custom designed and created Application Protocols Interchange (API) (see Figure 1-2). An API is generally non-reusable. As well, adding a new system to a system based on file exchanges would require writing and compiling a pair of new APIs for each of the existing systems. The situation can multiply very fast, becoming unwieldy even for enterprises that use only a few information systems. A second example of file transfer are work flow management systems that a user can query to retrieve particular information in a fixed and predetermined way.

Although this class of work flow managers comes close to our second level, global query; it tends to have some or all of the following limitations:

- Intelligence of what information is to be had is limited.
- Most available information exists in a format suitable to only a few select users, or rather specific technical knowledge is required to get desired information.
- Current solutions address pre-defined needs as opposed to supporting ad hoc inquiries on a casual basis.
- Systems are not changed easily to either re-configure or support a different process.
- Redundant information exists but accuracy between them is lacking.

Remove these limitations and global query with its level two capabilities results. Commercially available IT does not fully support global query unless the scope of systems is limited to, basically, a Local-Area Networked (LAN) low-volume database system. Figure 1-3 illustrates the need for level two capabilities not satisfied presently.

Level three capabilities of information management are similar to global query in certain functions. Both global query and information management require file transfer and global query capabilities. However, information management goes well beyond retrieving information to undertake the task of managing changes made to data, knowledge, and processes. As in the case of global query, traditional IT has similar limitations for managing such changes that extend beyond LAN environments; for example, the configurations (paths, methods, and contents) of

A TRUE ENTERPRISE SYSTEM

Functional requirements for any globally-distributed, enterprise database are three-fold:

1 FILE TRANSFER
Application to application read/write compatibility without unwieldy application protocol interchanges;

2 GLOBAL QUERY
An enterprise-wide search by a non-technical user returns all threads related to search term;

3 MANAGING INFORMATION & SYSTEM-LEVEL CHANGES
Changing data, rules, control, configuration, processes, and systems without down time, inflexible or slow data exchange, or inappropriate locking of shared resources.

Fig. 1-1: Three levels of inter-operability

CURRENT TECHNOLOGY INADEQUACIES OF FILE TRANSFER

APPLICATION PROTOCOAL INTERCHANGE (API) USES COUPLED CONNECTIONS FOR FILE TRANSFER

SYSTEM ADMINISTRATOR MUST PROVIDE N (N - 1) APIS TO CONNECT USERS

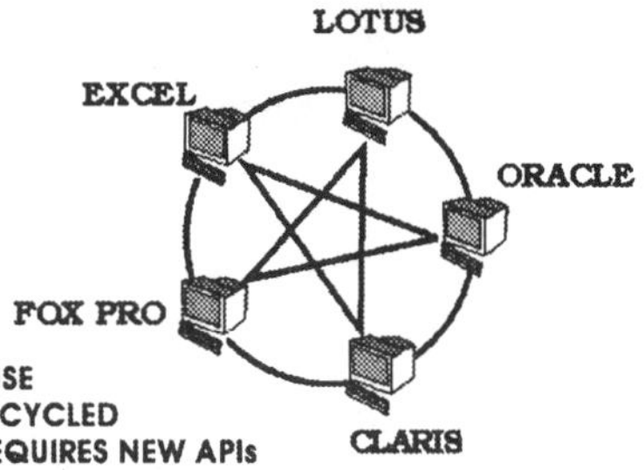

CHARACTERISTICS:

- APIs CONFIGURED FOR LOCAL USE
- CANNOT BE EXCHANGED OR RECYCLED
- NEW SOFTWARE ACQUISITION REQUIRES NEW APIs

AMOUNT OF CONVERSION WORK IS COMPOUNDED; FILE EXCHANGES ARE LIMITED FOR PRACTICAL REASONS TO STABLE, SMALL GROUPS.

Fig. 1-2: Typical file transfer is achieved through APIs.

CURRENT TECHNOLOGY INADEQUACIES OF GLOBAL QUERY

OPERATOR MUST ALREADY KNOW FILE NAMES, ALIASES, AND LOCATIONS OF ALL INFORMATION SOUGHT; DATABASE NOT INTELLIGENT ENOUGH TO LOCATE RELATED OR ALIASED INFORMATION.

ORDER: FIND EVERYTHING ON V-22 DEVELOPMENT PROGRESS

OPERATOR ASKS:

INDIANAPOLIS: DESIGN FILENAME:
??
SEATTLE: PWB DESIGN: FILENAME
??
PHOENIX: ELECTRONIC FAB: DELIVERY AND SPECS:
??
ORDER PROCESSING FILE:
??

THOROUGH GLOBAL SEARCH IMPOSSIBLE IN SHORT ORDER

Fig. 1-3: Commercial IT seldom allows for flexible global query capabilities.

CURRENT TECHNOLOGY INADEQUACIES OF MANAGING
DATA TO SYSTEM-LEVEL CHANGES

UPDATING AN INTERNATIONAL DATABASE

APPLICATIONS AND FILES IN DATABASE NOT USABLE BY NETWORKED OPERATORS DURING CONTENT CHANGE—EVEN IF CHANGES NOT CRITICAL.

SMALL CHANGES IN SYSTEM CONFIGURATION, PRE-DETERMINED PROCESSES, OR INFORMATION FLOW RESULT IN SYSTEM DOWN TIME AND RECOMPILATION OF CODE.

Fig. 1-4: Current IT technology cannot manage data or system changes globally.

updates must be fixed. Furthermore, it must shut down the current systems before new systems can be added on-line, or even just to overhaul some parts of the current systems. Figure 1-4 illustrates this situation.

The EIM technology available previously can be analyzed in the above context. The broad-based DAE (Distributed Application Environments) class technology deals with API and other inter-system interface tasks to provide a file transfer level of integration. A prime example is CORBA (Common Object Request Broker Architecture), which supports direct inter-operability for object-oriented systems. CORBA also provides gateway services for these systems to connect with relational or other traditional systems. This class of EIM technology lacks a global model of the enterprise and typically does not include much enterprise metadata (e.g. on-line contextual knowledge) in its inter-system configuration. Methods such as intelligent interfacing agents and rule-based shells are not supported in present commercial solutions, and are left to be implemented by database-class technology. In between DAE and database classes, data warehouse-class EIM's exist, such as IBM's Information Warehouse and Hewlett-Packard's WorkManager. Some limited global query capabilities, as mentioned above, are provided in addition to file transfers. The database-class EIM technology is exemplified by various HDDBMS (Heterogeneous Distributed Database Management Systems) results. While more elegant and complete, commercial HDDBMS's are less robust than the other two classes of EIM technologies; they tend to be limited to LAN environments and cater to low volume transactions. For example, HDDBM's are not amenable to transferring large engineering drawing files across continents. They also lack the ability to dynamically change inter-system processes and intra-system structures, nor can they incrementally build or group systems in the case of adding a new system to an existing HDDBMS environment. All of these gaps in technology are required for dynamic alignment as discussed in Section 1.1.

The value of an Enterprise Information Manager (EIM) that can provide shared access to enterprise data and knowledge through an intuitive graphical visualization system and support distributed and scalable client/server systems, multiple database technologies and legacy systems, can best be illustrated by a specific industrial case. Consider a multi-billion dollar world-wide enterprise whose objective it is to be the marketplace leader through excellence in products and services and superior service to the customer at the lowest industrial cost. Its products include heavy machinery, industrial systems and service activities. This enterprise employs over 30,000, 80% domestically and the remainder overseas. With regard to the necessity for sharing information, consider that there are over 20 manufacturing facilities, over 75 apparatus shops, over 100 sales offices, almost 200 engineering offices and almost 100 business associates/licensees in over 50 countries. A recent internal study uncovered a number of suspected, but not previously known, factors associated with the manner in which information was utilized. The factors they found concerning information usage and flow are completely in agreement with the above discussions concerning EIMs. Minimally speaking, access to required information throughout the business can easily save over five million dollars per year. With 10% usage from a population of 37,000 who work 240 days per year at a savings of only 15 minutes a day, they would easily realize savings in productivity and corresponding cycle reduction of 222,000 hours per year. Additionally, a large proportion of the information access requirements involve at least one other person, thereby multiplying additional opportunities for saving. The minimum base line savings in dollar alone is significant, but still does not recognize the extent of reduced cycle time and additional opportunities created with information integration.

1.3 THE METADATABASE TECHNOLOGY

The **Metadatabase model** is inspired by the principles of organic architecture using enterprise metadata, as discussed in Sections 1.1.4 and 1.1.5. As such, it is poised to support the EIM's dynamic alignment for enterprise integration and modeling. Its structure directly represents the design goal of effecting a logical layer for the enterprise to accomplish information integration. A high level overview is provided in this section that paves the way to the details elaborated in the balance of the book.

The concept of a Metadatabase has a few basic elements. First, it employs the full range of enterprise metadata (see Section 1.1.5) and manages the metadata as an independent, full-fledged database which can be distributed, hence the term Metadatabase. Second, it deploys the inter-system operating knowledge into a concurrent (rule-based) shell system to inter-operate multiple systems at all three levels (see Section 1.2) without requiring, yet allowing for, a global synchronizer.

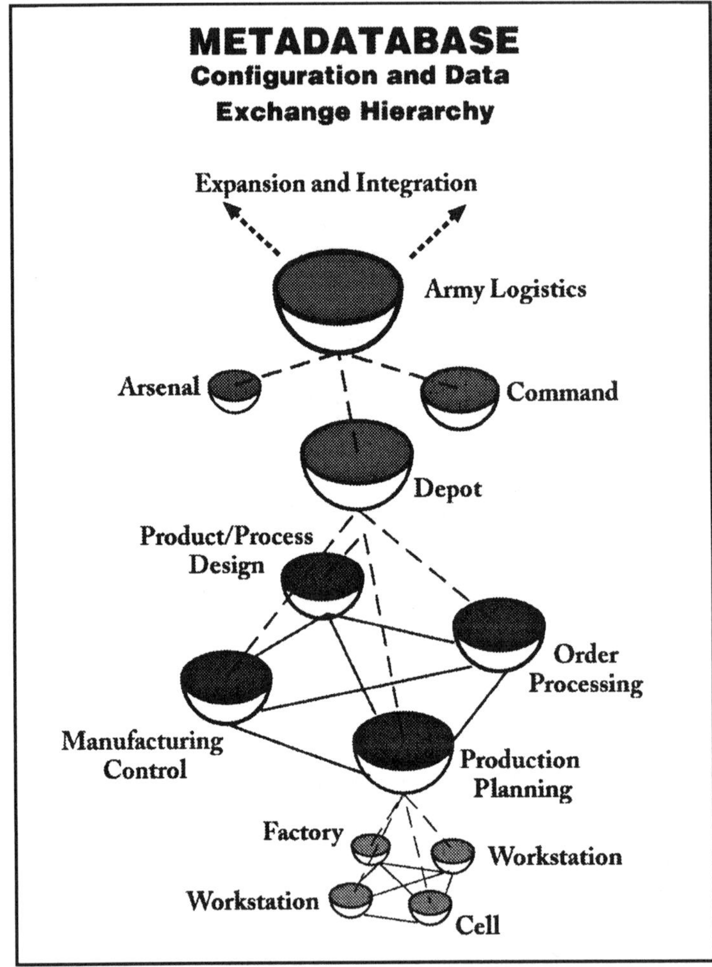

Fig. 1-5: The distributed Metadatabase architecture.

The Metadatabase acts not only as the repository of models but also as the Enterprise Information Manager (EIM), managing directly the enterprise metadata and then using the deployed metadata to indirectly coordinate the operation of local systems. In other words, the Metadatabase embeds the knowledge of all three levels of integration into local environments and allows those local systems to operate with this knowledge thereafter on their own. It intervenes only when the enterprise metadata is changed; for example, when introducing new systems or updating the previous dynamic alignments. In such a case, the Metadatabase EIM will update the peripheral metadatabase(s) and their shells which are distributed into local systems. These tasks are all accomplished on an on-line, non-disruptive, and automated basis.

An Army Logistics example is used below as a scenario to illustrate the proposed metadatabase technology. Figure 1-5 depicts an overview of the distributed Metadatabase architecture. Figures 1-6, 1-7 and 1-8 correspond to Figures 1-2, 1-3, and 1-4. These six figures suggest how the new Metadatabase EIM would improve the inter-operation of multiple systems at all three levels of integration: file transfer, global query, and information management.

Flow of information for Army logistics, which upholds the most rigorous requirements for response time, is literally a matter of life and death. The Army's intricate logistics issues are further compounded by the many kinds of Army entities (ranging from arsenals and depots to commands and bases), that are distributed across wide physical geography. These Army entities may also use a myriad of information systems that may not operate together seamlessly. Decision makers within this distributed environment would like to have access to integrated sources of information representing their own base or depot, as well as the entire distributed Army. They would further like to be able to change this data, have their changes automatically update the entire Army information network, and then have all affected Army processes instantly brought into line. This type of information management is called global query and events control. Having this control would enable a widely distributed enterprise to maneuver its entire heterogeneous operation within days in anticipation of future events, and, upon encountering adverse conditions, to change that course of action immediately. With such information control, changes made on the shop floor of an arsenal or a depot, distribution center, or command level would be registered in real time throughout the entire enterprise structure, eliminating the need for an exceptional communications effort from a central control.

Metadatabase technology would provide a comprehensive linkage between each Army locale, giving personnel the ability to search the global Army environment for particular pieces of data and to control global events. If one were, for instance, performing a search on the status of a weapon system, the search would return the information on the widget development at Arsenal A, the frame manufacture at Depot B, the subcontractor's schedule for the electronics PWB, and the schedule for assembly at Plant C. This information would be drawn in real-time from each Arsenal and Depot connected through the Metadatabase.

The strength of the proposed EIM's global query is matched by its ability to control events from a distance. Personnel may modify data on a global scale, such as would be required in changing the development schedule of the research, prototype, and manufacture of a new weapons system. Normally, changing the development of any distributed effort that involved an enterprise and multiple commercial contractors would begin a cascading effect: one Army arsenal would inform another by telephone until the chain of developers and contractors were informed. Each in turn would have to determine which of their local information systems required updating, locate the databases and implement the changes piecemeal. Finally, each would realign all local development processes to the new schedule to ensure consistency across a

FILE TRANSFER USING METADATABASE TECHNOLOGY

APPLICATION PROTOCOL INTERCHANGE (API) IS ALWAYS WRITTEN TO THE GLOBAL METADATABASE REPRESENTATION.

ONE API WRITTEN PER CONNECTION

IF AN API IS WRITTEN FOR FOX PRO, ANY CURRENT OR NEW USER WHO WANTS TO SWAP DATA WITH FOX PRO FROM ANY APPLICATION IN THE MDB CAN USE THE SAME FOXPRO API SIMPLY BY CHANGING THEIR LOCAL DATA EXCHANGE PREFERENCES — NO NEW CODE!

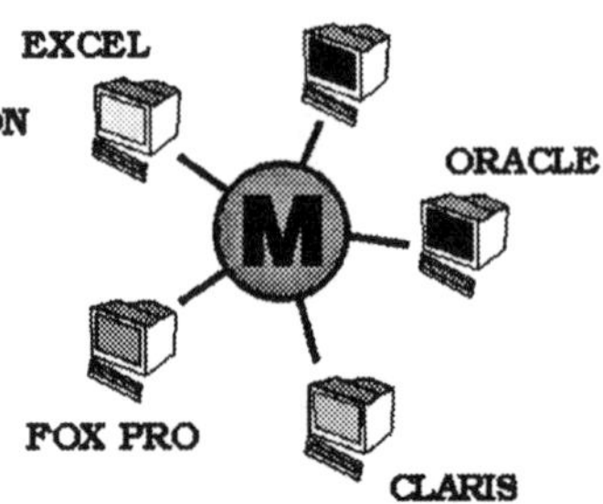

CONVERSION WORK DONE ONLY ONCE WITHIN GLOBAL MDB SYSTEM; AS MDB SYSTEM GROWS, FILE EXCHANGE GROWS MORE FLEXIBLE & SIMPLE.

Fig. 1-6: File Transfer using Metadatabase technology.

GLOBAL QUERY USING METADATABASE TECHNOLOGY

GLOBAL SEARCH STRING: V-22

[MDB RETURNS]
INDIANAPOLIS: DESIGN:
FILENAME: V22AR7.52
WANT TO SEE IT?

SEATTLE: PWB DESIGN:
FILENAME: FBW_B4.DSS

PHOENIX: ELECTRONIC FAB
DELIVERY AND SPECS: JULY 7
ORDER PROCESSING FILE:
LINE6/JULY16/ASDFO9.BO
....

OPERATOR CAN SEARCH FOR STRING IN SPECIFIED MDB REGIONS

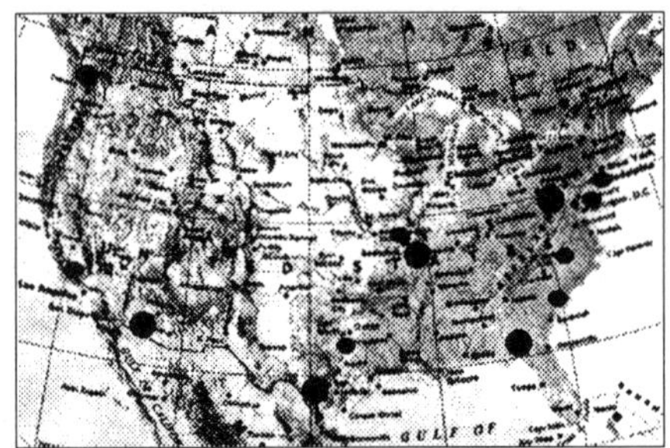

GLOBAL SEARCH RESULTS ARE ATTAINABLE BY NON-TECHNICAL USERS

Fig. 1-7: Global Query using Metadatabase technology.

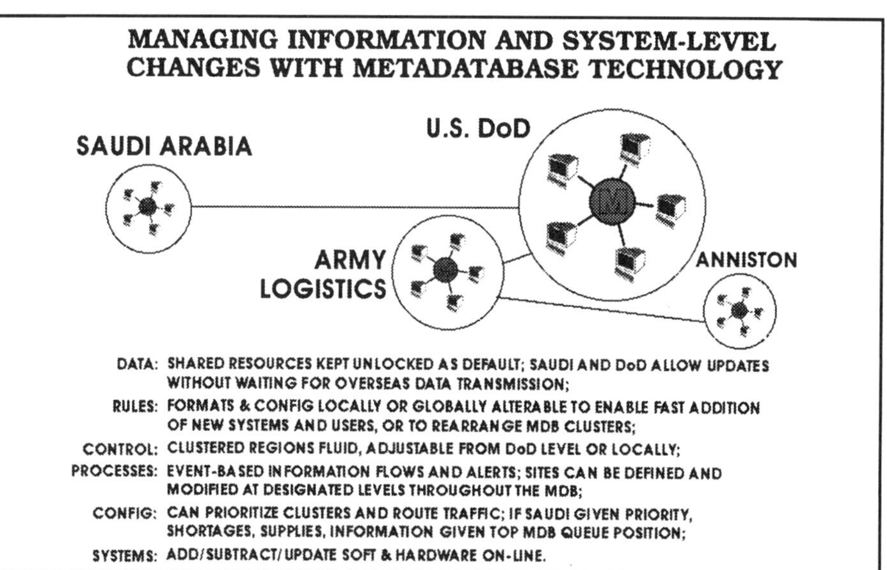

Fig. 1-8: Managing information and system changes with Metadatabase technology.

single arsenal or depot. In contrast, the Metadatabase would perform all of these repetitious and error-prone tasks on-line. Personnel (who were given such access privileges) would be able to change the global schedule associated with a particular weapon system in real time, thus simultaneously redirecting all Army efforts with a minimum loss of time in the transition.

Due to its rule-based structure, installation of the Metadatabase does not have to replace existing Army data structures; all depot and arsenal activity would continue undisturbed. However, the Metadatabase would add unique capability on top of current and future depot and arsenal data banks by allowing them to interact as one entity within the Metadatabase. Personnel with Metadatabase "management" access privileges could perform enterprise-wide searches, and modify the returned data to affect future events on a global scale. The Metadatabase is also expandable; its knowledge-based (using enterprise metadata) architecture and structure provides for computing growth within all arsenals and depots. All three types of networks are supported within the Metadatabase environment because of this expandability: Local Area Networks (LANs) that connect workstations to a server in a single locale, Wide Area Networks (WANs) that operate across regional distances, and single system mainframes. The above scenario represents the development goals of the Metadatabase technology. The major elements are disseminated in chapters in 7, 8, 9, and 10.

Acknowledgment

Mr. Alan Rubenstein of Rensselaer; Mr. John Manthorp, formerly of GE; and Mr. Jay Lieserson of IBM have given input to the discussions of industrial experiences in Sections 1.1.4 and 1.2. Ms. Tara Rosenberger edited Chapter 1, wrote the Army logistics example included, and created the figures. Ms. Debra Winchell word-processed the text of Chapter 1.

2

SYSTEMS ANALYSIS AND DESIGN

The strategic planning of IT for enterprise modeling (discussed in chapter 1) needs to be followed by systems analysis and design. Therefore, some common methods and techniques for information requirements analysis and database and knowledgebase design are discussed in this chapter. It also provides basic background to the information management technology that enterprise integration and modeling utilizes. The particular approach of metadatabase modeling is overviewed at the end of the chapter, and presented in detail in the next two chapters.

2.1 A SYSTEMS DEVELOPMENT FRAMEWORK

Information systems are typically developed in stages: (1) planning. (2) analysis. (3) design. (4) implementation. and (5) control. These five stages are customarily referred to as the system development life cycle, because control usually would precipitate planning and thus generate a new cycle. Sometimes this cycle is shortened by using a system prototyping approach to bring some parallelism into this otherwise sequential process and speed up the analysis and design. The planning to conceptual design stages are also referred to as enterprise modeling, which, at the enterprise level, specifies the goals and information requirements of the information systems being considered. A reference model that can serve both as a guideline and as a starting point to enterprise modeling would be invaluable for the effort. Other critical elements in any development project include commitment from top management and teamwork between functional and information professionals.

2.1.1 The Systems Development Life Cycle

Information Planning and Goal Setting. The objective here is to evaluate strategically problems and opportunities facing the enterprise's information systems to ensure congruency between its information goals and manufacturing policies. The need to start the life cycle at a strategic level stems squarely from the promises and impact of today's information technology. Solving information problems in an enterprise or solving an enterprise problem with information can lead to significant reengineering of existing processes at the enterprise level as well as at the functional level. Only strategic-level review and planning can determine, and implement, the right goals as the solution to these problems or opportunities. A ready example is the mundane systems of material requirements planning (MRP) and shop floor control in a manufacturing facility. Every one of these systems can be improved according to either of two premises: increments and integration. The optimal solution to MRP problems given the premise that current processes of production planning and shop floor control would not be changed is certainly different from a solution in which the given premise requires that the processes would change. Even if a project is relatively minor in scope and impact, it is still necessary to make sure if a project is relatively minor in scope and impact, it is still necessary to make sure that it follows the current policies and/or the existing enterprise model: if there are discrepancies, these should be made manifest and documented. The methodology for planning is a combination of traditional strategic planning, bottom-up problem-driven planning, and top-down opportunity driven planning as shown in Figure 2.1. The three sets of heuristics discussed in Section 1.1.3 of chapter 1 provide a framework for top-down planning.

Information Requirements Analysis. Structured systems analysis techniques such as Data Flow Diagrams and Integrated Computer-Aided Manufacturing (ICAM) Definitional (IDEF0) method are commonly used for information requirements analysis. The object is to determine the functional processes, data resources, and knowledge resources necessary for the missions of the planned system. Both DFD and IDEF0 depict these requirements. These methods are discussed in Section 2.2 below. A feasibility study is usually conducted at this stage. A cost-benefit analysis is also desirable but hard to perform in most cases, because reliable metrics and measures are difficult to come by for enterprise information systems. This analysis can be applied to either status quo systems or new systems. The Two-Stage Entity-Relationship (TSER) model discussed later in this chapter and also in chapters 3 and 4 supports information requirements analysis and its integration with systems design.

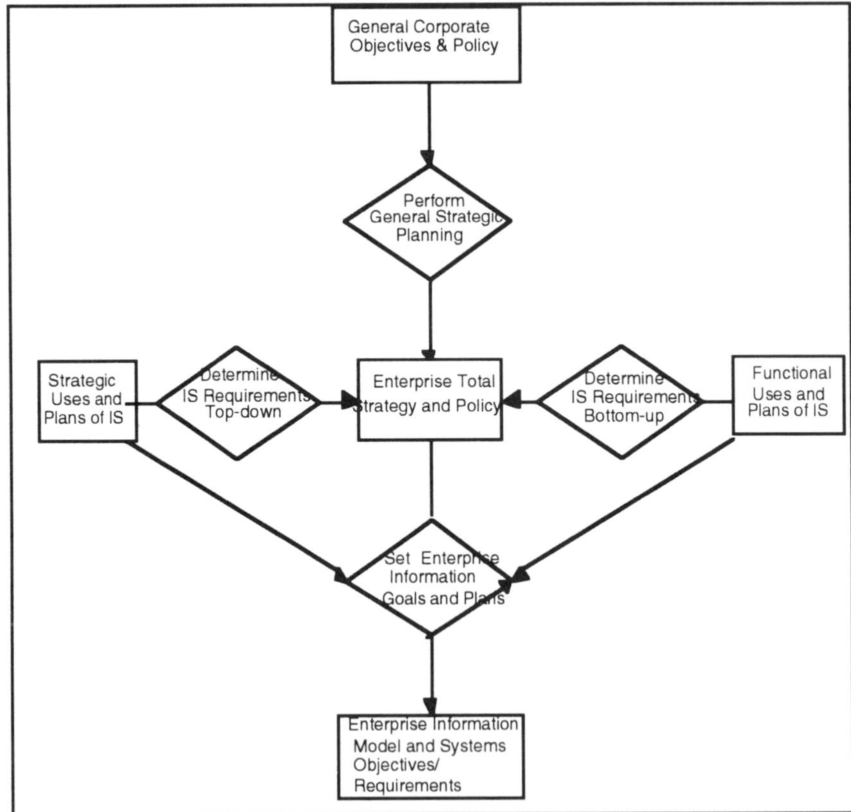

Fig. 2.1. An overview of information planning

Systems Design. High level design for the planned system can be considered part of an iterative process of systems analysis and design, whereby old processes and systems are reengineered and new ones are designed as their information requirements are analyzed. Once the information requirements are finalized, system design is focused on developing data models for data resources, knowledge models for knowledge resources, and application models for functional processes, which, respectively, lead to databases, knowledge-based and decision support systems, and custom application programs. Methods and techniques commonly used for this include (1) semantic data modeling, conceptual database design, and particular database or file system design for data resources; (2) knowledge acquisition and engineering, decision and knowledge-base modeling, and particular expert or decision support systems design for knowledge resources; and (3) application modeling, software engineering, and user interface for particular application software systems design. It should be noted that decision support and expert systems can be deployed either to modulize and manage certain classes of control and processing logic (knowledge resources) for particular application programs or to perform some applications themselves. Databases, on the other hand, are strictly developed to integrate and but manage data resources for, ideally, the enterprise as a whole. The TSER model provides a particular approach to designing databases as well as modeling their integration for an enterprise.

Software Development and Systems Implementation. The detailed design of the planned system is implemented first through software and other information technology and then in the organization. The technical implementation is accomplished through software engineering, coding, and installation; this whole process, well known in the profession, requires careful project management. The organizational implementation, on the other hand, is basically an art requiring delicate nurturing on the human side of the systems. Essentially, successful implementations seem to use one or more of the following strategies: (1) early involvement of the users in the development life cycle of the planned system (i.e., engineers, technicians, and managers can participate in the identification of information problems and opportunities as well as in the analysis of information requirements and systems design), (2) intensive education and open communication about the intended changes and the planned systems, and (3) pilot installation for helping the users gain familiarity and experience with the new systems. Without user cooperation, any information system efforts would likely fail, as is always the case with the introduction of any major new technology, be it robotics, TQM, or CIM.

Systems Operation and Control. Systems operation and control present the most critical challenge to both systems and their managers. The focus is performance monitoring, feedback, and adaptation. The monitoring must be based on adequate metrics and measurement of performance, which can only come from the enterprise model (especially its goals) and users' satisfaction. Feedback implies an accountability of the system design that permits a cause-and-effect analysis for the monitored results. Adaptation may fall into two categories: fine-tuning or incremental changes versus a striving for overhaul or even new systems. Adaptation generates another phase of planning and hence another cycle of development.

Rapid Prototyping. The above life cycle is not too different from the product development life cycle and is certainly subject to the same need for abbreviation as the latter does. An alternative to the sequential life cycle is the rapid development of a prototype: the prototyping should embody the tasks of all stages of the cycle. In practice, rapid prototyping is usually employed to facilitate early integration of planning, analysis, and design and especially to verify the concept and feasibility of the enterprise model before the full system is constructed. In this sense, the rapid prototyping approach to information systems development is similar to the engineering paradigm of prototyping for new product development.

2.1.2 A Reference Model

The notion of a reference model for enterprise integration efforts is formally articulated in the ESPRIT's CIM Open Systems Architecture (CIMOSA) project, although there have been a few sources in academia and industry in both Europe and North America that independently investigated the topic at the time. CIMOSA calls for a family of reference models, including generic models, models for particular industries, and models for specific domain enterprises. Ideally, these three sets of models would be consistent vertically across levels (form generic to particular) and horizontally across individual models in terms of their content structures. A common set of constructs is employed that includes function view, information view, resources view, and organization view for the content structures. It was hoped that through the use of an internally consistent family of reference models for all enterprises, standards would be easier and more effective to maintain, thereby securing the foundation for open systems architecture. Industry also has its vendors (e.g., IBM and Digital) working on proprietary reference models coupled with their own integration products, but few of these efforts have yet resulted in actual models available to common users. A theory-based reference model was developed in 1990 at Rensselaer Polytechnic institute, (Troy, NY.). Based on this model and the actual practice for enterprise information integration, several principles are derived as follows:

Enterprise Perspective. Transcend organization boundaries and look into the natural and underlying processes of the enterprise including customer, vendor, and manufacturer.

Core Information Model. Adopt a particular enterprise model which covers the basic information requirements for integration as a starting point for the development of the complete model. This approach tends to save time, effort, and hence money.

Systems Integration. Examine the information flows and connect information systems that have common flows form the enterprise perspective; specifically, connect design with production and business, and production with customer and vendor.

Parallel Processes. Analyze the internal information flows of existing systems or processes to uncover commonalty among them, then reengineer these processes into smaller unit processes that are connected through their common flows; in other words, maximize the parallelism of all processes throughout the enterprise. For example, perform scheduling, routing, and loading concurrently.

Integration. Integrate (logically, not physically) all common data resources for the shared use of the enterprise as a whole.

Knowledge Enhancement. Develop new classes of knowledge resources and utilize knowledge-based techniques to effect integration of parallel processes.
Concurrent Architecture. Implement the whole environment in a manner that allows for heterogeneity (in software and hardware), distribution, and local autonomy; in other words, pursue multiple and open systems.
On-line Enterprise Model. Employ metadata technology to implement the enterprise model for information management tasks throughout the life cycle, where the model itself may be distributed.
Feedback Loops. Create sufficient feedback flows for integration, e.g., use in-process verification to link production back to design to close up the loop initiated by, for instance, design manufacturability.
Visual Interface. Invest as much effort into acquiring a good user interface that is robust and intuitive as into developing the system itself; ideally use visualized interfacing environments throughout (especially for systems used by non-technical or low-education personnel).

2.2 SYSTEMS ANALYSIS TECHNIQUES

Modeling for information requirements is a key to the development of all manufacturing information systems, regardless of their level and functional domain. The two most commonly used techniques for modeling information system requirements are arguably IDEF and the data flow diagram (DFD).

2.2.1 IDEF: ICAM Definitional System

The integrated computer-aided manufacturing project launched by the Air Force in the late 1970s developed an enterprise modeling system called ICAM definition or IDEF. This system consists of IDEF0 (read IDEF zero) and a few other components for the modeling of integrated manufacturing systems with IDEF0 performing structured systems analysis at the functional-level and others performing entity-relationship data modeling, process simulation, and database design. However, only IDEF0 has received wide and common acceptance in the industry. IDEF0 is based on the structured analysis and design technique (SADT), which is a graphical diagramming method developed in the 1970s.

The basic constructs of IDEF0 are the following, which are symbolized in Figure 2.2.

1. *Activity-subject.* The functional elements of the system; always labeled by a phrase starting with a verb and decomposable.
2. *Input.* The logical or physical objects to be turned into the output of the activity.
3. *Output.* The logical or physical objects turned out by the activity.
4. *Control.* The logical means of the activity, such as control algorithms. design specs, or process plans.
5 *Mechanism.* The physical means of the activity, such as workstations and automatic guided vehicles.

Note that outputs from a box may become inputs or controls (or mechanisms) for other boxes and that input, output, and control define the interface of a box. All

Note that outputs from a box may become inputs or controls (or mechanisms) for other boxes and that input, output, and control define the interface of a box. All inputs to a box should generally sum up to its outputs, logically and physically. The inclusion of mechanism is optional.

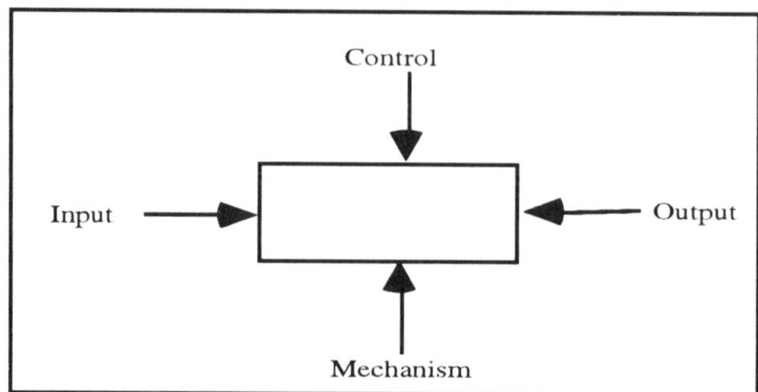

Fig. 2.2. The basic construct of IDEF0

The modeling methodology entails an iterative and "zoom-in, zoom-out" type of detailing hierarchy. Specifically, an IDEF0 model begins with a context diagram showing the whole system being modeled as a black box, i.e., a single activity-subject with its input, output, control, and mechanism. The purpose of the context diagram is to depict the scope and boundary of the model. The box is decomposed into levels of detailed IDEF0 submodels, with each submodel showing several boxes connected through their input, output and control arrows and pertaining to a particular subject at the level immediately higher than it. The boxes in all submodels at all levels are carefully numbered according to the decomposition hierarchy to maintain a logical order. Once decomposed, a subject is fully and completely replaced by its submodels; its existence is merely a matter of convenience for presentation, communication, and record keeping. The decomposition of the context diagram into level 1 is obviously mandatory; further decomposition, however, is a choice of modeling, dictated only by need. When decomposing one box at a level, the other boxes at the same level can either also be decomposed or can stay undecomposed, it is purely a modeling choice. At the completion of this decomposition process, collecting all submodels at the leaves of the decomposition tree should amount to a complete model without having to involve any higher-level boxes from which the submodels are decomposed.

A set of IDEF diagrams that models a CIM system is included. Figure 2.3 shows the manufacturing facility and the production system at a higher level than Figure 2.4, which focuses mainly on shop floor and cell system activities. Figure 2.4 is not a direct decomposition from Figure 2. 3. To illustrate a rigorously coordinated modeling effort, three IDEF0 diagrams are provided (Figures 2.5, 2.6, 2.7), which, respectively, depict the decomposed submodels for the MRP, SFC, and PP activities in Figure 2.3. All three diagrams are interconnected through common inputs, outputs, and control (e.g., the output of the "Store PP Data" activity in Figure 2.7 appears as input to the "Store Shop Floor information" activity in Figure 2.6 and to the “Maintain Static MRP Data" activity in Figure 2.5). By combining these common input, output, and control flows, a single IDEF0 diagram would emerge from these three submodels. One more IDEF0 is included to show order entry activities (Figure 2.8). When put together, a core CIM model in IDEF0 is presented.

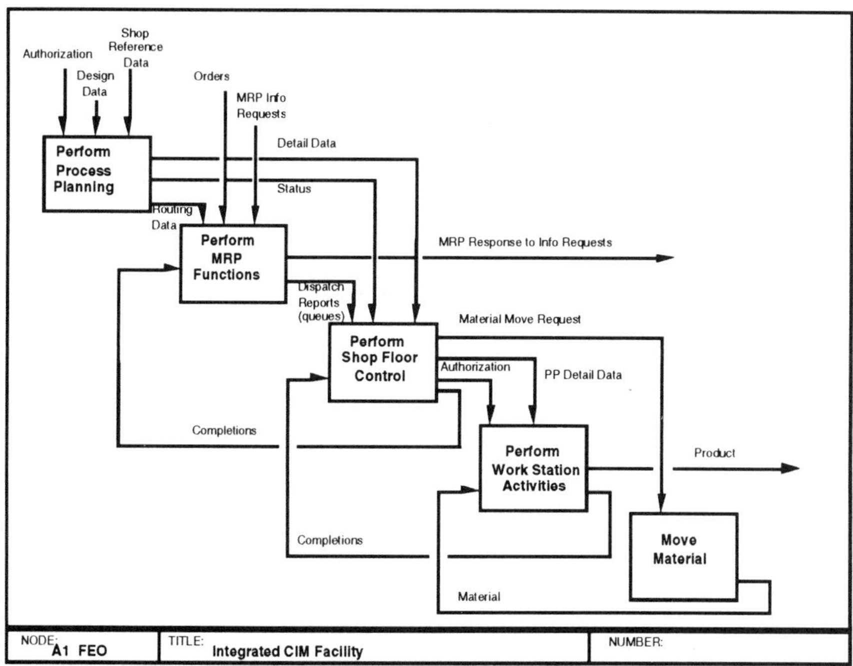

Fig. 2.3. Integrated CIM Facility

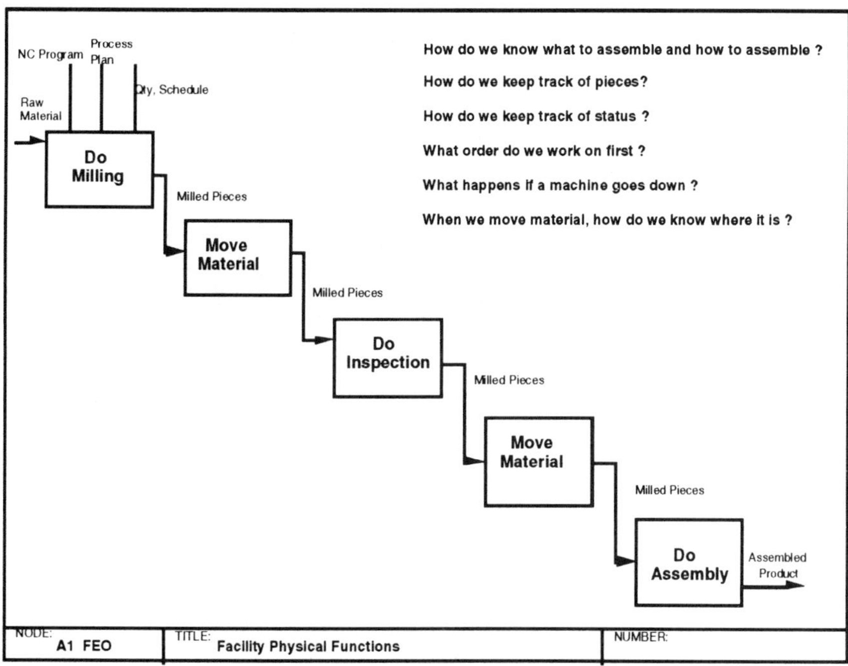

Fig. 2.4. The need for a shop floor information system

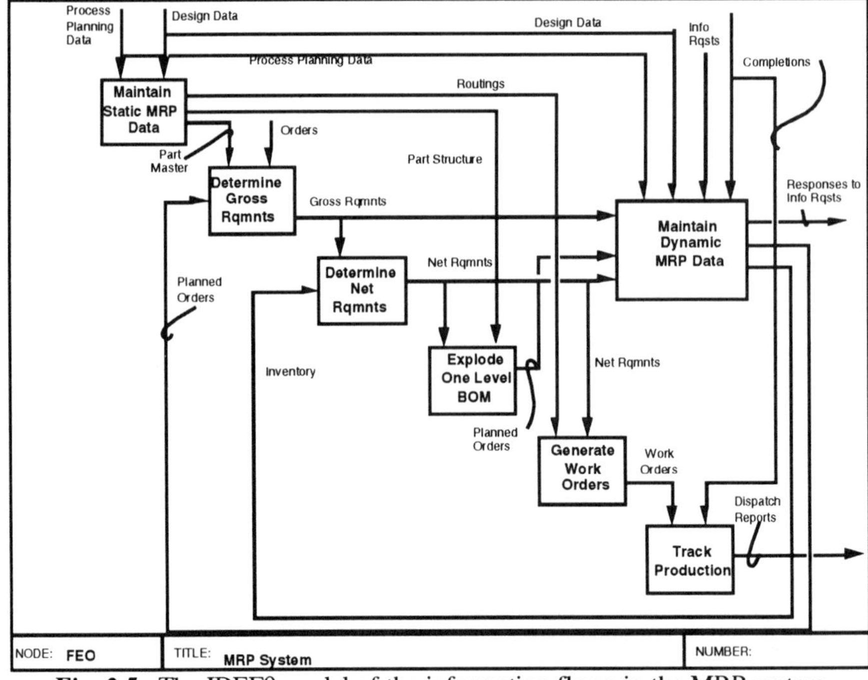

Fig. 2.5. The IDEF0 model of the information flows in the MRP system

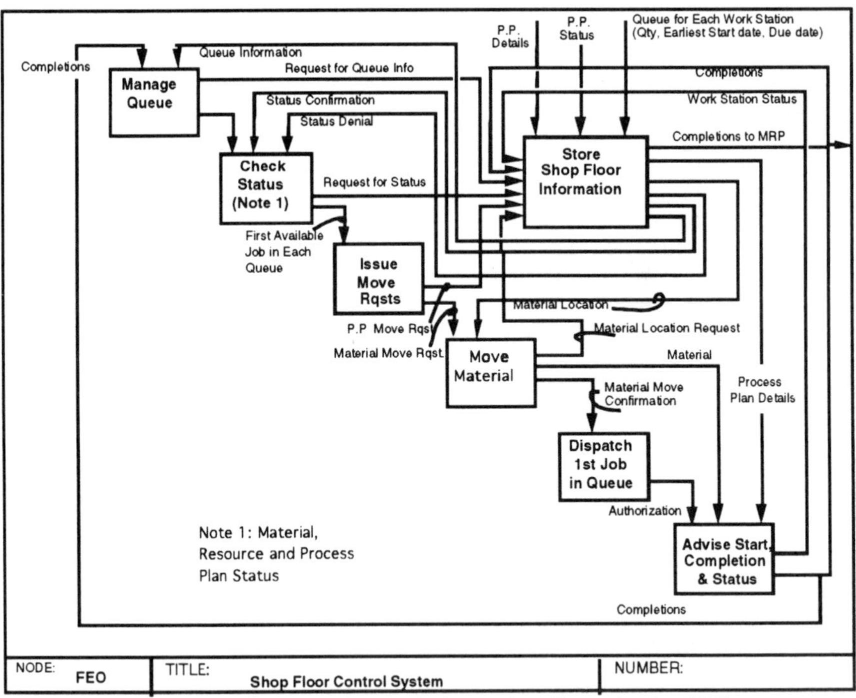

Fig. 2.6. The IDEF0 model for the information flows in the SFC system.

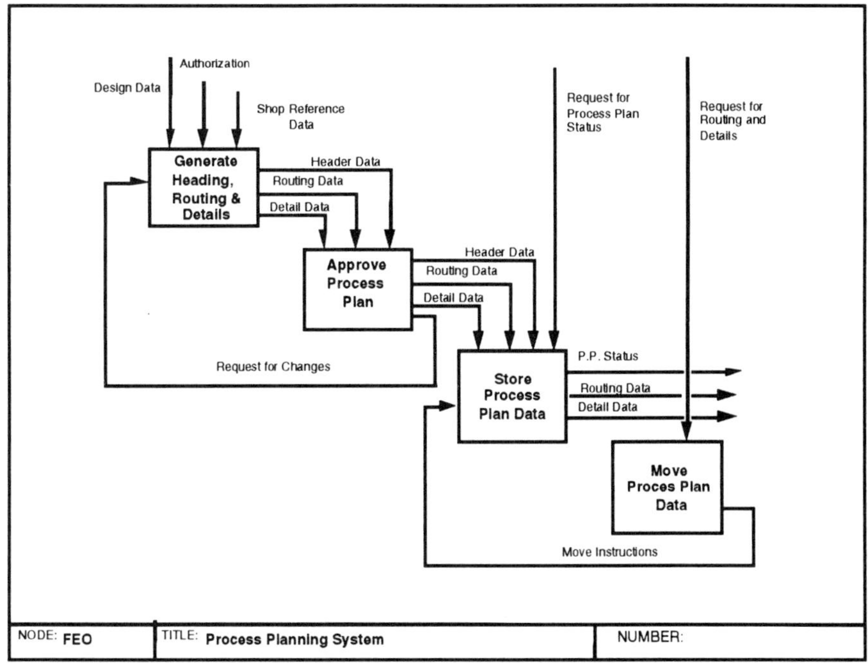

Fig. 2.7. The IDEF0 model of the information flows for the PP system

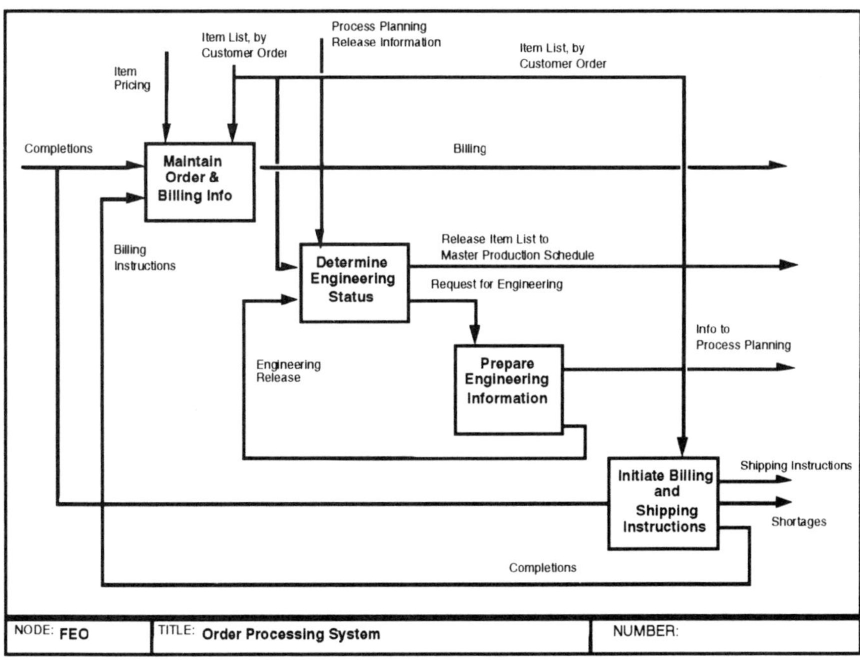

Fig. 2.8. Order processing system

2.3.2 Data Flow Diagram

DFD is another commonly used structured systems analysis technique in information systems modeling. In fact, DFD might command more popularity in the information systems profession as a whole than IDEF0 or SADT, although IDEF0 is arguably the choice for many large manufacturers, due to the ICAM effort. DFD's basic modeling constructs consist of external entity, process, data flow. and data store.

External entities represent sources and destinations of the system's data flows from the users' perspective; they, in effect, establish the scope and boundary for the system. The system proper is centered around the definition and declaration of processes. Each process has both input and output in the form of data flows, which might require storage in files or databases for time-phased use. The off-line storage of data flows is data store. Like IDEF0, DFD's constructs are fairly intuitive. Its modeling methodology also calls for the same iterative process as IDEF0 (discussed above). One of the principal differences between these two models is the fact that DFD's flows focus on data and explicitly represent data stores, while IDEF0's input and output are more general. In DFD, the logical procedures required to execute each process are contained in the process and are specified outside the diagrams as the process logic, as opposed to being separately represented as control in IDEF0. A context diagram is not always needed with DFD, because its external entities usually suffice the purpose. Instead, a level-zero business model is required to overview the system concerned. This model is a regular DFD consisting, usually, of 3 to 8 (aggregate) processes with all data stores hidden.

Two DFD examples are shown in Figures 2.9 and 2.10, depicting the same manufacturing facility under two different strategies: make-to-stock (MTS) versus assemble-to-order (ATO). From an information systems' perspective, the major differences are clearly (1) the need for inventory data resources in MTS and (2) the need for shorter time frames for the processes (i.e., knowledge resources) in ATO. The difference in data resources is visible in the DFDs. However, the difference in knowledge resources would become evident only when the logic of processes was fully specified. In the diagrams, squares represent external entities, arrows represent data flows, and rectangles with one end open represent data stores. The large, rounded rectangles are processes. Decomposition would be carried out on a process-by-process basis virtually identical to the decomposition of IDEF0 activities.

Listed below are some rules and heuristics to help avoid common errors in DFD modeling. Some modeling logic is also provided, which is not particular to DFD and is applicable to IDEF0 as well.

DFD definitional

1. All information flows must either originate or terminate at a process or both originate and terminate at a process.

2. Use a verb to define a process and a noun for everything else.

3. Bi-directional information flows indicate that the contents of the flow in either direction are identical, thus separate one-way flows must be used if the contents are different.

4. The DFD hierarchy is a "Zooming" mechanism not a pyramid, thus only the lowest layers or nodes are "real" and they must add up to a single, consistent diagram.

5. Each layer should not consist of more than eight processes or less than four.

6. All information flows must be meaningfully labeled unless they are clearly implied by a flow.

7. Physical systems, organizations, or material flows should appear either as external data store (whole content), entities or as footnotes in processes; only their information contents can be modeled as processes, data stores, or data flows.

8. All processes must have both input and output.

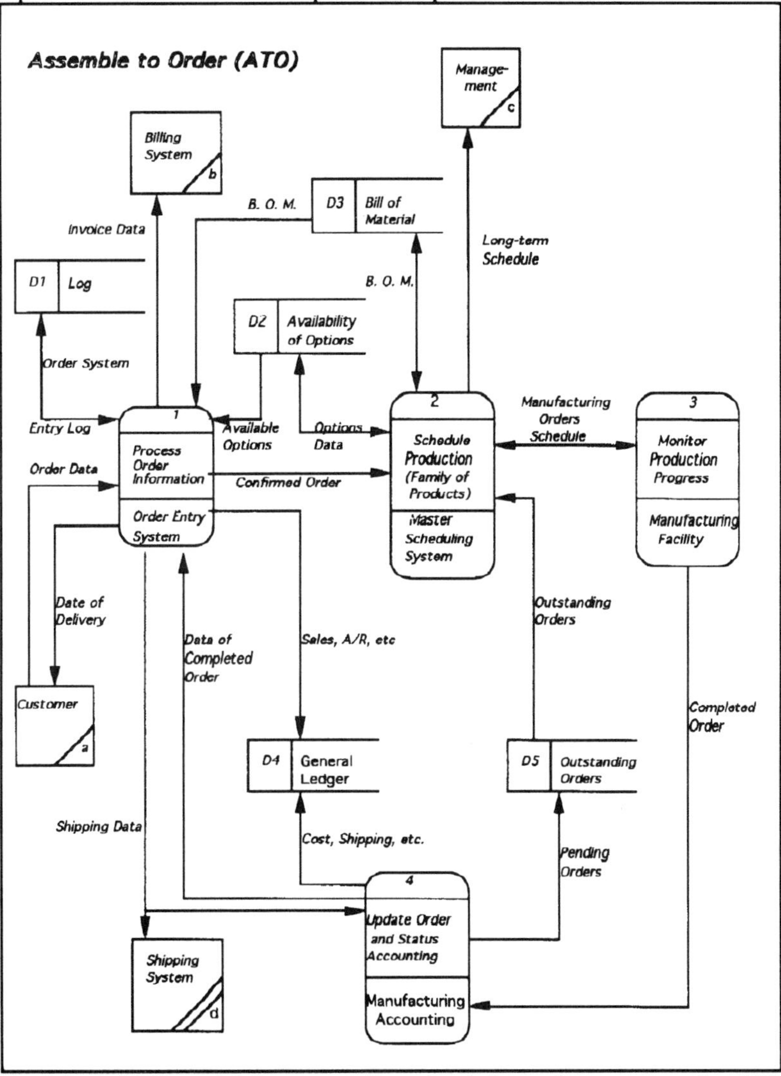

Fig. 2.9. A DFD model for a manufacturing information system using MTS

Fig. 2.9. A DFD model for a manufacturing information system using MTS

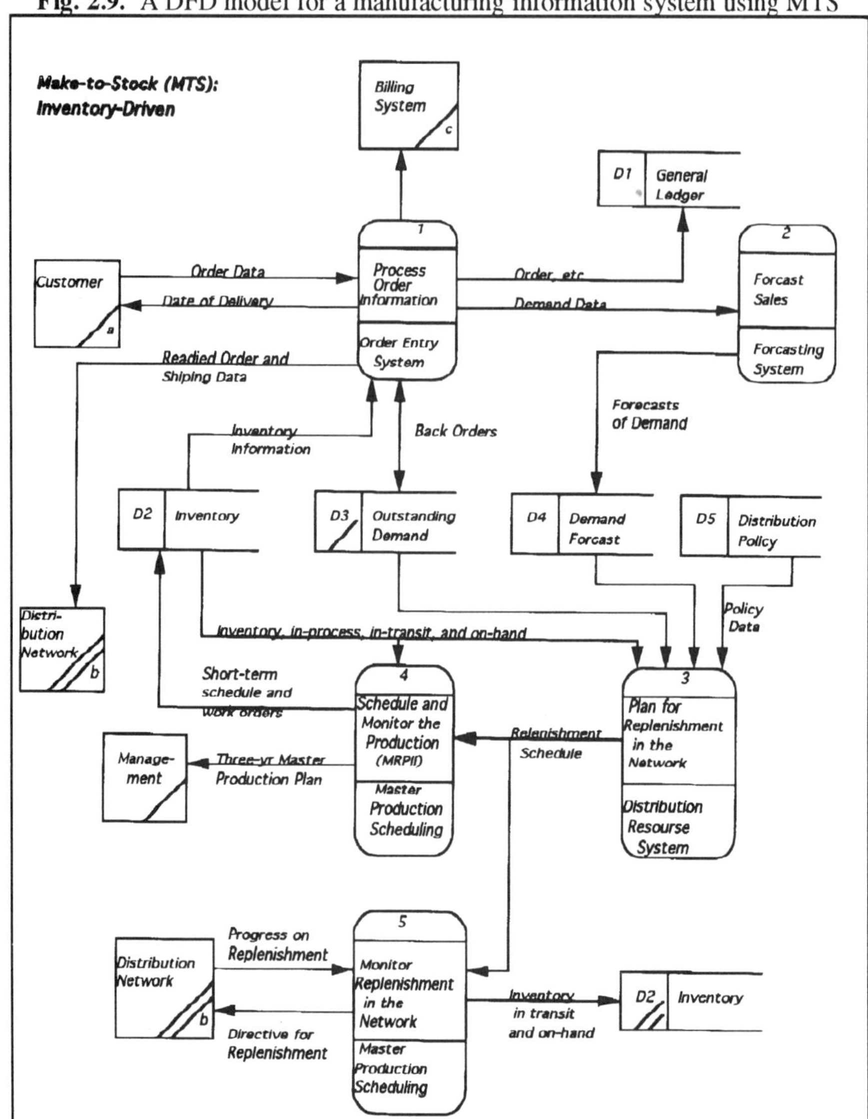

Fig. 2.10. A DFD model for a manufacturing information system using MTS

Modeling Logical

1. The modeling effort must be centered around developing processes; everything else follows.

2. A process should correspond to an application program, not a subroutine or a step in a routine; this determines when the decomposition should stop.

3. The read- and write-only data stores must be balanced in the whole model so that no unintentional dead ends exist.

4. There should not be any transitional processes (those that have only one input and one output), except perhaps in high level conceptual representations.

5. The 'business" cycle for a mission or job should be complete and shown clearly in the model (e.g., requests should be completed with response).

6. The model should show clear system logic (i.e., planning, executing, monitoring, and controlling the basic functions).

7. The model should show a clear enterprise cycle (i.e., origins, destinations, authority, stages-tasks, and the like).

8 The model should show clear mandate or use (e.g., the "plot," the statement, and the purpose of knowing all of these processes, data stores, and data flows).

Both IDEF0 and DFD owe their strengths to graphical modeling capabilities, which enable the user to make succinct visual statements of the system concerned. Both are similar in philosophy, methodology, and many technical aspects. There are, however, important differences. Foremost is the fact that IDEF0 includes both logical and physical elements of a system, whereas DFD focuses exclusively on logical elements (for application software development). Thus IDEF0 can be said to be more general and natural for systems in which the visibility of physical elements in the model is preferred, either for completeness or for concerted representation of both information and facility, as in manufacturing. Usually, a DFD can be readily derived from the logical part of an IDEF0 model. They can also be mapped into the TSER model.

2.3 INFORMATION MANAGEMENT TECHNOLOGY

The backbone of information management is the database systems; which, coupled with decision support and expert systems, account for the bulk of systems development effort discussed above. Simply put, databases manage and process the data resources for the enterprise, while decision support and expert systems are concerned with knowledge resources for particular processes or activities in the enterprise. The main difference between decision support systems and expert systems is that the former employ mathematically based decision models to represent structured knowledge, and the latter use knowledge-based technology such as production rules to implement unstructured knowledge. When IDEF0 or DFD is used to determine information requirements, data resources are typically found in IDEF0's inputs and outputs and DFD's data stores and data flows. Likewise. knowledge resources are derived from IDEF0's controls and DFD's process logic. In practice, however, neither IDEF0 nor DFD alone can provide sufficient contents for data and knowledge modeling; additional efforts (e.g., semantic data modeling) are usually required, independent of the IDEF0 or DFD modeling conventions. The Two-Stage Entity-Relationship (TSER) method provides an integrated modeling approach that supports both information requirements analysis and database and knowledgebase design. In fact, it encompasses the goals of DFD, IDEF0, and semantic data modeling for enterprise information modeling.

2.3.1 Database Systems

The key concept of databases is data integration based on a three-schema model. The model is illustrated in Figure 2.11. Conceptually, all data resources are consolidated into a repository using certain file structures (internal schema) that are transparent to all users (and, ideally, to hardware, too). Users, on the other hand, view only the portion of data that concern them in their own preferred ways as if these data were structured exclusively for their software environment (external schema). The integration takes place with the conceptual schema, which is the community representation of the consolidated data resources and is precisely the heart of the database model. All three levels of representations are linked through internal mappings and managed by the software called database management system (DBMS), which is the operating system of databases. The three-schema architecture allows heterogeneous user groups all to share the same data resources without imposing a single standard end-user software or sacrificing control needed for data integrity, consistency, and security. The separation of end users' views form the real structures of data facilities tremendously the database system's ability to add, delete, and modify user groups and views with no disruption to the system. This property is referred to as data independence. Data independence with respect to hardware is also desired but much harder to accomplish.

Depending on how the conceptual schema is constructed, there are three major types of databases; hierarchical-network, relational, and object oriented. Hierarchical-network databases have become obsolete in the present market but still account for a significant portion of all databases installed to date due to their venerability. They focus on determining the semantically meaningful entities and relationships for the user groups at large and then represent them in computationally optimal data structures and access paths using pointers and indexes. Relational systems, on the other hand, employ rigorous, set-theoretic dependency theory to decompose and reshuffle users' views into generic and simple tables (normalized relations) for the community, and develop powerful query languages to allow users manipulate these tables in any way with little concern whatsoever to access paths.

Thus relational systems are more flexible than hierarchical-network systems -- a property that has rendered the relational systems the leading technology in databases, until the advent of industry-grade object oriented systems. Object-oriented databases use data abstraction and typing to organize individual data objects (e.g., a part or an employee) into a class hierarchy, where each class is a family characterized by properties common to all of its subclasses (inheritance), to achieve efficient and effective data management (e.g., a change to class properties will automatically be "inherited" by all objects belonging to this family of class and subclasses). This approach has certain similarity with the network model when it comes to the storage and retrieval of persistent data objects. Furthermore, its data abstraction-based class hierarchy compares with the dependency theoretic integrity rules of relational systems in a strikingly similar way, too. Object-oriented databases, however, do benefit from a rigorous model (data abstraction) and a powerful software technology (object-oriented programming), both of which the hierarchical-network systems lack.

Therefore, the o-o database is able to encapsulate routines into objects to improve re-usability of software programs. It seems that relational systems still enjoy more flexibility and will continue to fare well in areas where ad hoc query is important and where data objects tend to be highly repetitive in structures, such as business and production planning functions. Object-oriented systems, on the contrary, will continue to do well in areas like engineering design and, perhaps, production control where individual data objects tend to be unique and their use more structured (predetermined views). The situation can change when either views are developed for object oriented systems, or hybrid technologies emerge into maturity.

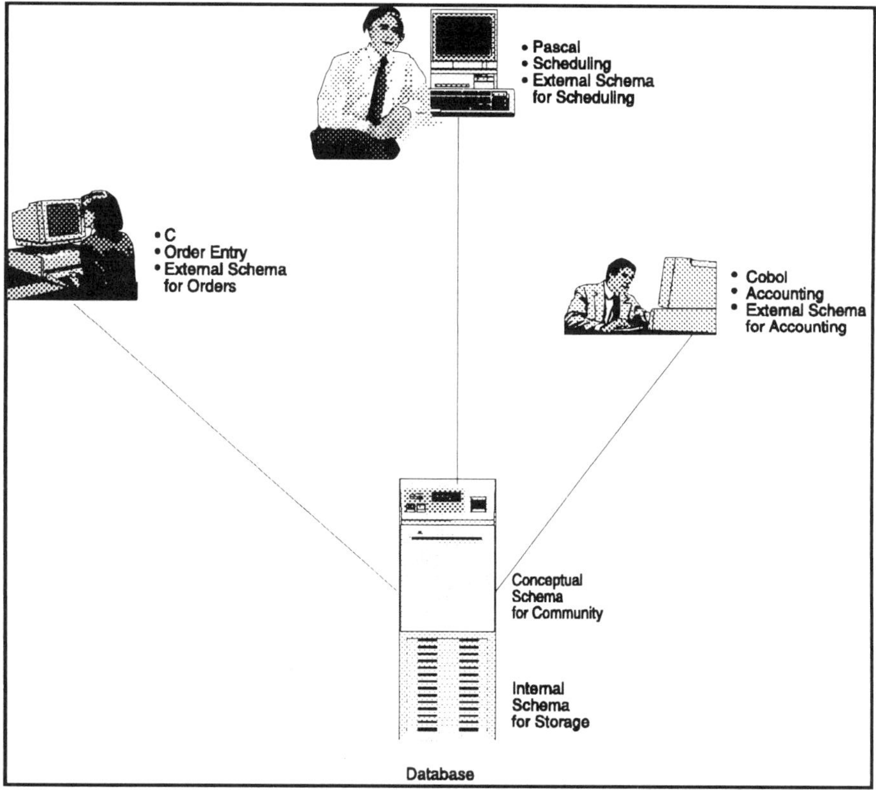

Fig. 2.11. Database: unified repository supporting heterogeneous applications.

Although databases are traditionally centralized with a single physical repository of data, distributed systems have become prominent recently. These systems feature multiple physical sites with the database dispersed or copied over these sites, but they are still centrally controlled by a management system. The advantages of distribution are mainly convenience to users, better performance for local applications, and higher level of security (backup). To maintain global consistency is the big challenge. More useful and challenging is a new breed of environments in which multiple database systems running on different software and hardware platforms are intended to work together in an autonomous and concurrent manner. Available results on this class of systems are still sparse. From this particular perspective, the metadatabase technology can be interpreted and evaluated as a solution to the multiple databases problem.

2.3.2 Decision Support and Expert Systems

Most expert systems use rule-based technology; others use a frame-based approach that is practically identical to object-oriented programming. The basic architecture is shown in Figure 2.12. The rule base contains knowledge (acquired from experts on the application domain) expressed in the form of production rules (a subset of first order logic). The inference engine works on the rules and searches for answers corresponding either to input conditions or to users' queries. The fact base is essentially a database internal to the system. Rule-based systems can be developed on a relatively small scale using off-the-shelf expert system shells. The key is to acquire knowledge from human experts and properly engineer the knowledge into rules.

Decision support systems (DSS) are characterized in essence through (1) the use of analytical decision models and (2) powerful user interfaces, both of which are customized for specific users concerning particular problems. Other than the difference in the underlying technology each uses, i.e., analytical decision models versus knowledge-based methods, decision support systems and expert systems appear to be more alike than different. A DSS ideally assists the users (presumably decision makers) to formulate decision problems and presents decision information in adequate forms for the users. Available technology tends to limit these systems to providing such abilities to only highly focused decision problems in rather well defined application domains. As shown in Figure 2.13, one salient element is the model base, the other is the problem formulator. When both elements are limited to simple capability, a decision support system becomes quite similar to a decision model-based application program that possesses well conceived customized user interface for particular user groups.

2.3.3 The Two-Stage Entity Relationship Model

The Two-stage Entity-Relationship (TSER) method is fully presented in chapter 4. We describe in this section a software implementation of the method. The resulting software is an information modeling CASE tool encompassing the following generic concepts: entity-relationship model, object-oriented paradigm, rule-based method, process representation, and to support (near-automated) databases and rule-based systems design.

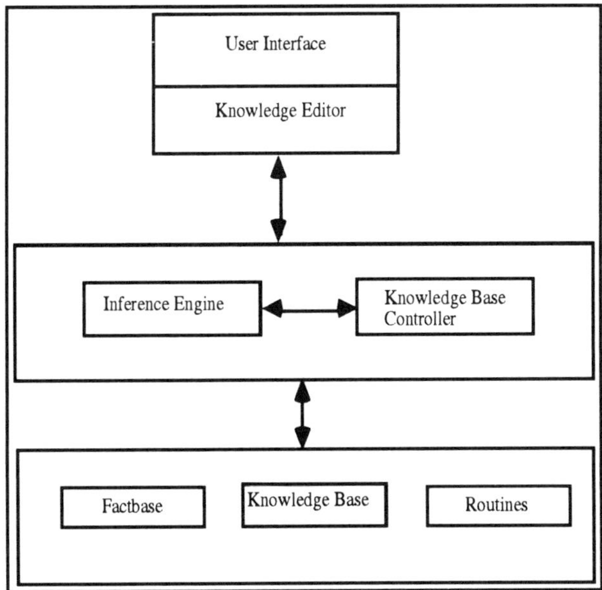

Fig. 2.12. A typical expert system shell architecture

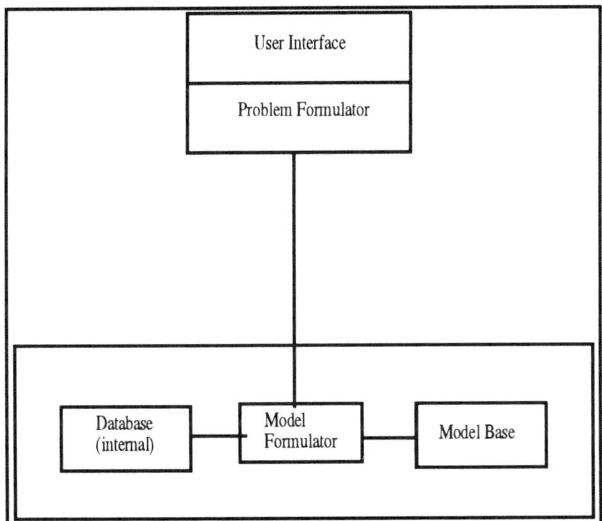

Fig. 2.13. Major elements of decision support systems

The Functional (Semantic) Modeling Constructs

The first stage features user-oriented semantic-level constructs for object-hierarchy and processes representation. They are used for system analysis and information requirements modeling; referred to in TSER as the Functional (or SER) Level Modeling Constructs; and employed exclusively for capturing semantics. The constructs include the following :

Subject:

Subject

Primitives: Contains data items (attributes), functional dependencies (among data items), *intra*-SUBJECT rules (triggers, events, and dynamic definitions of data items belonging to a single SUBJECT), and association hierarchies (explodes as well as generalizes and aggregates SUBJECTs).

Description: Represents functional units of information such as user views and application systems, and is analogous to activity or object/frame.

Context:

Primitives: Contains *inter*-SUBJECT rules (characterized by references to data items belonging to multiple SUBJECTs), typically includes directions of flows for logic (decision and control) and data (communication, etc.). It is allowed to contain only descriptive rules used for holding together a set of SUBJECTs or SER models that otherwise do not have direct associations.

Description: Represents interactions among SUBJECTs and control knowledge such as business rules and operating procedures and is analogous to process logic.

The Structural (Normalized) Modeling Constructs

The second stage is concerned with providing a neutral normalized representation of data semantics and production rules from functional model for logical database design; and referred to in TSER as the structural (or OER) model. There are four basic constructs described below.

Operational Entity (OE):

Entity

Description: Entities; identified by a singular primary key and (optional) alternative keys and non-prime attributes, and implies Entity Integrity : no component (attribute) of a primary key may accept null value, and no primary key (as a whole) may accept duplicate values.

Plural Relationship (PR):

Description: Association of entities; characterized by a composite primary key and signifying a many-to-many and independent association, and implies Associative Integrity : each of the PK's component attributes must be a PK of some Entity and its values in the PR must match that in the Entity.

Functional Relationship (FR):

Description: A many-to-one association that signifies characteristic traits or composition relationships (corresponding to the grouping type of association of SUBJECTs). FRs represent the referential integrity constraints implied by the existence of foreign keys.

The arrow side is called the *determined* side and points to either an OE or a PR, while the other side is called the *determinant* and is also linked to either an OE or a PR. The primary key of the *determined* side is included as a non-prime attribute (i.e., a foreign key) of the *determinant* side. Referential Integrity : the value of every foreign key in the *determined* must either be null or be identical to some PK value in the *determinant*.

Mandatory Relationship (MR):

Description: A one-to-many *fixed* association of OEs that signifies derived and inheritance relationships (corresponding to the classification type of association of SUBJECTs). MRs represent the existence-dependency constraint, and are symbolized as a double diamond with direction.

The "1" side is linked to the *owner* OE while the arrow side points to the *owned* OE. Existence Dependency : when the *owner* instance is deleted, then all *owned* instances associated will it must also be deleted; and there is a foreign key implied in the *owned* whose value must match exactly the *owner*'s PK value.

Although TSER has its own unique design and methodology, it is, nevertheless, compatible with three common perspectives of modeling that the user may choose to employ; all of which lead to the same data and knowledge capabilities that the system offers. These perspectives are:

• Entity-Relationship: The user considers the information model as mainly consisting of (high-level, semantic) entities and behaviors. The difference with the traditional E-R model is that the user does not further separate entities from relationships nor defines their types, at the user-oriented modeling stage (the first). The system will later determine these definitions using all of the semantics provided and normalize the semantic entities into structural entities and relationships according to the dependency theory (the second stage). The behaviors are represented using production rules, where those which are internal to the entities are embedded therein and those which are external (i.e., involving multiple entities) are grouped accordingly and exposed independently. The TSER construct SUBJECT is used for the semantic entities and the construct CONTEXT for external behaviors. The other two basic TSER constructs, ENTITY and RELATIONSHIP, are, in this perspective, used by the system at the second stage.

• Object-Oriented: The user considers the information model in terms of objects and behaviors. TSER supports the modeling of objects in the same way as called for by the O-O paradigm, except that it offers two additional features. First, the user may choose to separate out the external behaviors (such as control/information flows and other contextual knowledge that interact different objects) and expose them for global representation and management. Second, the user may choose to have these objects normalized by the system (at the second stage) and thereby relax the concerns of data structure design at the semantic modeling stage (the first). SUBJECT represents objects in this perspective and CONTEXT models external behaviors (internal rules are embedded into objects).

• Process-Activity: The user considers the information model as made up with activities and information flow/work flow controls. Compared to functional modeling techniques such as Data Flow Diagram and $IDEF_0$, activities via TSER have the choices of associating data resources with the processes that use them (or associating the processes with the data resources that they need) into a neat encapsulation unit , using SUBJECT. The contextual knowledge concerning the flows among activities need not be forced into any single activity but globally exposed and modeled through CONTEXT. (Utilities are provided in TSER to translate DFD into SUBJECT and CONTEXT). After this stage, activities are normalized into ENTITY and RELATIONSHIP (the second stage).

Acknowledgement

Mr. Alan Rubenstein of Rensselaer created the IDEF diagrams in Section 2.2.1.

3

EXAMPLES OF INFORMATION MODELING

A few prototypical examples of using the TSER method (see Section 2.3.3 for an overview and chapter 4 for full discussion) to model enterprise information and design databases and knowledgebases are included. These examples illustrate the logic of TSER, and also provide some practical designs that may be used as some elements of a core reference model for realistic systems design projects.

3.1 THE MODELING METHODOLOGY

From the perspective of an information modeling methodology, the TSER method actually encompasses a variety of modeling perspectives including data modeling, knowledge modeling, and functional modeling that combines both. The set of constructs for functional modeling is comprised of SUBJECTs and CONTEXTs and is used to represent data semantics and knowledge as viewed from an application level or systems analysis perspective. These constructs may be employed in their entirety or just subsets of them, depending on the perspective and tasks intended. These possibilities are compared to certain traditional notions as shown in Table 3.1. Performing traditional data modeling tasks for, say, relational database design would not require CONTEXTs (or even the intra-subject knowledge). A model using SUBJECTs alone would suffice the requirements of semantic data modeling for this purpose, and then lead to the normalized structure (OER) through the attendant mapping algorithms. Similarly, SUBJECTs could be made virtual (without CONTEXTs), serving only as certain reference points for CONTEXTs in rulebase modeling to recognize and group rules. When, on the other hand, both SUBJECT and CONTEXT are used, the resulting model would encompass what is usually referred to as functional models of structured systems analysis. The structural modeling constructs are made of one type of entity and three special types of relationships that refine the representation of data and production rules captured in the functional model of logical design. They, too, may be decoupled from the functional constructs and used for modeling in their own right. In this manner, they can be compared to the traditional Entity-Relationship model except for the rigorous definitions employed in TSER. These definitions ensure proper data structures and integrity rules for the design of databases or rulebases, or their combination.

In the usual case where the models of more than one system are being developed, a three-step process for basic global information modeling is used. First, a functional model (hierarchy) for each application system is created; second, each model is mapped to its corresponding structural model; and third, the several structural models are consolidated into a single global structural model using dependency-theoretical principles (e.g., normalization). When systems integration is actively formulated on top of this basic model, step 2 would be expanded to provide a single functional model. That is, the several functional models would be integrated into a global functional model by creating and populating *inter*-application

CONTEXTs with the control knowledge and operating rules that define the interactions among application systems. This process represents the traditional top-down modeling in the common life cycle of systems analysis and design.

Table 3.1 The TSER Modeling Portfolio

Constructs	Perspective	Comparable Methods
Subject (used alone)	Data Modeling	Semantic Data Models and Object-Oriented Models
Context (used alone)	Knowledge Modeling	Process and Flow Models, and Rule-Base Models
Subject and Context	Functional Modeling	Functional Models (e.g., DFD and IDEF0)
Entity and Relationships (used directly)	Data Modeling	Entity-Relationship Models

Paradigm translation, on the other hand, is based on bottom-up reverse engineering. This process, however, will piggy-back on the top-down capability of TSER. In essence, reverse engineering calls for a general guideline whose specificity depends largely on the particular systems to be translated in reverse engineering. The general guideline employs TSER functional constructs to represent the local models and then proceed from there following the usual (top-down) methodology. For example, base relations/object classes, views, or data files would be represented as subjects, with additional data semantics being modeled into functional dependencies, intra-subject rules, or contexts. Relational systems, object-oriented systems, and other Entity-Relationship models are clearly amenable to being modeled as SUBJECTs. The above logic is depicted in Figure 3.1 below, which includes both top-down modeling and reverse engineering approaches.

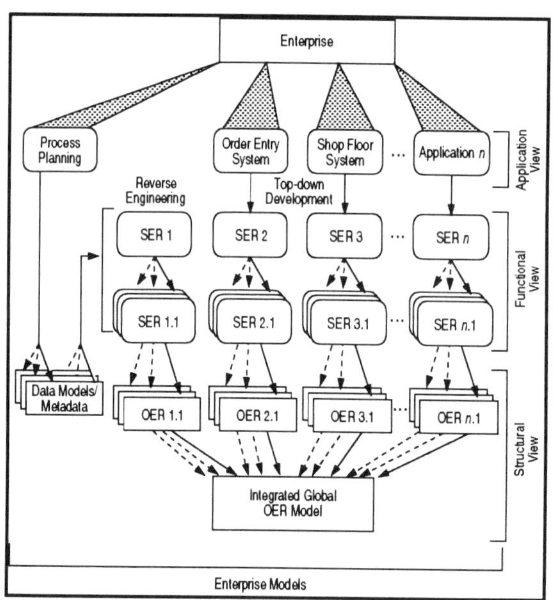

Fig. 3.1. The Information Modeling Methodology Using TSER

3.2 A SIMPLE HOSPITAL EXAMPLE

The basic mechanism of TSER is illustrated in a simple hospital information system where all information resources are put into one subject. The semantics of these data items are represented using the concept of Functional Dependency, which defines the determinant data item(s) on which certain other item(s) uniquely depends - the latter being clustered around, derived from, or identified by the former. An example is that patient-ID determines ("-->") patient address and date-of-birth. Note that neither address nor date-of -birth determine (or uniquely identify) patient-ID since there could be multiple patients who have the same address or date-of-birth. Similarly, the *combination* of patient-ID, surgeon-ID, and Date-of-surrey determines a unique surgery, but the individual elements of this group on their own do not.

In this first example, a hospital is modeled from the perspective of surgeries performed on patients, and hence a single subject (SER) of surgery is formed in the first stage. The system then determines a primary key for the subject and decomposes it into basic entities and relationships (OER) according to the dependency theory of data normalization ; this is the second stage. An Oracle schema is generated for the OER model afterwards. The SER, OER and the Oracle schema generated for this model are given in Figures 3.2a, b, and Table 3.2 respectively.

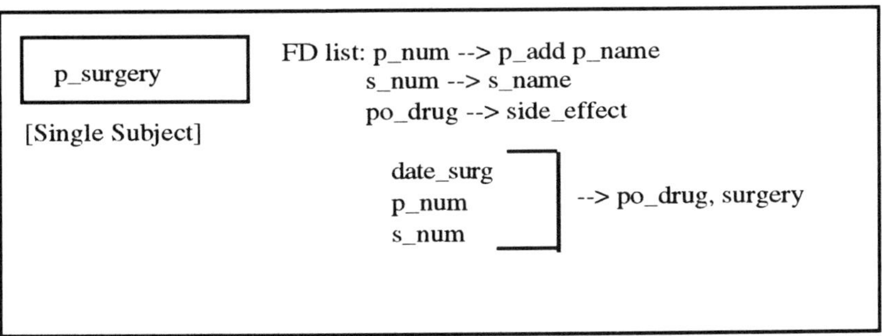

Fig. 3.2a. The single-subject SER model for the hospital

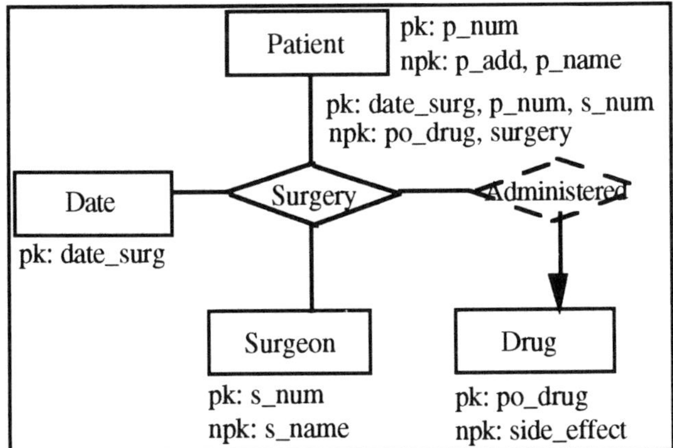

Fig. 3.2b. The OER model for the hospital

Table 3.2 The Oracle schema definitional statements for the hospital

```
SET AUTOCOMMIT ON;
        REMARK RELATIONS FOR OEs

CREATE TABLE date_surg
  (date_surg CHAR(10) NOT NULL);

CREATE UNIQUE INDEX date_surgNDX ON date_surg
  (date_surg);

CREATE TABLE p_number
  (p_num CHAR(10) NOT NULL,
   p_add CHAR(60),
   p_name CHAR(30));

CREATE UNIQUE INDEX p_numberNDX ON p_number
  (p_num);

CREATE TABLE s_number
  (s_num CHAR(10) NOT NULL,
   s_name CHAR(30));

CREATE UNIQUE INDEX s_numberNDX ON s_number
  (s_num);

CREATE TABLE po_drug
  (po_drug CHAR(20) NOT NULL,
   side_effect CHAR(30));

CREATE UNIQUE INDEX po_drugNDX ON po_drug
  (po_drug);

        REMARK RELATIONS FOR PRs

CREATE TABLE p_surgery
  (date_surg CHAR(10) NOT NULL,
   p_num CHAR(10) NOT NULL,
   s_num CHAR(10) NOT NULL,
   po_drug CHAR(20),
   surgery CHAR(30));

CREATE UNIQUE INDEX p_surgeryNDX ON p_surgery
  (date_surg, p_num, s_num);

REMARK ASSOCIATE CONSTRAINTS :

   REMARK Value of attribute date_surg in p_surgery relation must match
   REMARK Value of primary key date_surg in date_surg relation

   REMARK Value of attribute p_num in p_surgery relation must match
   REMARK Value of primary key p_num in p_number relation
```

```
REMARK Value of attribute s_num in p_surgery relation must match
REMARK Value of primary key s_num in s_number relation

        REMARK EXISTENCE DEPENDENCE CONSTRAINTS :
        REMARK REFERENTIAL INTEGRITY CONSTRAINTS

REMARK Every value of the foreign key po_drug in p_surgery relation must
REMARK either be null or match some value of the primary key
REMARK of the po_drug relation.

        REMARK  ORACLE SCHEMA HAS COMPLETED
SET AUTOCOMMIT OFF;
```

3.3 AN OBJECT-ORIENTED EXAMPLE

The simple hospital is reformulated according to the object-oriented paradigm. Inheritances are defined in contexts, including the type of inheritance and the contents. The modeling could stop at this stage (Figure 3.3a); but could also proceed to the next, OER stage (Figure 3.3b) to obtain a common representation that is readily compatible with the global representation of other systems (if any) in the hospital enterprise.

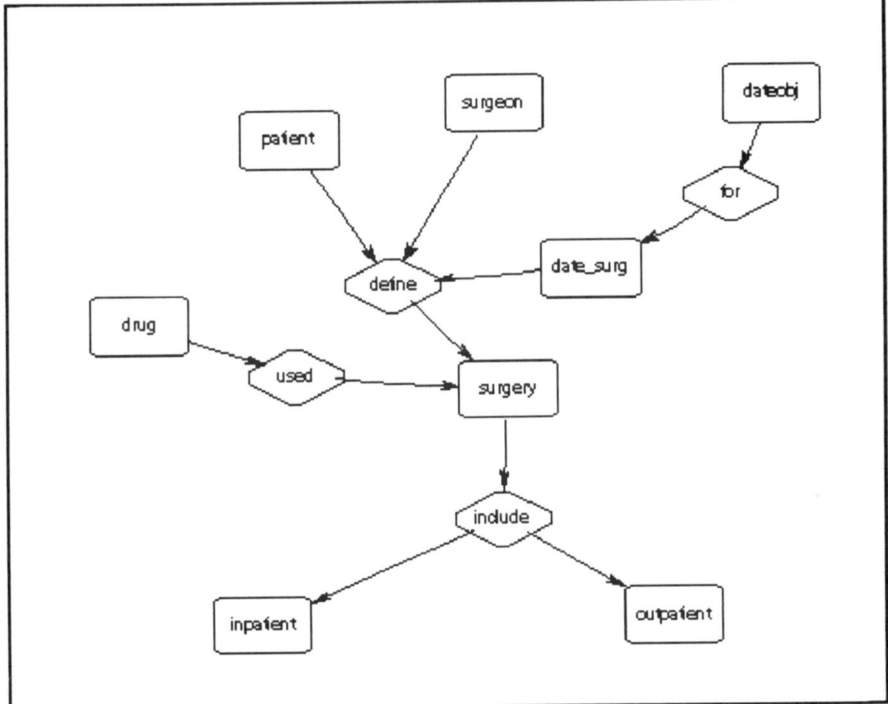

Fig. 3.3a. The object-oriented SER for the Hospital

Table 3.3 SUBJECTs, Inheritance and Data Items for the O-O example

Subject	Inheritance	Data Items
Patient	self	address, pid, pname
surgeon	self	sid, sname
date	self	date1
date_surg	referential; from Date	sdate$date
inpatient	full; from Surgery	lenofstay, pid, psadrug$drug, sdate$date, sid, surg
outpatient	full; from Surgery	pid, psadrug$drug, rate, sdate$date, sid, surg
drug	self	drugname, sideeffect
surgery	partial; from Patient, Date, Surgeon, and Drug	pid, psadrug$drug, sdate$date, sid, surg

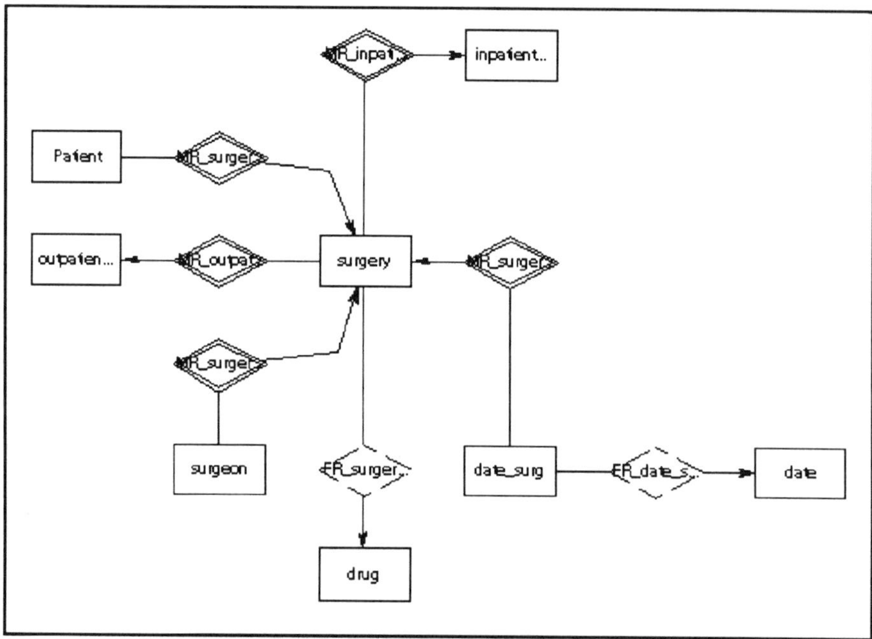

Fig. 3.3b. The common OER representation for the O-O SER

Although the single subject modeling is not necessarily impractical, a model that uses several subjects is evidently more flexible and informative. Thus, a realistic modeling example involving several applications of an information system is presented below.

3.4 A BANKING EXAMPLE

In this example seven reports required of a typical branch of a bank are modeled as seven subjects. A virtual context connects the seven subjects - see Figure 3.4a. The reports (subjects) with their data items and functional dependencies are given below. The resulting OER is shown in Figure 3.4b.

3.4.1 The Semantics

Branch Manager Report (Exception)

The data elements representing the entities of this report are:
BRANCH-NO, BRANCH-NAME, BRANCH-ADDR, MGR-NAME, ACCT-NO, ACCT-TYPE,
CID, CUSTNAME, X-DATE, X-TIME, X-TYPE, AMOUNT, REASON-CODE, ACTION-CODE, REMARKS.

The FD relationships between the data elements are:

1. BRANCH-NO ---> BRANCH-NAME, BRANCH-ADDR, MGR-NAME. For a given BRANCH-NO there is only one BRANCH-NAME and BRANCH-ADDR (branch address), and also only one MGR-NAME (manager name).
2. ACCT-NO ---> ACCT-TYPE, BRANCH-NO, CID. For a given ACCT-NO (account number)
there is only one ACCT-TYPE (account type). But there may be many accounts of the same type. This is a one-to-many mapping.
3. CID ---> CUST-NAME. A given CID (customer identification number) uniquely identifies the CUST-NAME (customer name).
But there may be many customers with the same name. This is also a one-to-many mapping.
4. ACCT-NO*X-DATE*X-TIME ---> X-TYPE, AMOUNT. The ACCT-NO (account number) with X-DATE (transaction date) and X-TIME (transaction time) uniquely identify the transaction. The X-TYPE (transaction type), and the AMOUNT are uniquely determined.
5 ACCT-NO*REASON-CODE ---> ACTION-CODE, REMARKS. The action to be taken (ACTION-CODE) and the REMARKS to be registered for an exception are dependent on the REASON-CODE and on the ACCT-NO (account number), that is, on the customer for whom an exceptional action has to be taken.

Branch Manager Report (Weekly Exception Summary)

The data elements representing the entities of this report are:
BRANCH-NO, BRANCH-NAME, BRANCH-ADDR, MGR-NAME, REASON-CODE, DSTRPT, DENDRPT, NO-X-TOTAL, NO-ACCTS-TOTAL, AMT-TOTAL.

The FD relationships between the data elements are represented below.

6. BRANCH-NO ---> BRANCH-NAME, BRANCH-ADDR, MGR-NAME
7. BRANCH-NO.*DSTRPT*DENDRPT*REASON-CODE ---> NO-X-TOTAL, NO-ACCTS-TOTAL, AMT-TOTAL.

Branch Loan Status

The data elements representing the entities of this report are:

BRANCH-NO, BRANCH-NAME, BRANCH-ADDR, MGR-NAME, LOAN-NO, LOAN-TYPE, LOAN-ASSGND, TOTAL-LOAN-COLLECTED, TOTAL-LOAN-TO-BE-COLLECTED, INTEREST, BRANCH-NO.

Tie FD relationships between the data elements are represented below.

8. BRANCH-NO ---> BRANCH-NAME, BRANCH-ADDR
9. LOAN-NO ---> LOAN-TYPE, LOAN-ASSGND, TOTAL-LOAN-COLLECTED, TOTAL-LOAN-TO-BE-COLLECTED, INTEREST, BRANCH-NO, CID.\

Teller Cash Drawer

The data elements representing the entities of this report are: -

BRANCH-NO, BRANCH-NAME, BRANCH-ADDR, TELLER-NO, TELLER-NAME, DATE, COH-SOD, COH-EOD, CASH-RECD, CASH-DISPENSED, CHECKS-RECD-US, CHECKS-RECD-OTHER, CHECKS-RECD-TOTAL, AMT-RECD-US, AMT-RECD-OTHER,
AMT-RECD-TOTAL, CHECKS-DISPENSED-TOTAL, NET-FLOW, AMT--CHECKS-DISPENSED-TOTAL.

The FD relationships between the data elements are represented below.

10. BRANCH-NO ---> BRANCH-NAME, BRANCH-ADDR
11. TELLER-NO ---> TELLER NAME
12. TELLER-NO*DATE ---> BRANCH-NO, COH-SOD, COH-EOD, CASH-RECD, CASH-DISPENSED, CHECKS-RECD-US, CHECKS-RECD-OTHER, CHECKS-RECD-TOTAL, AMT-RECD-US, AMT-RECD-OTHER, AMT-RECD-TOTAL, CHECKS-DISPENSED-TOTAL, NET-FLOW, AMT-CHECKS-DISPENSED-TOTAL.

Teller Audit Report

The data elements representing the entities of this report are:

BRANCH-NO, BRANCH-NAME, BRANCH-ADDR, TELLER-NO, TELLER-NAME, DATE, AUDIT-REASON, NO-X-TYPE1, NO-X-TYPE2, LARGEST-AMT-TYPE1,
LARGEST-AMT-TYPE2.

The FD relationships between the data elements are represented below.

13. BRANCH-NO ---> BRANCH-NAME, BRANCH-ADDR
14. TELLER-NO ---> TELLER-NAME
15. TELLER-NO*DATE ---> BRANCH-NO, AUDIT-REASON, NO-X-TYPE1, NO-X-TYPE2, LARGEST-AMT-TYPE1, LARGEST-AMT-TYPE2

INQUIRY Transaction

The data elements representing the entities of this report are:

ACCT-NO, ACCT-TYPE, BALANCE, CID, CUST-NAME, CUST-ADDR, CUST-TEL-NO, CUST-DOB.

The FD relationships between the data elements are represented below.

16. ACCT-NO ---> ACCT-TYPE, BALANCE
17. CID ---> CUST-NAME, CUST-ADDR, CUST-TEL-NO, CUST-DOB
18. CUST-NAME*CUST-DOB ---> CID

DEPOSIT/WITHDRAWAL Transaction

The data elements representing the entities of this report are:

ACCT-NO, ACCT-TYPE, BALANCE, BRANCH-NO, BRANCH-NAME, BRANCH-ADDR, X-DATE, X-TIME, X-TYPE, X-NO, AMOUNT, TELLER-NO, PASSBOOK-LINE-NO.

The FD relationships between the data elements are represented below.

19. ACCT-NO ---> ACCT-TYPE, BALANCE, BRANCH-NO
20. BRANCH-NO ---> BRANCH-NAME, BRANCH-ADDR
21. ACCT-NO*X-DATE*X-TIME ---> X-TYPE, X-NO, AMOUNT, TELLER-NO, PASSBOOK-LINE-NO

Rules

In addition to data modeling, the IBMS also provides facility for including inter- and intra-subject production rules. Two such rules are encountered in the first report , the Branch Manager Report (Exception) report; that the automatic loan account "Checking Plus" may be overdrawn or a savings account exceeds the balance of $100,000, which is the maximum amount insured by the Federal Deposit Insurance Company. The way IBMS would handle these rules is by incorporating them as intra-subject rules for the given subject (Daily_Mgr_Rpt). The two rules and their TSER syntax are as follows:
(a) If a "Checking Plus" account is overdrawn, charge $15.00 to the account and inform the customer.

(b) If a savings account exceeds the balance of $100,000, inform the customer.

IBMS Syntax: IF [Expression] THEN [Action]

IF (AMOUNT < 0) AND (ACCT-TYPE="Checking Plus") THEN
AMOUNT:=AMOUNT - 15.00; INFORM(CUSTNAME);

IF (AMOUNT > 100000) AND (ACCT-TYPE="Savings")THEN INFORM(CUSTNAME);

3.4.2 The Models

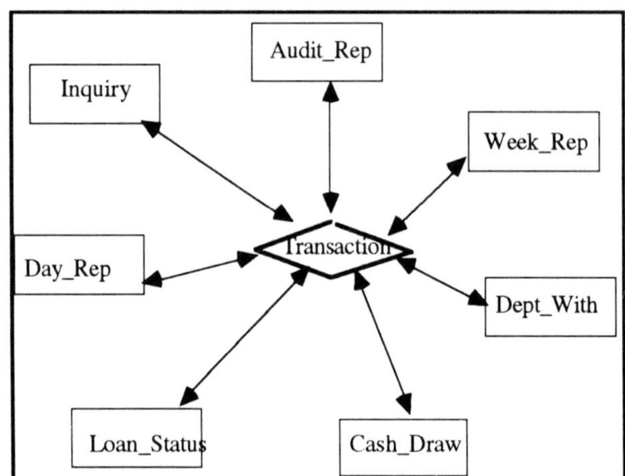

Fig. 3.4a. The SER model for the bank

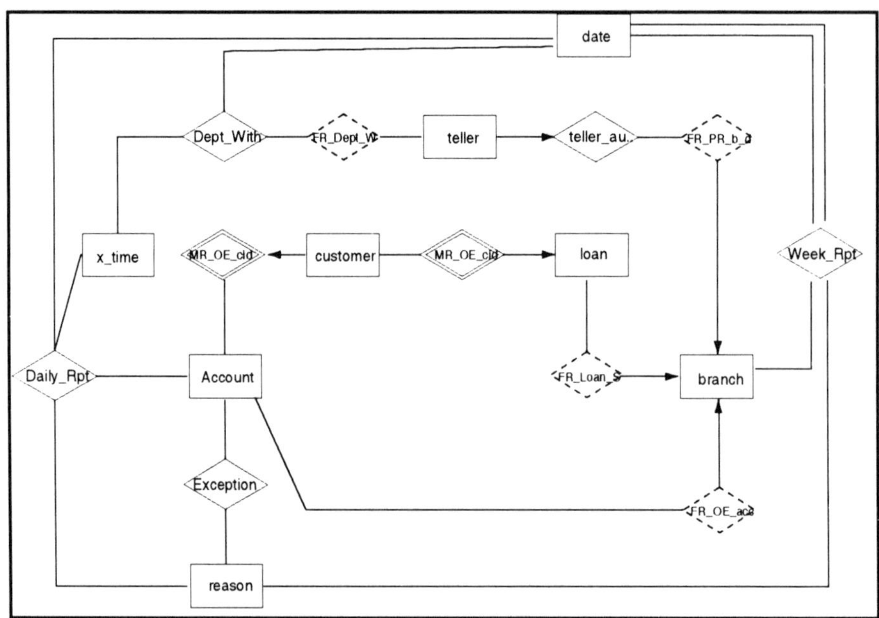

Fig. 3.4b. The OER model for the bank

3.5 A CIM EXAMPLE

In the above examples, there have been only one level of SER modeling and the possibility of doing process/activity decomposition via TSER has not been illustrated. The following example focuses on developing a multi-level functional model using SUBJECT decomposition. The details of this model and its normalization into an integrated OER model for CIM is shown in Chapter 10, where the role of this model as a core information model to facilitate CIM information integration is discussed.

In this example, five major functions (see Figure 3.5) of a CIM enterprise are modeled. Both data resources and contextual knowledge are included, as supported by TSER. Each of these functions are shown as a single subject in the level 1 CIM system, but are also individually detailed into level 2 and level 3 models. At the leaf level, all subjects would then be mapped into OER submodels which can be integrated either for individual functional systems (such as product design) or for an integrated CIM model, or both. Figures 3.6(a) - 3.6(d) show these level 2 SER models and Figure 3.7 provides one example of level 3 SER model for a particular subject in Figure 3.6(a). The data resource contents of these subjects are tabulated at the end of the models (see Table 3.4), while the knowledge resources are included in the core model in Chapter 10.

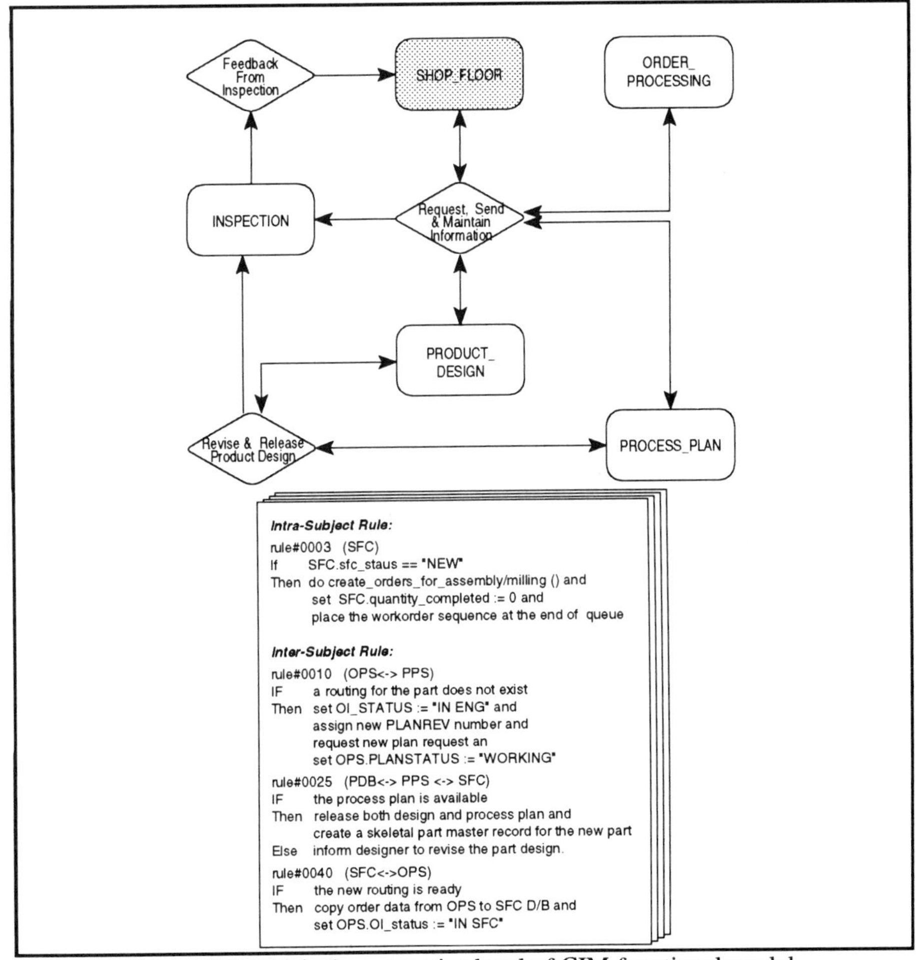

Fig. 3.5. Level 1: the enterprise level of CIM functional model

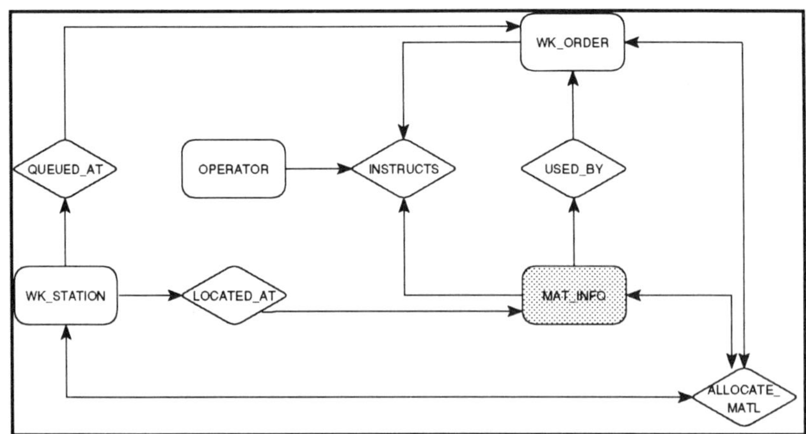

Fig. 3.6a. Level 2: Shop Floor Control System

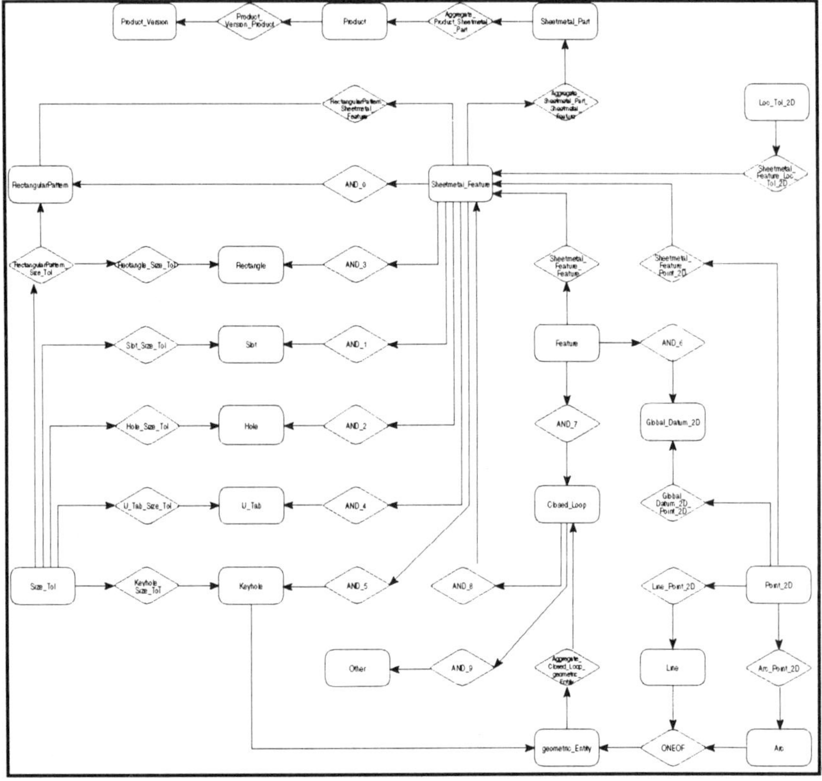

Fig. 3.6b. Level 2: the Product Design System (PDB)

Fig. 3.6c. Level 2: the Order Processing System (OPS)

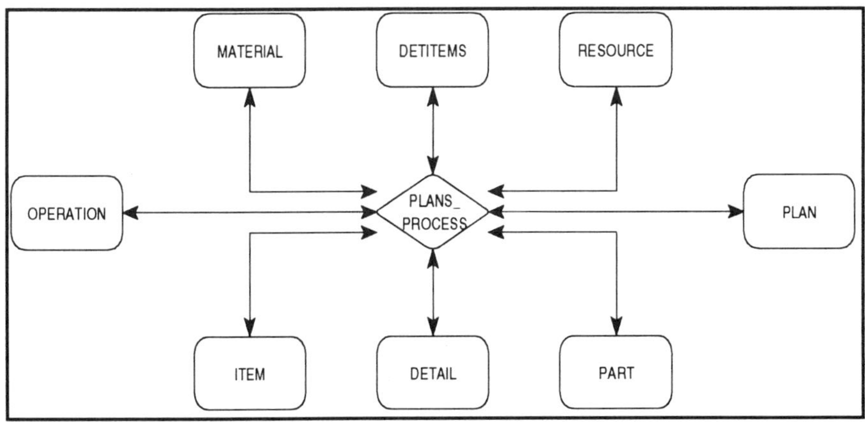

Fig. 3.6d. Level 2: the Process Plan System (PPS)

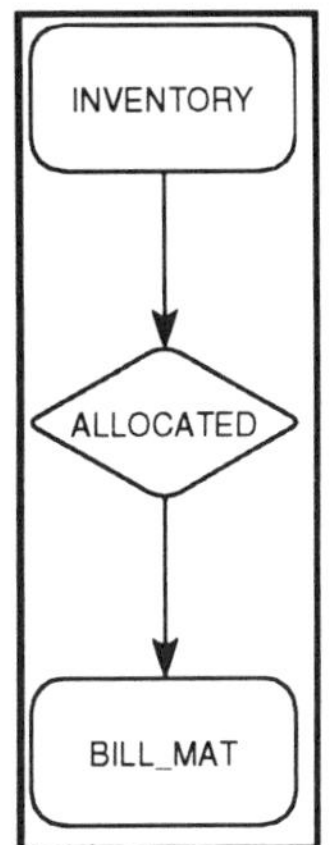

Fig. 3.7. Level 3: MAT_INFO

Table 3.4 Data Items and Functional Dependencies

Appl.	**SUBJECT**	**FDs**
OPS	CUSTOMER	(CUST_ID) -> (CUST_NAME, B_ADDRESS, S_ADDRESS)
	ORDER	(CUST_ORDER_ID) --> (OD_STATUS, CUST_ID, DATE_DESIRED) (PART_ID) --> (COST, DESCRIPTION) (CUST_LINE_ID) --> (CUST_ORDER_ID,PART_ID, QUANTITY, OI_STATUS, DATE_SCHED)
SFC	MAT_INFO	No FDs. Super-subject encompassing subjects BILL_MAT and INVENTORY
	BILL_MAT	(PART_ID_ASSEM, PART_ID_COMP) --> (BOM_QUAN)
	INVENTORY	(PART_ID_COMP, PART_ID, WS_ID) --> (NUM_NOT_ALLOC, NUM_ALLOC)
	WK_STATION	(WS_ID) --> (WS_NAME)
	OPERATOR	(PART_ID, SEQ_ID, PAGE, LINE) --> (TEXT)

	WK_ORDER	(WO_ID) --> (WO_QUAN, TYPE, NUM_COMPLETED, ORDER_ID, NUM_SCRAPPED, PART_ID, WS_Q_ORDER) (WO_ID, SEQ_ID) --> (STATUS, END_DATE, WS_ID, START_DATE_SCHED, END_DATE_SCHED) (WO_ID, SEQ_ID, NUM) --> (END_TIME, START_TIME, END_TIME_SCHED, START_TIME_SCHED)
PPS	MATERIAL	(MATCODE) --> (YSTRENGTH, TSTRENGTH, RHN, BHN, MATDESC, MATWEIGHT, STUNIT, MCHABLITY)
	ITEM	(ITEMID) --> (ITEMTYPE, ITEMDSC, LOCATION)
	RESOURCE	(RESID) --> (TONNAGE, MAXX, MAXZ, MAXY, HP, RESTYPE, DEPARTMENT, HOURLYRATE, MAXWEIGHT, RESDESC)
	PART	(PARTID) --> (PARTDESC) (PARTREV) --> (SOURCECODE, ABCCLASS, HEIGHT, CYCLCNTCLS, WIDTH, PARTID, UNITMEASUR, LENGTH, MATCODE, UNITS, RECORDTYPE)
	PLAN	(PARTREV) --> (PARTID) (PLANREV) --> (PLANNER, ROUTING, PLANSTATUS, TTLDIRECT, PLANNRCODE, EFFSTART, SSTKTRSHR, PLANDATE, PARTREV, GTCODE, INSTKTRSHR)
	OPERATION	(OPID) --> (PLANREV, RESID, CYCLETIME, RESPEROP, OPDESC, TRANSITHRS, SUTIME) (PARTREV) --> (PARTID) (PLANREV) --> (PARTREV)
	DETAIL	(DETAILID) --> (MFGTEXT, OPID, DETAILDESC) (OPID) --> (PLANREV) (PARTREV) --> (PARTID) (PLANREV) --> (PARTREV)
	DETITEMS	(DETAILID) --> (OPID) (DETAILID, ITEMID) --> (QUANTITY) (OPID) --> (PLANREV) (PARTREV) --> (PARTID) (PLANREV) --> (PARTREV)
PDB	Feature	(feature_ID) --> (feature_ID)
	Point_2D	($Point_2D) --> (x, y)
	Line	($Line) --> (start_Point, end_Point)
	Arc	($Arc) --> (center_Point, start_Point, end_Point)
	geometric_Entity	($geometric_Entity) --> ($Line, $Arc)

	Closed_Loop	($geometric_Entity, $Closed_Loop) --> (geo_List$U$L) ($Closed_Loop) --> (feature_ID)
	Other	(other_ID) --> ($Closed_Loop)
	Global_Datum_2D	($Global_Datum_2D) --> (feature_ID, origin, x_Datum)
	Sheetmetal_Feature	($Sheetmetal_Feature) --> ($Closed_Loop, centerpoint, theta_Rot, datum_Feature, location_Tol, gT_Position_Flag, gT_Position_Tol)
	Loc_Tol_2D	($Loc_Tol_2D) --> (x_Tol_Plus, x_Tol_Minus, y_Tol_Plus, y_Tol_Minus)
	Size_Tol	($Size_Tol) --> (plus minus)
	Hole	($Hole) --> ($Sheetmetal_Feature, diameter, diameter_Tol, gT_Circularity_Flag, gT_Circularity_Tol)
	Slot	($Slot) --> ($Sheetmetal_Feature, s_length, s_width, size_Tolerance, gT_Profile_Flag, gT_Profile_Tol)
	Rectangle	($Rectangle) --> ($Sheetmetal_Feature, height, width, height_Tol, width_Tol, corner_Radius, corner_Radius_Tol, corner_Radius_Flag)
	U_Tab	($U_Tab) --> ($Sheetmetal_Feature, height, width, height_Tol, width_Tol, gap, gap_Tol, corner_Radius_Flag, corner_Radius, corner_Radius_Tol)
	Keyhole	($Keyhole) --> ($Sheetmetal_Feature, circleDiameter, slotDiameter, k_length, circle_Tol, slot_Tol, length_Tol, corner_Radius_Flag, corner_Radius,corner_Radius_Tol)
	RectangularPattern	($RectangularPattern) --> ($Sheetmetal_Feature, no_OF_Columns, no_OF_Rows, x_Pitch, y_Pitch, stagerFlag, pitch_Tol, patternType)
	Sheetmetal_Part	($Sheetmetal_Feature, $Sheetmetal_Part) --> (plate_Charact$L) ($Sheetmetal_Part) --> ($Sheetmetal_Part)
	Product	($Sheetmetal_Part, product_ID) --> (components$L) (product_ID) --> (product_ID)
	Product_Version	($Product_Version) --> (product)

3.6 A PROJECT MANAGEMENT EXAMPLE

TSER provides facilities for supporting paradigm translation. One of these facilities is to import data flow diagrams and translate them into SER. Certain conventions are required, which are implemented into the DFD provisions of the CASE tool of TSER. Therefor, a modeler could choose to use DFD in lieu of SER for the tasks of functional modeling and later engage TSER for database design and integrated modeling. The modeling of a project management system illustrates this process below.

In this example, a DFD model is developed first and shown in Figure 3.8(a) and (b). The DFD model in 3.8(b) is then mapped into SER using the built-in facility - see Figure 3.9(a). A more refined SER model is given in Figure 3.9(b), which is resulted by manually consolidating some subjects that are virtually identical. The OER model is given in Figure 3.10.

Fig. 3.8(a) The level 1 DFD for the project management system

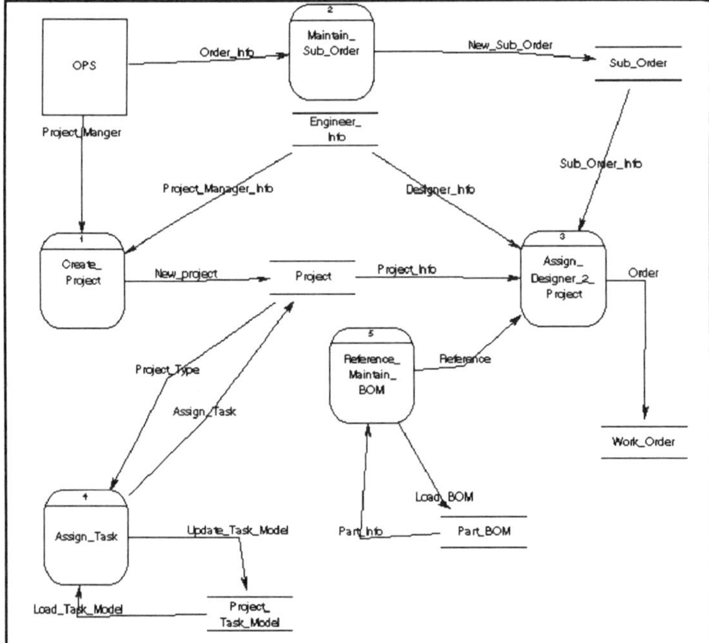

Fig. 3.8(b) The level 2 DFD for the project management system

Data Store Definition

Datastore Name: Project
Description: *Basic* Project Information

Items: enddate, prj_id, prj_manager, prj_name, prj_status, start_date, prj_type, order_id, task_id, task_status;

Internal Structures:
Entity Name: prj_struct
Description: Project structure
Primary Identifier: prj_id:
Non-Primary Aflributes:end_date, orderJd, prj_manager, prj_name, prj_status, prj_type,
start_date;

Entity Name: Project_Task_Status
Description: One project is composed of multiple tasks. Tliis structure represents project-task
Primary Identifier:prj_id, task_id;
Non- Primary Attributes :task_status;

Datastore Name: Project_Task_Model
Description: Sample Task Processing Model

Items: prj_type, task_desc, task_id, task_name, task_relseq:
Internal Structures:
Entity Name: Defaul_Proj_Type
Descripuon: Pre-defined process classified by project type
Primary Identifier:prj_type, task_id;
Non-Primary Attributes: task_rel_seq:

Entity Name: Task_Table
Description: Pre-defined basic task information
Primary Identifier:task_id;
Non-Primary Attributes :task_desc, task_name;

Datastore Name: Part_BOM
Description: Basic part_ information for designing

Items: part_id, part_cost, part_desc, part_name, part_property, part_spec, part_type, spec_change, part _child_id, part_parent_id;

Internal Structures:
Entity Name: Part
Description: Detailed part_ information
Primary Identifier:part_id'

Non-Primary Attributes:part_cost, part_desc, part_name, part_prnpeny, part_spec, part_type,
spec_change:

Entity Name: Assembly
Description: A parent-child relation for part
Primary Identifier:part__child_id, part_parent_id;
Non-Primary Attributes :parUchildJd, partparenUid;

Datastore Name: Work_Order
Description:

Items: designer_id, part_id, pri_id, end_date, start_date, order_comment, order_satus;

Internal Structures:
Entity Name: Assign_Designer_Work
Description:
Primary Identifier:designer_id part_id:
Non-Primary Attributes:end_date, order_comment, order_satus, prj_id, standate;

Datastore Name: Sub_order
Description:

Items: order_id, partid, sub_order_id, sub_order_ststus;
Internal Structures:
Entity Name: Sub_Order
Description:
Primary Identifier: sub_order_id;
Non-Primary Attributes: orderid, part_Jd, sub_order_status;

Datastore Name: Engineer_Info
Description: Project manager & designer

Items: department, designer_id, designer_name, passwd;

Internal Structures:
Entity Name: engineer_struct
Description:
Primary Identifier:designer_id;
Non-Primary Attributes:department, designer_name, passwd;

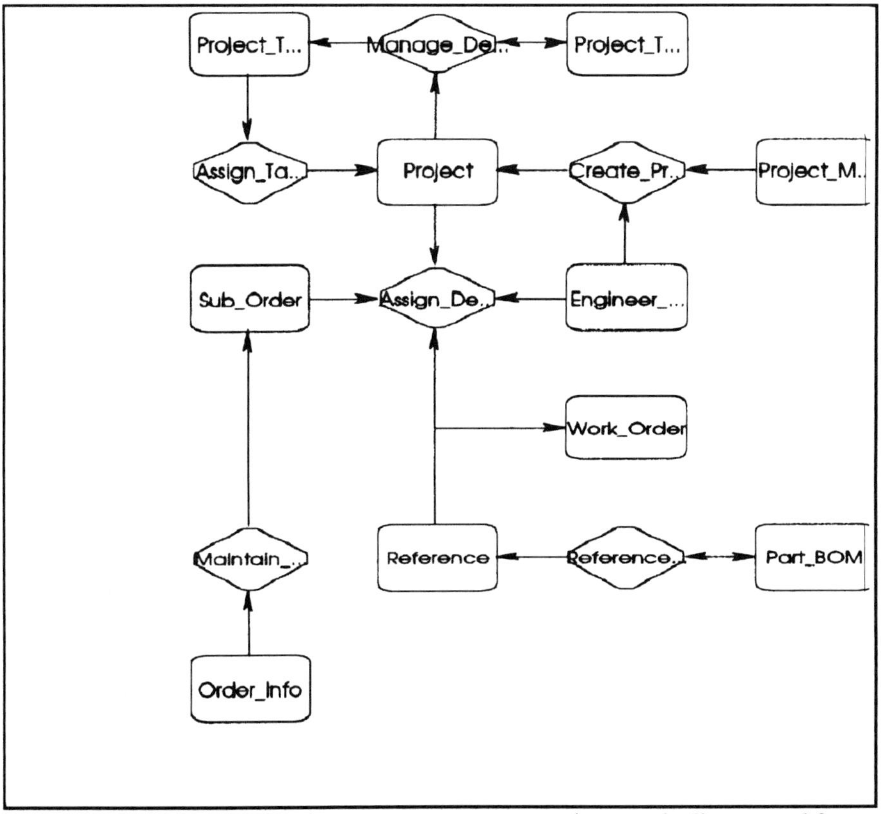

Fig. 3.9(a). SER for the project management system (automatically mapped from the DFD).

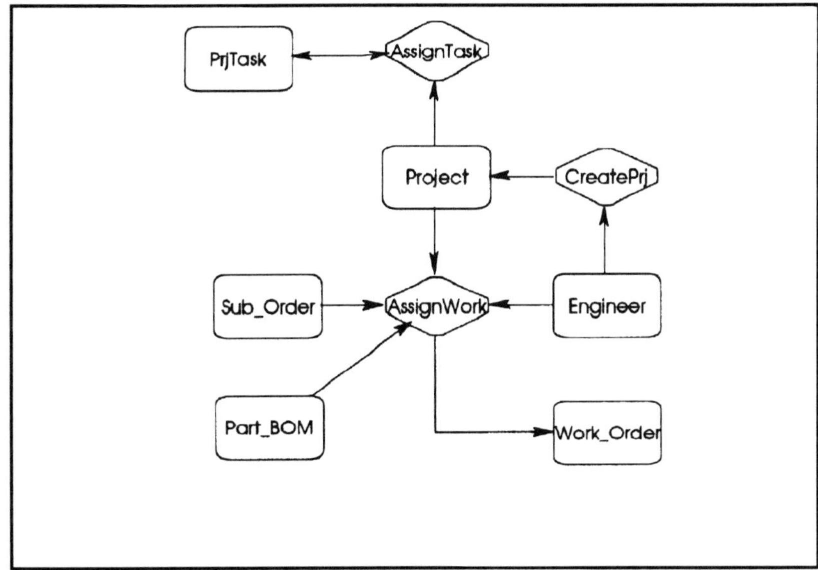

Fig. 3.9(b). SER for the project management system (manually modified).

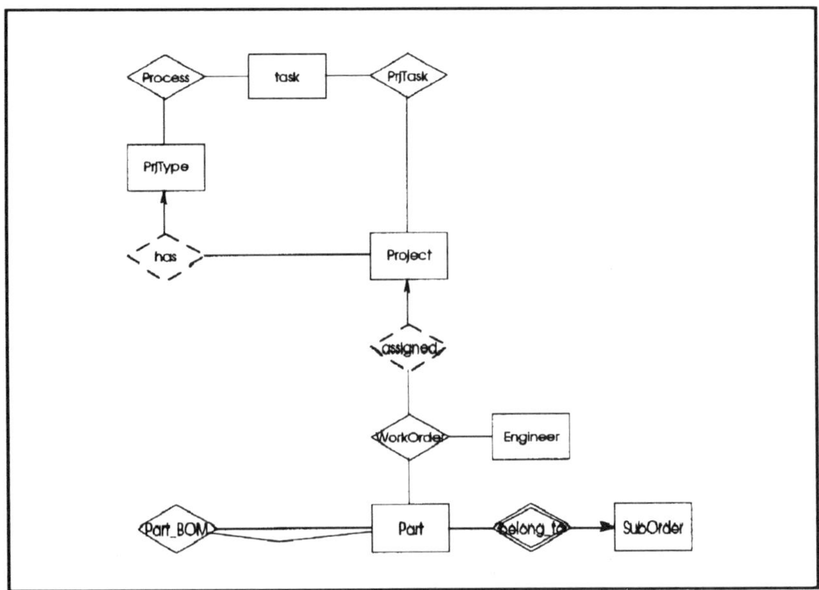

Fig. 3.10. OER for the project management system

Acknowledgment

Mr. Myung-Joon Jung developed the project management example in Section 3.6. In addition, Mr. Jangha Cho compiled data semantics for the CIM example in Section 3.5, Mr. Yicheng Tao compiled the TSER model for the O-O example in Section 3.3, and Mr. Somendra Pant compiled the data semantics for the Hospital example in Section 3.2 and the Banking example in Section 3.4. Both the Hospital and the Banking examples are based on similar examples in S. Atre, *Database: Structured Techniques for Design, Performance, and Management,* Wiley Interscience, 1980.

4

AN ENTERPRISE MODELING METHOD

The concepts discussed in chapter 1 need clearly an enterprise modeling method to facilitate their implementation in actuality. From the perspective of information integration, the method required can be formulated as one of meta-models dealing with multiple data and knowledge systems. This chapter presents such a method. The examples in chapter 3 also are some modeling cases illustrating the software implemntation of the method. All four types of enterprise metadata discussed in Chapter 1 are supported.

4.1 META-MODEL : THE CONCEPTUAL SCHEMA FOR INTEGRATED MULTI-MODEL ENVIRONMENTS

Business databases, manufacturing databases, and engineering design databases have traditionally followed different paths of evolution and espoused different paradigms, although they are all based on the same information technology. To compound the situation further, each paradigm has also prompted a number of different modeling tools since the advent of Computer-Aided Software Engineering (CASE). The integration of manufacturing functions must deal with the full scope of paradigm translation problem facing business, manufacturing and engineering design databases pertaining to the enterprise. Current strategies commonly employed by companies range from the formation of the so-called strategic alliances to reduce the number of different systems involved, all the way to the adoption of a common standard for all systems. The problem with a common standard is, ironically, the lack of a standard that is acceptable to the industry, suitable to all requirements, and adaptable to changing technology. The strategic alliance approach tends to rely on "hand-shaking", i.e., developing peer-to-peer solutions on an ad hoc basis, and hence is prone to suffering from the sheer size of (potential) number of pairs and is vulnerable to change to the contents of the models as well as to the compositions of the alliance.

Therefore, the notion of using a meta-model to anchor these paradigm translations has emerged recently. It can be traced back to the early IRDS work in U.S. Bureau of Standards and the CIMOSA project in EC under the ESPRIT consortium, among others. Major ongoing industry-led efforts under ISO include PDES community's project on developing a general information model for product design and process planning , and the IRDS community's endeavor under ANSI for formulating an encompassing framework involving common data and knowledge representation methods and ontology . Considering their all-encompassing nature, these visions may turn out to more likely be high-level reference models than particular meta-model solutions that can be immediately implemented for the needing manufacturing enterprises. In any case, many manufacturers can use compact solutions that are non-overwhelming in effort, reasonable in cost, and yet sufficiently support their integration needs. A particular meta-model system using the Two-Stage Entity-Relationship (TSER) method and the Metadatabase model is developed to provide a compact solution for this purpose.

The substantiation of the meta-model concept in this system spans three levels:

(1) At the modeling (or metadata) level, the meta-model is a neutral paradigm serving as the common representation method that all paradigms are translated into.

(2) At the models integration (or metadata management) level, the meta-model is a generic metadata schema abstracting and structuring all models into an integrated enterprise metadatabase.

(3) At the information management (or data instances) level, the meta-model is the integrated enterprise model contained in the metadatabase.

Clearly, the meta-model system is envisioned to not only support CASE tools management and paradigm translation per se, but also utilize the resultant metadata capabilities to directly facilitate the management of application information systems across the enterprise. The above concept is illustrated in Figure 4.1, where the Paradigm Translation Knowledge Kernel contains mapping knowledge for a layered mapping approach progressing from particular tools to their generic paradigms, then to the common core, as depicted in Figure 4.2.

The basic advantages of this meta-model approach are that, the complexity of the translation problem is simplified from n-square (pairwise connection) to n, where n is the number of representations involved, through the use of such an enterprise conceptual schema. The impact of any change to existing application models and systems, or addition of new ones, on the rest of the enterprise is also minimized. The feasibility of the system is demonstrated in a prototype discussed in Chapter 6.

The TSER method provides the meta-model at the first, modeling level; while the Metadatabase model which is itself represented using TSER avails the second (through its schema) and the third (through its instantiation) levels of meta-model. This completeness is a unique characteristic of the meta-model: it provides a seamless integration of functionalities at all levels as well as a logical synergism of these metadata concepts. In comparison, virtually all other results in the field fall either in the category of information modeling (level one plus aspects of level two) or in multiple-databases management (level 3 plus aspects of level 2. The value of such an integrated solution for the enterprise information integration problems is sufficiently documented in the metadatabase literature. TSER alone, as a meta-modeling method, offers an implementation-proven compactness if not comprehensiveness in the field. As discussed above, we believe that a major contribution in compactness that facilitates the actual implementation and therefore fosters the real integration is needed.

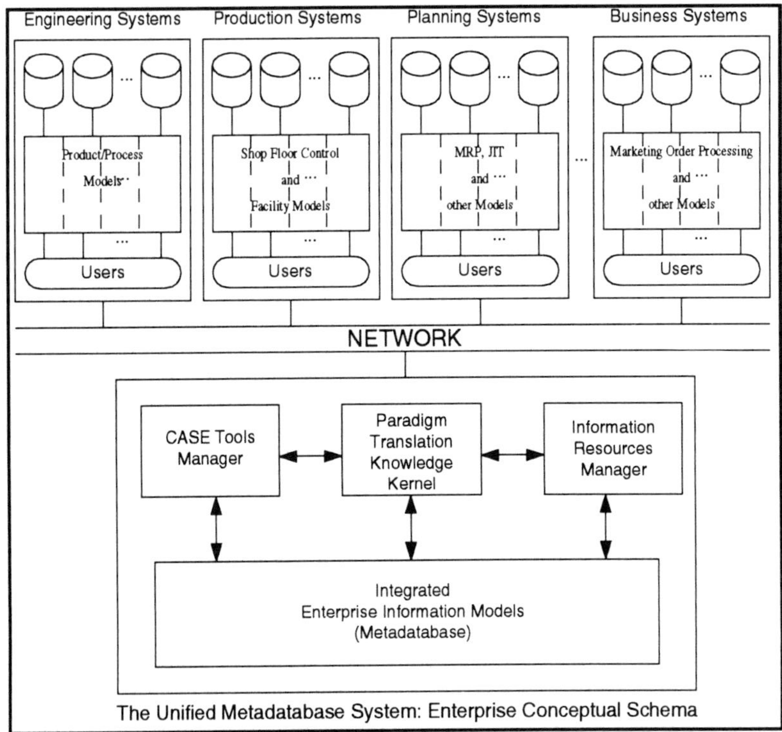

Fig. 4.1. Enterprise Information Integration Using Meta-Models

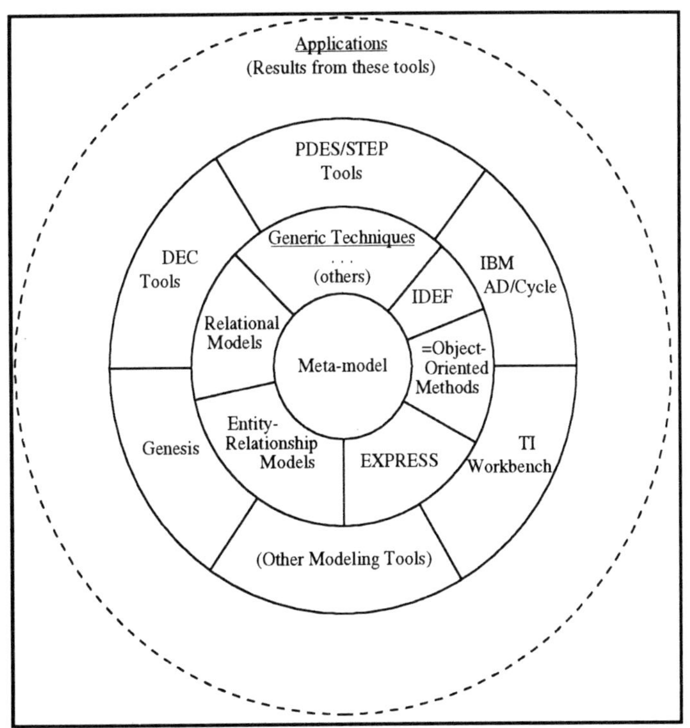

Fig. 4.2. The Paradigm Translation Knowledge Kermel for Layered Mapping

4.2. THE TWO-STAGE ENTITY-RELATIONSHIP (TSER) APPROACH TO META-MODELS

The perfect but unlikely meta-model evidently must support all conceivable paradigms now and in the future. A little more realistic expectation is that an ideal method would satisfy several requirements that can be derived from the literature and the above vision. The requirements include (1) the ability to represent major classes of knowledge concerning manufacturing processes in operating, control, and decision areas, (2) the inclusion of all pertinent models from a multi-stage analysis and design life cycle, (3) the neutral accommodation of heterogeneous data views (especially relations and object hierarchies), and (4) the unified representation of the full content of these metadata.

Concerning the representation of knowledge, a major element of these classes of knowledge is "flows" or dynamics that can be characterized with digraphs, such as data flows and control flows in the model. These global flows cannot be sufficiently represented through any implicit methods that embed knowledge into an encapsulation around data types. Such encapsulation methods are amenable mainly to localized triggers, contingency definitions, and other similar application logic. A combination of encapsulation and digraph techniques using certain generic primitives would suffice the need.

An objective for combining multi-stage models is isomorphism. That is, the mapping from a model at one stage of the life cycle to a model at the next stage should be complete and accurate. A corollary of this isomorphism is a reversible modeling process where, after the initial development of systems has long been completed, the information models that resulted from the initial analysis and design can be recovered from the metadatabase.

On the issue of data representation, a clear need is to encompass heterogeneity as exemplified by the relational approach and the object-oriented paradigm, two recent alternative models. It is evident that each has revealed certain unique but fundamental elements of the science of data modeling that have to be considered by any general model. In particular, the relational approach has, among other things, established the dependency theory for data integration (i.e., removal of redundancy) and the principle of separating applications and user views from common data structures; while the object-oriented paradigm asserts (or reasserts) the data abstraction hierarchy and integration of certain classes of transactions with data modeling.

There is probably no ideal method existing presently that satisfies all of the above requirements. However, the meta-model scope and structure aim directly at *subjects* of databases and their *contexts* for information integration, leading to a particular representation method which is discussed below.

4.2.1. The Modeling Method : TSER

The Two-Stage Entity-Relationship (TSER) model was first developed to integrate some tasks of system analysis with database design in complex enterprises and was later expanded to include knowledge representation. It entails two levels of modeling constructs devised respectively for semantics-oriented abstractions (i.e., the functional constructs defined below) and cardinality-oriented (normalized) representations (i.e., the structural constructs defined below) of data and production rules. The constructs allow for top-down system development, as well as bottom-up design, i.e., reverse engineering of existing applications or software packages into the TSER constructs. There are rigorous TSER algorithms which map from semantic to structural models and these algorithms ensure that the resulting structures are in at least third normal form. TSER algorithms also integrate views, thus allowing systematic consolidation of any number of data models. The integrity constraints built into the TSER constructs are used to facilitate the management and control of the metadatabase.

The Functional (Semantic) Modeling Constructs

The first stage features user-oriented semantic-level constructs for object-hierarchy and processes representation. They are used for system analysis and information requirements modeling; referred to in TSER as the Functional (or SER) Level Modeling Constructs; and employed exclusively for capturing semantics. The constructs include the following :

Subject:

Subject

Primitives:
Contains data items (attributes), functional dependencies (among data items), *intra*-SUBJECT rules (triggers, events, and dynamic definitions of data items belonging to a single SUBJECT), and association hierarchies (explodes as well as generalizes and aggregates SUBJECTs). A (sub-) subject may be associated with one or many (super-) subjects in the hierarchy. Specific types of association include : **Full inheritance** (is-a, mandatory relationship; used for classification), **Partial Inheritance** (related-to, plural relationship, may be function-defined; used for grouping), **Referential Inheritance** (attribute type, functional relationship; used to define the domain or data type of an attribute), **Composing Inheritance** (part-of, mandatory relationship; used for construction such as complex objects), and **Process** (no inheritance — no integrity implications on information management).

Description:
Represents functional units of information such as user views, forms, and application systems, and is analogous to frame or object or activity. The process type of association is found in the representation of flows where a subject is decomposed (but not inherited) for modeling convenience; while the other types are typical of inheritance hierarchies in semantic representations.

Context:

Context

Primitives:

Contains *inter*-SUBJECT rules (characterized by references to data items belonging to multiple SUBJECTs), typically includes directions of flows for logic (decision and control) and data (communication, etc.). It is allowed to contain only descriptive rules used for holding together a set of SUBJECTs or SER models that otherwise do not have direct associations. Also contains definitional or declarative statements, especially those for the types of association (e.g., inheritance) - see Subject.

Description:
Represents interactions among SUBJECTs and control knowledge such as business rules and operating procedures and is analogous to process logic. Depending on the type of association, two modeling planes are represented through this unifying construct: one for subjects that are associated through inheritance (hierarchy) and the other for process organization (decomposition).

Note:
(1) The full contents (as applicable) must be specified for all SUBJECTs at the leaf level of the SUBJECT hierarchy. The class hierarchy implies integrity rules for applications, but its presence is not required.
(2) Rules are constructed in the form of (a subset of) predicate logic where all clauses must only consist of the logical operators and the data items that have been declared or defined in the SUBJECTs (except for certain key words such as *do* and *execute*.). A data item may be defined to represent an executable routine, algorithm, or mathematical expression.
(3) The three types of association of Subjects may exist simultaneously in a model and thereby create three abstraction plains for Subjects; namely, (i) generalization and strong aggregation (the classification type), (ii) ad hoc aggregation (the grouping type), and (iii) simple decomposition similar to Data Flow Diagram and IDEF (the process type).

The Structural (Normalized) Modeling Constructs

The second stage is concerned with providing a neutral normalized representation of data semantics and production rules from functional model for logical database design; and referred to in TSER as the structural (or OER) model. There are four basic constructs described below.

Operational Entity (OE):

Entity

Description:
Entities; identified by a singular primary key and (optional) alternative keys and non-prime attributes.
Entity Integrity - no component (attribute) of a primary key may accept null value, and no primary key (as a whole) may accept duplicate values.

Plural Relationship (PR):

Description:
Association of entities; characterized by a composite primary key and signifying a many-to-many and independent association.

Associative Integrity - each of the PK's component attributes must be a PK of some Entity and its values in the PR must match that in the Entity.

Functional Relationship (FR):

Description:

A many-to-one association that signifies characteristic traits or composition relationships (corresponding to the grouping type of association of SUBJECTs). FRs represent the referential integrity constraints implied by the existence of foreign keys. The arrow side is called the *determined* side and points to either an OE or a PR, while the other side is called the *determinant* and is also linked to either an OE or a PR. The primary key of the *determined* side is included as a non-prime attribute (i.e., a foreign key) of the *determinant* side.

Referential Integrity - the value of every foreign key in the *determined* must either be null or be identical to some PK value in the *determinant*.

Mandatory Relationship(MR):

Description:

A one-to-many *fixed* association of OEs that signifies derived and inheritance relationships (corresponding to the classification type of association of SUBJECTs). MRs represent the existence-dependency constraint, and are symbolized as a double diamond with direction. The "1" side is linked to the *owner* OE while the arrow side points to the *owned* OE.

Existence Dependency - when the *owner* instance is deleted, then all *owned* instances associated will it must also be deleted; and there is a foreign key implied in the *owned* whose value must match exactly the *owner*'s PK value.

Note:

(1) In both top-down design and reverse engineering, the structural model is typically *derived* automatically from the functional model by using the TSER normalization and mapping algorithms.

(2) While there usually are multiple functional models representing different views or application systems of an enterprise model, there always exists only one integrated structural model for the global system.

In sum, underlying these constructs at both stages are two types of primitives: data items and predicate logic. Therefore, the basic structure of TSER metadata is characterized by (1) data representation as relations, (2) knowledge representation in the form of production rules, and (3) the two representations being tied via data items.

4.2.2. The Meta-model for Information Modeling

The translation of usual paradigms into TSER would be best comprehended by first examining the inner working of TSER as a modeling paradigm itself. From the perspective of an information modeling methodology, the TSER method may be described as follows. There are actually a variety of modeling perspectives supported by TSER, including data modeling, knowledge modeling, and functional modeling that combines both. The set of constructs for functional modeling is comprised of SUBJECTs and CONTEXTs and is used to represent data semantics and knowledge as viewed from an application level or a systems analysis perspective. These constructs may be employed in their entirety or just subsets of them, depending on the perspective and tasks intended. To illustrate how SUBJECTs and CONTEXTs may be employed separately to perform some major tasks for data or knowledge modeling, they are compared to certain traditional notions in Table 4.1. Perform traditional data modeling tasks for, say, relational or object-oriented database design would not require CONTEXTs (or even the intra-subject knowledge). A model using SUBJECTs alone would suffice the requirements of semantic data modeling, and then lead to the normalized structure (OER) through the attendant mapping algorithms. Similarly, Subjects could serve as only certain reference points for recognizing and grouping rules via Contexts in rulebase modeling. When, on the other hand, both SUBJECT and CONTEXT are used, the resulting model would encompass what is usually referred to as functional models of structured systems analysis. Again, in the case of TSER, the functional level model would include data semantics and knowledge which would then be structured into normalized combined representations, i.e., the structural level model. The structural modeling constructs are one type of entity and three special types of associations that refine the representation of data and production rules captured in the functional model of logic design. They, too, may be decoupled from the functional constructs and used for modeling in their own right. In this manner, they can be compared to the traditional Entity-Relationship model except for the rigorous definitions in TSER. These definitions ensure proper data structures and integrity rules for the design of databases or rulebases or their combination.

In the usual case where the models of more than one system are being developed, a three-step process for basic global information modeling is used. First, a functional model (hierarchy) for each application system is created; second, each model is mapped to its corresponding structural model; and third, the several structural models are consolidated into a single global structural model using dependency-theoretical principles (e.g., normalization). When systems integration is actively formulated on top of this basic model, step 2 would be expanded to provide a single functional model. That is, the several functional models would be integrated into a global functional model by creating and populating *inter*-application CONTEXTs with the control knowledge and operating rules that define the interactions among application systems. This process represents the traditional top-down modeling in the common life cycle of systems analysis and design.

Table 4. 1. The TSER Modeling Portfolio

Constructs	Perspective	Comparable Methods
Subject (used alone)	Data Modeling	Semantic Data Models and Object-Oriented Models
Context (used alone)	Knowledge Modeling	Process and Flow Models, and Rule-Based. Models
Subject and Context	Functional Modeling	Functional Models (e.g., DFD and IDEF0)
Entity and Relationships (used directly)	Data Modeling	Entity-Relationship Models

Paradigm translation, on the other hand, is based on bottom-up reverse engineering. This process, however, will piggy-back on the top-down capability of TSER. In essence, reverse engineering calls for a general guideline whose specificity depends largely on the particular systems to be translated in reverse engineering. The general guideline employs TSER functional constructs to represent the local models and then proceed from there following the usual (top-down) methodology. For example, base relations, views, or data files would be represented as subjects, with additional data semantics being modeled into functional dependencies, intra-subject rules, or contexts. File systems, Relational systems, and other Entity-Relationship models are clearly compatible to be modeled as SUBJECTs. Translating Object models into TSER is accomplished in Section 4.4. The above logic is depicted in Figure 4.3, which includes both top-down modeling and reverse engineering approaches.

4.2.3. The Metadatabase Conceptual Schema Using TSER

The Metadatabase is constructed from combining all models and views in Figure 4.3, along with other classes of metadata such as software and hardware resources. All of these combined metadata are organized according to a conceptual schema which is the meta-model for models (or metadata resources) integration. The populated metadatabase directly participates in the management of enterprise information and facilitates the integration of local systems. Therefore, the metadatabase becomes a data instance level meta-model not only to support CASE tools and other passive metadata applications, but also to effect functionalities needed in global query processing and systems interactions.

The development of this generic metadatabase schema is reported in Chapter 7. In a nutshell, the schema follows directly the generic logic of TSER and contains all three classes of views (application, functional, and structural) plus resources views (see Figure 7.3). Its structure is also based on TSER modeling constructs (a class of self-descriptiveness). The design is generic excepting Software and Hardware Resources, which are extensible depending on particular enterprises. Therefore, once created, the meta-schema will stay stable and the addition or deletion of models will become merely metadata transactions inserting into or removing from the metadatabase.

4.3. BASIC MAPPING ALGORITHMS OF TSER

There are two basic groups of mapping algorithms supporting TSER as a modeling method. The first derives normalized structures from the functional model and the second uses the resulting structures to design database schema, including relations and integrity rules, object-oriented hierarchies, and CODASYL data structures. In addition, the rules that are captured in the functional model (Context and Subject) are also grouped into a persistent rulebase model associated with the data structures that use them/they use. This grouping is performed directly according to the schema of the rulebase; which is developed using the same principles of the metadatabase schema and the same dependency theory that the structural mapping for database design employs. In addition to these two basic groups are algorithms that perform paradigm translations for specific target models.

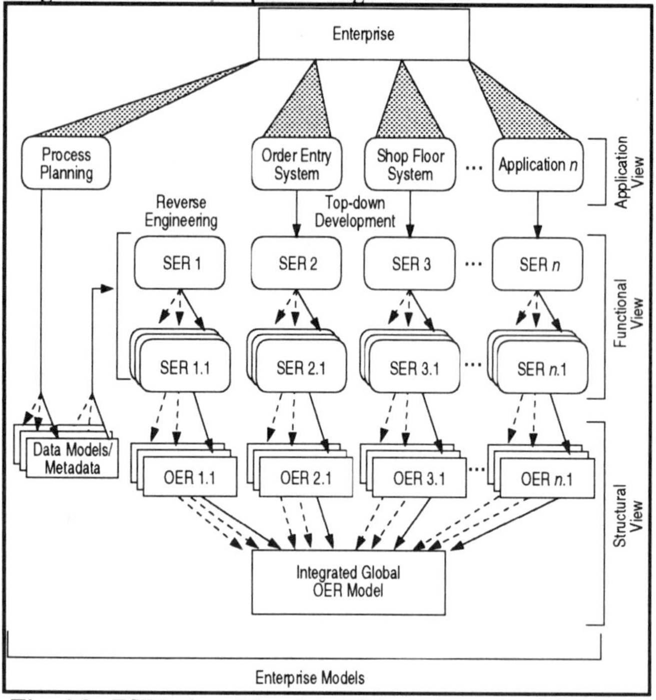

Fig. 4.3. TSER As a Meta-Model for Information Modeling

4.3.1. Functional-to-Structural Mapping Algorithm

The mapping process is carried out in three main steps. The first step, called DECOMPOSITION, creates a submodel for each SUBJECT in the hierarchy (excepting the process type of association - or, decomposition plain, where only the leaf level SUBJECTs are substantive for mapping) and analyzes its basic cardinality. The second, NORMALIZATION step, improves and simplifies the data structures within each submodel based on dependency theory. Finally the third step, CONSOLIDATION, links and merges these submodels to produce an OER model corresponding to the SER in the input. The global variables used by the three steps are categorized as follows:

A. *Fields* : which represent the fundamental (generic or worldlike) objects.. The value of a field can be either a simple atom such as the name of an entity or relationship, or a group of atoms such as the attributes of an entity or relationship. These fields are the following:

NAME : represents the name of a structure (entity or relationship).
KEY : the primary key of a structure.
ALTKEY : the alternate keys.
NONKEY : the non-key attributes of a structure.
TYPE : A designation telling whether the structure is an OE, PR, MR, or FR.
INVOLVEDIN : A list of the entities and relationships involved in a PR, or associated with an OE.
OWNER, OWNED : used only in MR structures to denote the owner and owned side of an MR, respectively.
DETERMINANT, DETERMINED : used only with FR structures to denote the determinant and the determined sides of an FR, respectively.
FDS : a list used only in the SE's to contain the list of all the functional dependencies among its attributes.
PR-DANT : a list used to contain the list of all composite determinants in FDS which are partially involved with key attributes.

B. *Structures* : Two fields or more are grouped together to form a structure, which can be a semantic entity or an operational entity/relationship. There are six major types of structures :

SE : represents a Subject; it has four fields : NAME, KEY, NONKEY, and FDS.
OE : represents an entity, consisting of five fields : NAME, TYPE, KEY, NONKEY, and INVOLVEDIN.
PR : represents a plural relationship. It contains the same fields as an OE.
MR : represents a mandatory relationship, consisting of the fields: NAME, TYPE, KEY, OWNER, and OWNED.
FR : represents a functional relationship using four fields : NAME, TYPE, DETERMINANT, and DETERMINED.
GROUP : this structure is used only in the Normalization step. It represents a collection of non-key attributes related to each other by a FD. It consists of two fields: DANT for the determinant side and DED or the determined side of a FD.

C. *Lists* : Groups of structures sharing some properties are linked together to form lists. The major lists used in the mapping algorithms are:

SER : list of all the Subjects in the input.
SM : list of Subjects and Contexts in a submodel.
SMS : list of all the submodels.
OER : the results of the mapping, which is a list of all the entities and relationships in the OER model.
GROUPS : a list whose elements are of type GROUP.
ASS-ATT : a temporary list, used to keep track of the non-key attributes already assigned to the OE's created during the decomposition.

The DECOMPOSITION Step

An SE having a composite primary key (PK) is recognized as an association of some generic entities. Thus, it is decomposed into a plural relationship (PR) and certain operational entities associated with it. The PR inherits the name and the primary key of a particular OE in the relationship. Then the non-key attributes of the SE in question are assigned among the PR and its OE's according to the functional dependencies (and also be asserted by the semantic rules in the knowledge base). However, if the SE's PK is singular, it is identified as an OE. The result of this process in either case is declared as a submodel. This information of submodels provides an access path for information production. Procedure for this step is given below:

```
Procedure DECOMPOSITION (SE);
begin
        PK:=SE.KEY;
        AK:=SE.ALTKEY;
        NPK:=SE.NONKEY;
        FD:=SE.FDS;
        PR-DANT:=Get_PR-DANT(SE.FDS);
        if Length(PK) > 1 then
        begin               /* case of composite key */
                PR:=create('PR');
                PR.NAME:=SE.NAME;
                PR.KEY:=PK;
                ASS-ATT:=NIL;
                Dants:=FirstSet(PR-DANT);
                while Dants ≠ NIL do
                        SubPR:=create('PR');
                        SubPR.NAME:=Naming('PR', Dants);
                        SubPR.KEY:=Dants;
                        SubPR.NONKEY:=AssignAtt(Dants, NPK, FD);
                        Insert(SubPR, SM);
                        Dants:=NextSet(Dants, PR-DANT);
                end;
                K:=First(PK);    /* start with the first component in PK */
                while K ≠ NIL do
                begin                   /* for each component in the PK an OE is created */
                        OE:=Create('OE');
                        OE.NAME:=Naming('OE',K);      /* give the OE a name */
                        OE.KEY:=K;
                        OE.NONKEY:=AssignAtt(K, NPK, FD);
                        OE.INVOLVEDIN:=PR.NAME;
                        PR.INVOLVEDIN:=AddList(PR.INVOLVEDIN, OE.NAME);
                        UpdatePR_Involved(OE, PR-DANT, PK, SM);
                        Insert(OE, SM);          /* Store OE's in corresponding submodel */
```

```
                                    K:=Next(K, PK);                  /* proceed to
the next component in PK */
                        end;
                        PR.NONKEY := Difference(NPK, ASS-ATT);
                        Insert(PR, SM);
                end;
                else                /* case of singular PK, just one OE is created in
that SM */
                begin
                        OE:=Create('OE');
                        OE.NAME:=SE.NAME;
                        OE.KEY:=PK;
                        OE.NONKEY:=NPK;
                        Insert(OE, SM);
                end;
end;
```

The NORMALIZATION Step

After decomposition, the next step is to identify the OE's and OR's that are embedded in the data abstraction in a submodel. Therefore, the second step decomposes the structures further to ensure at least the Boyce-Codd normal form(BCNF) for all OE's and the third normal form for all OR's. In fact, if multi-valued dependencies are properly represented as a one-to-one FD between the multiple attribute group (many-to-many) and itself, then the results of this normalization will be at least in the fourth normal form. It first unbundles the nested FD structures (if any) in the PR via the definition of new PR's, then removes the transitive functional dependencies (TFD) by representing them through functional relationships(FR's). At the end, it compiles all the relationships as necessary to include the semantic information.

Procedures NESTEDRELATIONS (ER) and TFD (ER) are devised for the further decomposition, but they are omitted from here due to space considerations; This decomposition is performed recursively, using two list for the same model: namely, TSM, which contains the OE's and PR's to be checked for TFD's, and SM which stores an OE or OR only if it does not contain any TFD.

All the relationships in a submodel after the normalization are compiled according to both the modeling rules and the operating knowledge (e.g., fixed associations between entities). The TSER system, when implemented, guides the user to make decisions based on the semantic rules. Examples include deciding when a PR or a FR should be declared as an MR; or providing a singular identifier for a PR; or converting an MR into an OE. These rules are a part of the modeling knowledge in the knowledge base. This normalization step is summarized in the procedure below:

```
Procedure NORMALIZATION (SM);
begin
        TSM:=NIL;               /* TSM is a temporary submodel to alternate
results */
        ER:=First(SM);
        while  ER ≠ NIL do      /* second normal form */
```

```
        begin
                        if  ER.TYPE  =  'PR'
                                then NESTEDRELATIONS(ER)
                                else  Insert(ER, TSM);
                        ER:=Next(ER, SM);
        end;
        SM:=NIL;
        ER:=First(TSM);
        while  ER ≠ NIL do          /* third normal form */
        begin
                        TFD(ER);
                        ER:=Next(ER, TSM);
        end;
        RelationCompilation(SM);            /* compilation of the relationships */
        Insert(SM, SMS);            /* store the SM contents and information in
SMS */
                                                        /* to be used in the
third step */
end;    /* procedure NORMALIZATION */
```

The CONSOLIDATION Step

The objective of this step is to produce the final OER model by connecting all submodels. This connection is made according to the modeling rules and the classification-specific knowledge in the knowledge base. Some of the rules include : (1) merging, respectively, the identical entities and relationships whose PKs are identical, (2) creating FR's through foreign keys, and (3) creating MR's or FR's between the submodels corresponding respectively to a superSE and its subSE according to association types (i.e., MR's for classification types and FR's for grouping types). All entities and relationships will be consolidated using certain heuristics to simplify their structures. The overall mapping algorithm is as follows:

```
Program SER->OER Mapping
begin
        SMS:=NIL;
        OER:=NIL;
        Input(SER);
        if    exists    Inheritance    relationships    in    SER
                                            /*  association  types  are
"classification" or "grouping" */
                        then for each SE in SER             /* the whole hierarchy
tree*/
                        else    for  each  SE  in  leaf  level  of  SER
                                                                /*    exists
Decomposition relationships only */
                                do
                                begin
                                        SM:=NIL;
                                        DECOMPOSITION(SE);
                                        NORMALIZATION(SM);
                                end;
        CONSOLIDATION(SMS);
```

Output(OER);
end.

The user (database designers) may modify the OER model derived by TSER to, e.g., obtain higher normal forms for data structures. These modifications can also be represented by virtue of the OER construct according to the definitions of OE, PR, FR, and MR. In any case, the finalized OER will, on the one hand, retain complete connection with the SER thereby allowing "zoom-in and zoom-out" between any levels of abstraction; it will also, on the other hand, lead to a complete schema design for target (or local) database systems.

4.3.2. Additional Algorithms : Models Integration, Rulebase Mapping, and Metadatabase Creation

The above mapping algorithms can be applied to two or more functional (SER) models as well. These multiple SER models may be results of paradigm translation from object-oriented, relational, or other entity-relationship models; they may also be other TSER applications (see Figure. 4.3). The CONSOLIDATION step will be executed to consolidate these models two at a time, after each is completely mapped to the structural model (OER). Additional metadata such as equivalence of data items across models will be employed in the step.

On the knowledge side, the rules in Contexts and Subjects will be further represented according to a rulebase model. This model relates all rules to data items comprising Entities and Relationships. The rulebase model is discussed in Section 4.3.4.

Finally, TSER extends to create the metadatabase conceptual schema (see Figure 4) for the enterprise models, and populate the metadatabase. This conceptual schema can be implemented in a number of paradigms just as any other OER model by using the algorithms discussed next.

4.3.3. CODASYL, Relational, and Object-Oriented Models Creation

The TSER models are translated directly into the CODASYL, relational, and object-oriented models, where only the latter needs the functional model (SER). A general framework for paradigm translation into the object-oriented models is outlined below.

Algorithm M1 : Mapping of TSER into Object-Oriented Models.

<u>Step 1.a</u> : SER -> O-O (option (a))

* Create an Object Class for every Subject, containing all attributes and knowledge.

* Create an Object Class hierarchy corresponding to the inheritance relationships among Subjects (i.e., association types "classification" and "grouping").

* Go to Step 2.

<u>Step 1.b</u> : SER+OER -> O-O (option (b))

* Create Object Classes from the OER model using Algorithm M2.

*   Create an Object Super-Class for each Subject, containing only an object identifier and (all) intra-subject knowledge.

*   Create a class hierarchy associating these Object Super-Classes according to the inheritance relationships among Subjects.

*   Create an inheritance (the classification type of association) between each Object Super-Class and the Object Classes created above from the OER model that corresponds to its Subject.

Step 2 : Distribution of inter-Subject rules into Object Classes.

*   Rules in every Context are incorporated into Object Classes according to the data items referenced in their condition clauses :

*   If the data items referenced in a rule belong mostly to a particular Subject, then the rule is incorporated into the Object Class corresponding to the Subject; otherwise use a tie breaker.

The structural model (OER) provides normalized data structures for implementation in any database. While directly leads to a relational model, it also fully characterizes a CODASYL model and avails a sound design for persistent objects at the foundations of objects class hierarchies.

Algorithm M2 : Mapping of OER into CODASYL, Relational, and Object-Oriented Models.

Step 1: Convert each Relationship (along with its participating Entities) individually into the target model according to the mapping rules depicted in following graphs.

Step 2 : Declare appropriate integrity constraints according to the OER structure :

(a)   For relational models: implement the key integrity rule for the OE's, and the referential integrity rule for the OR's.

(b)   For CODASYL models: implement the regular, mandatory, and fixed membership classes for FR's, PR's, and MR's, respectively.

(c)   For object-oriented models: implement the association types into appropriate inheritance rules available in the models/systems.

Step 3 : Implement the rules in the software environments (this step is implementation-specific).

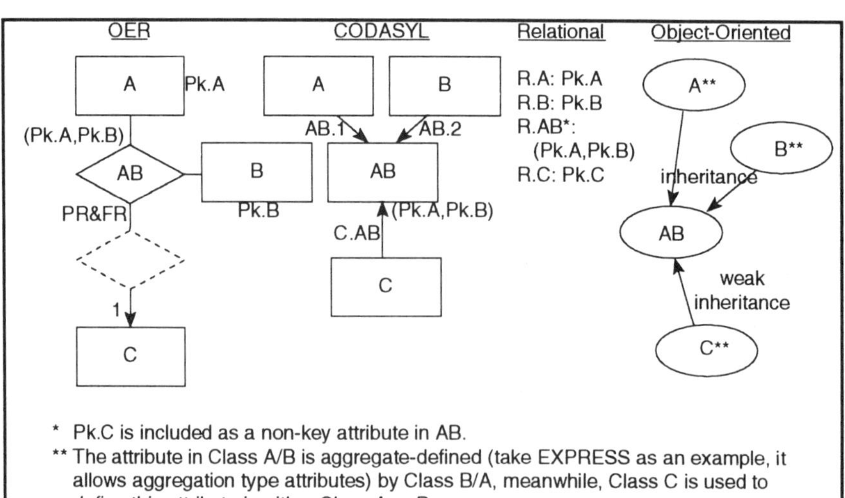

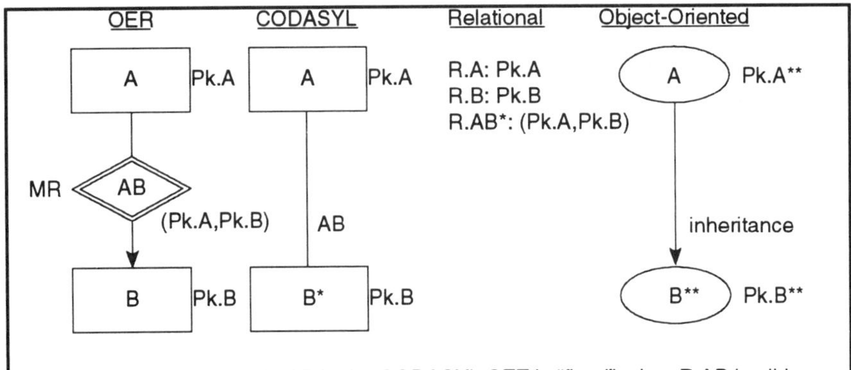
OER
CODASYL
Relational
Object-Oriented
A
Pk.A
A
Pk.A
R.A: Pk.A
R.B: Pk.B
R.AB*: (Pk.A,Pk.B)
A
Pk.A**
MR
AB
(Pk.A,Pk.B)
AB
inheritance
B
Pk.B
B*
Pk.B
B**
Pk.B**
* The membership of B in AB in the CODASYL SET is "fixed", also, R.AB is all-key.
** The membership of B is inherited, therefore is "fixed"; also, if Pk.A and Pk.B are system created primary keys, the the attribute should be eliminated, in this sense, they become all-key.

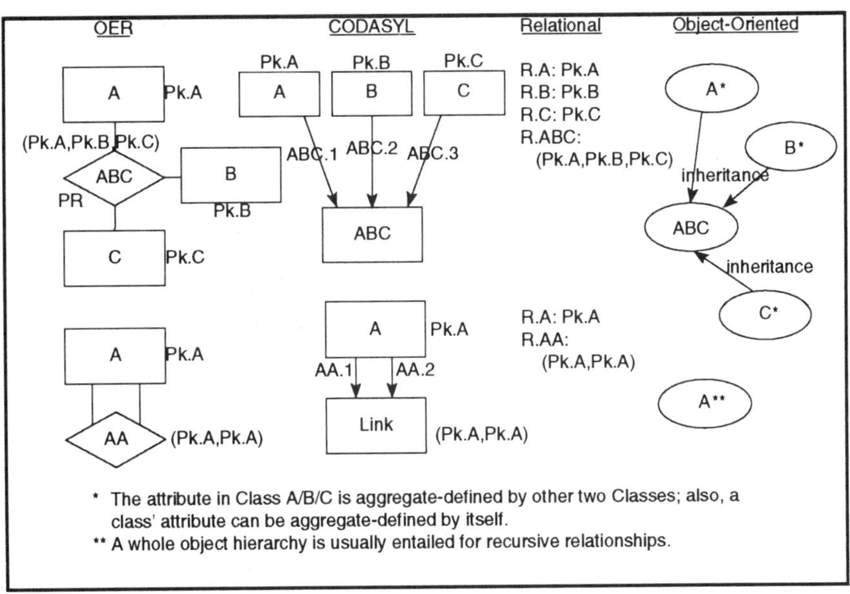
OER
CODASYL
Relational
Object-Oriented
A
Pk.A
(Pk.A,Pk.B,Pk.C)
ABC
PR
B
Pk.B
C
Pk.C
Pk.A
Pk.B
Pk.C
A
B
C
ABC.1
ABC.2
ABC.3
ABC
R.A: Pk.A
R.B: Pk.B
R.C: Pk.C
R.ABC:
(Pk.A,Pk.B,Pk.C)
A*
B*
inheritance
ABC
inheritance
C*
A
Pk.A
AA
(Pk.A,Pk.A)
A
Pk.A
AA.1
AA.2
Link
(Pk.A,Pk.A)
R.A: Pk.A
R.AA:
(Pk.A,Pk.A)
A**
* The attribute in Class A/B/C is aggregate-defined by other two Classes; also, a class' attribute can be aggregate-defined by itself.
** A whole object hierarchy is usually entailed for recursive relationships.

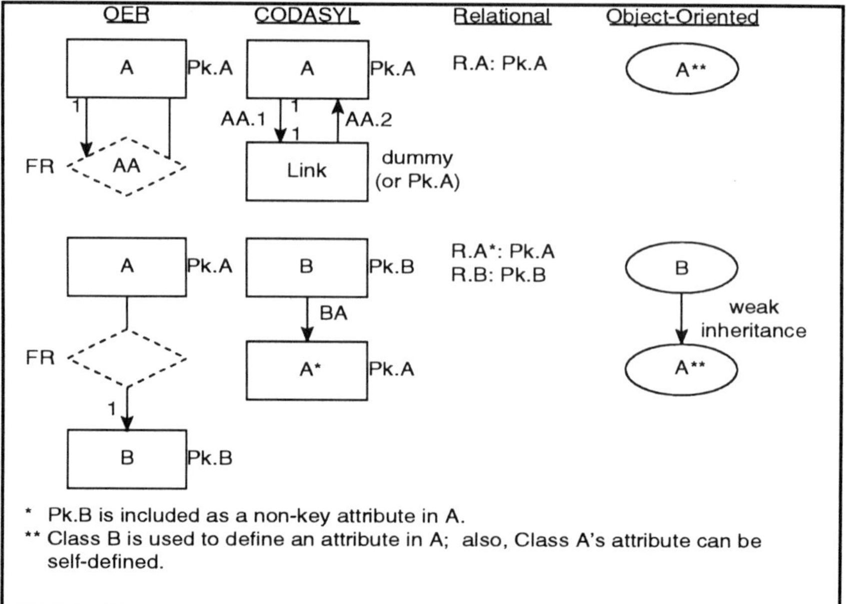

Fig. 4.4. Illustration of Algorithm M2

The general algorithm M2 can be illustrated with specific examples which cover comprehensively the various (primitive) cases found in an OER structure. These examples are shown in Figure 4.4.

4.3.4. Rulebase Model Creation

The rulebase model is anchored in three basic results established in the literature: (1) the metadatabase model for overall metadata integration, (2) the TSER model for information modeling primitives (metadata classes), and (3) the expression grammar, along with predicate logic, for production rule structures. The basic approach used in modeling knowledge in the metadatabase combines ideas from production rules, frames, and object-oriented representations, through the TSER modeling methodology. The basis of this derivation is the specific grammar of rules that we constructed from general results in the field. It is shown as G_1 and G_2 below.

G_1: (1) <Rule> ::= IF <Condition> THEN [<Action>]$^+$
(2) <Condition> ::= <Expression>
(3) <Action> ::= <Declarative-Statement> | <Assignment-Statement>| <Procedure-Call>
(4) <Assignment-Statement> ::= <Action-Ident> := <Evaluated-Fact>
(5) <Procedure-Call> ::= Procedure-name([<Parameter-List>]*)
G_2: (1) <Expression> ::= <Fact> <Operator> <Fact> | <Fact>
(2) <Fact> ::= <Evaluated-Fact> | <Declarative-Statement>
(3) <Evaluated-Fact> ::= <Simple-Fact> | <Composed-Fact>
(4) <Simple-Fact> ::= Constant | Item | <User-Ident> | <Action-Ident>
(5) <User-Ident> ::= Identifier

(6) <Action-Ident> ::= Identifier
(7) <Composed-Fact> ::= <Function-call> | <Expression>
(8) <Function-call> ::= Function-name([<Parameter-List>]*)
(9) <Parameter-List> ::= <Parameter>[, <Parameter-List>]*
(10) <Parameter> ::= <Fact>
(11) <Declarative-Statement> ::= <Simple-Fact> Verb <Simple-Fact>

TSER constructs are employed to represent the different components of the rulebase according to G1 and G2, and are consolidated into an overall normalized model shown in Figure 4.5, which is, in turn, incorporated into the meta-model in Figure 7.3 to represent contextual knowledge of enterprise models. The result of this consolidation also constitutes a generic structure for the rulebase model. This model can be implemented using commonly available database technology (such as relational databases) and routines/files manager plus an inference engine.

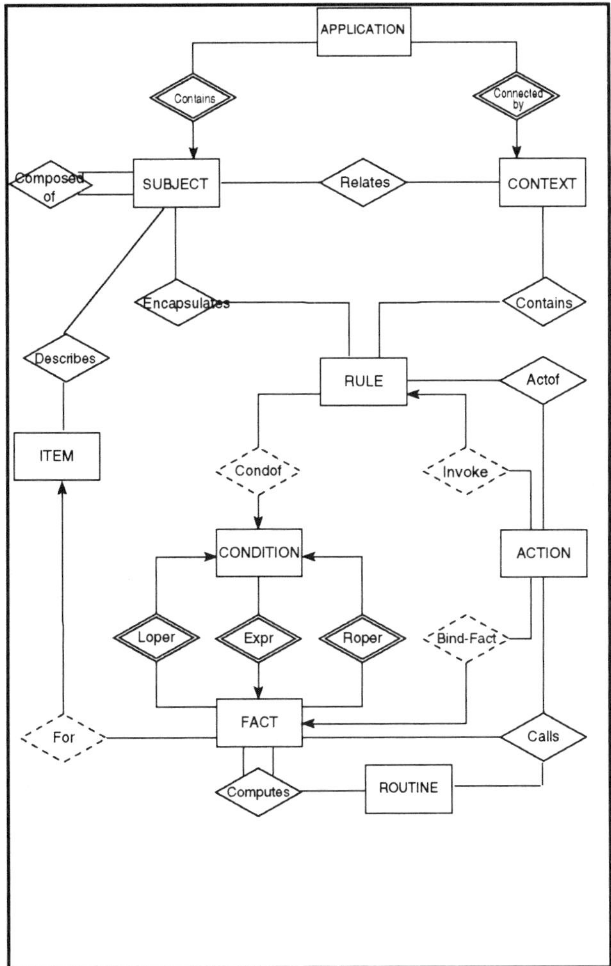

Fig. 4. 5. The Rulebase Model

4.4. PARADIGM TRANSLATION : THE STEP/EXPRESS CASE

EXPRESS is an information modeling language developed for product design and engineering databases under the auspices of ISO/STEP endeavors. It combines the traditional Entity-Relationship paradigm into the latest object-oriented paradigm with rules . The design also reflects a mix of data modeling construct with certain software engineering concepts for programming. As a result, EXPRESS is more powerful and complicated than one would expect for an object-oriented data definitional language. A reverse engineering success on EXPRESS paves the way for similar efforts on other object-oriented systems and entity-relationship models in the field.

4.4.1 The Mapping

EXPRESS is based on an extensible object-oriented semantic association knowledge model. It supports the basic association types of generalization and aggregation among the primitive objects, called entities. Generalization association is specified as "SUPERTYPE <classes/entities>" or "SUBTYPE <classes/entities>", and aggregation association is in the form of "instance_variable <aggregation>, key <identifier>." The class/entity properties can be inherited through the generalization association. Behavioral properties of a class/entity are specified as methods and rules. Also, in EXPRESS, there are two major categories of item definition. One is the item defined by **non-aggregation** type, i.e., items declared as real, integer, Boolean, Entity...etc. The other is the items defined by **aggregation** type, i.e., items declared as array, list, bag, set...etc. While the first category is straight forward, the second can be used to imply aggregate-defined entity/object hierarchy. This category actually represents multiple/plural relationships among entities from a usual data modeling perspective. The inheritance mechanism is the major characteristic of object-oriented concept. In EXPRESS, there are two ways to define the inheritance relationship between entities. The first is by using the keyword SELECT, which allows a child-entity's attributes inherited from one of its parent-entities. The second is by using the keyword SUBTYPE or SUPERTYPE, which allows a child-entity's attributes inherited from several parent-entities.

A general algorithm mapping an EXPRESS model into the TSER model is given below.

Algorithm RM1 : EXPRESS -> TSER

Step 1 : Convert the object definition into Subject.

* Create a Subject for each Entity.
* Create a Subject for each Type/Selection Type.

Step 2 : Model the specific item definition.

* Create Placeholder Identifier for each Subject if there is no UNIQUE (key declaration) item(s) in Entity.
* Create same items in Subject for those items declared through non-aggregation type in Entity.
* Declare FR's for those items declared through non-base type in Entity; also declare those items equivalent to non-base type's key

* Declare PR's for those items declared through aggregation type in Entity.

Declare FD's as "(key, aggregation type's key) <-> (key, aggregation type's key)" for PR-related items; and as "key -> other non-key items" in Subject.

Step 3 : Model the inheritance constructs.

* Duplicate Super-Subject's key in Sub-Subject for inheritance relationships (SUPERTYPE/SUBTYPE, or SELECTION).

* Declare FD's as "Sub-Subject's key -> Super-Subject's key".

Step 4 : Model the methods/rules and other special definitions.

* For methods that return a value : define a data item representing each method and model the method itself as an expression to be fired by a rule, according to the grammars of the rulebase model in Section 3.3;

* For other methods : model them as rules with all variables classified into data items that correspond to Subjects (names and attributes) and those that are other facts (also according to the rulebase model).

* Create from methods and rules Inter-Subject rules for each Subject, according to the SUBJECT definition.

* Create from methods and rules Intra-Subject rules in Contexts, according to the CONTEXT definition.

* Identify UNIQUE keyword and update declared items, FD's, equivalence table in Subject if necessary.

* Identify INVERSE keyword and update PR/FR declaration if necessary.

To illustrate this procedure, we first present an EXPRESS schema taken from a sheet metal design database, then show the result of its reverse engineering into TSER. Several comments follow. As shown in the example, each object/entity (e.g. Feature and Point_2D) is mapped to a Subject at the functional level. Most instance_variables (e.g., feature_ID, x, y, etc.) are attributes of a Subject. When converting the semantic meaning for the inheritance constructs, the generalization association is represented by a mandatory relationship (MR) and parent-entity's key (e.g., Feature's feature_ID) is added as a foreign key to child-entity (e.g., Close_Loop). Concerning methods (not shown in the above EXPRESS example) that return a value can be treated as derived data items and the function itself will be referred to by firing a rule. All other methods and rules can be mapped to operating rules of a Subject. Some special definitions should also be considered while converting EXPRESS into other models. One such definition is the keyword UNIQUE, which allows an object to have a key in entity, thus, can be used to define functional dependencies and the primary key for a Subject. Another is the keyword INVERSE, which allows some relationship constraints between entities, thus, implies necessary relationship modifications between Subjects.

4.4.2 The Example

A Sheet Metal EXPRESS Model

```
SCHEMA SheetmetalObjects;

ENTITY Feature;
        feature_ID: INTEGER;
        UNIQUE single: feature_ID;
END_ENTITY;

ENTITY Point_2D;
        x: Real;
        y: Real;
END_ENTITY;
```

```
ENTITY Line;
        start_Point: Point_2D;
        end_Point : Point_2D;
END_ENTITY;

ENTITY Arc;
        center_Point: Point_2D;
        start_Point : Point_2D;
        end_Point : Point_2D;
END_ENTITY;

TYPE
        geo_Type = SELECT(Line,Arc);
END_TYPE;

ENTITY Closed_Loop
        SUBTYPE OF (Feature);
        geo_List: LIST\[0:100] OF
geo_Type;
END_ENTITY;

...

ENTITY Sheetmetal_Feature
        SUBTYPE OF Closed_Loop);
        centerpoint : Point_2D;
        theta_Rot : REAL;
        datum_Feature : Feature;
        location_Tol : Loc_Tol_2D;
        gT_Position_Flag: BOOLEAN;
        gT_Position_Tol : REAL;
END_ENTITY;

ENTITY Loc_Tol_2D;
        x_Tol_Plus : REAL;
        x_Tol_Minus: REAL;
        y_Tol_Plus : REAL;
        y_Tol_Minus: REAL;
END_ENTITY;

...

ENTITY Sheetmetal_Part;
        plate_Charact : LIST 1:?] OF
Sheetmetal_Feature;
END_ENTITY;

ENTITY Product_Version
        product : Product;
END_ENTITY;

ENTITY Product;
        product_ID : STRING(5);
        components: LIST [1:?] OF
        Sheetmetal_Part;
        UNIQUE single : product_ID;
        INVERSE versions : SET[1:?]
OF Product_Version FOR product;
END_ENTITY;

END_SCHEMA;
```

The SER Model converted from the EXPRESS Example

```
SUBJECT Feature
ITEMS: feature_ID : INTEGER;
FD's : feature_ID <-> feature_ID;
END_SUBJECT;

SUBJECT Point_2D
ITEMS: $Point_2D : String;
        x : Real;
        y : Real;
FD's : $Point_2D -> (x, y);
END_SUBJECT;

SUBJECT Line;
ITEMS: $Line : String;
        $geo_Type : String;
        start_Point : String;
        end_Point : String;
FD's: $Line -> (start_Point, end_Point);
        $Line -> $geo_Type; // MR
efinition
Declare : FR
        Two FR between (Line,
Point_2D) due to items "start_Point" and
"end_Point"
        Equivalence :
                (start_Point,
$Point_2D)
                (end_Point,
$Point_2D)
END_SUBJECT;

        ...

SUBJECT geo_Type
ITEMS: $geo_Type : String;
FD's: $geo_Type <-> $geo_Type;
```

END_SUBJECT

SUBJECT Closed_Loop
ITEMS: $Closed_Loop : String;
feature_ID : INTEGER;
$geo_Type : String;
FD's: ($Closed_Loop, $geo_Type) <-> ($Closed_Loop, $geo_Type)
$Closed_Loop -> feature_ID; (MR)
Declare : PR
name of all key relation are "geo_List"
END_SUBJECT

...

SUBJECT Sheetmetal_Part
ITEMS: $Sheetmetal_Part : String;
$Sheetmetal_Feature : String;
FD's:
($Sheetmetal_Part, $Sheetmetal_Feature) <-> ($Sheetmetal_Part, $Sheetmetal_Feature)
Decalare : PR
name of all key relation are "plate_Charact"
END_SUBJECT

SUBJECT Product_Version
ITEMS: $Product_Version: String;
product: String;
FD's: $Product_Version -> product;
Declare: FR
One FR between (Product_Version, Product) due to item "product"
Equivalence :
(product, product_ID)
END_SUBJECT

SUBJECT Product
ITEMS: product_ID: String;
$Sheetmetal_Part : String;
versions : String;
FD's: product_ID -> versions;
(product_ID, $Sheetmetal_Part) <-> (product_ID, $Sheetmetal_Part)
Declare : PR
name of all key relation is "components"
Equivalence :
(versions, $Product_Version)
** product_ID becomes the key of this subject due to "UNIQUE" definition
** one PR has been replaced to be FR due to "INVERSE" definition
END_SUBJECT

A structural model (OER) of the object example is shown in Figure 4.6. Note that some of the relationships do not correspond directly to the original objects; but rather, they represent certain semantic information derived from objects that need to be represented in the metadatabase. For instance, start_Point in Line and Arc is associated with the equivalence definition start_Point = Point_2D. Similarly, plate_Charact in Sheetmetal_Part serves as a representation of the association between sheetmetal parts and features.

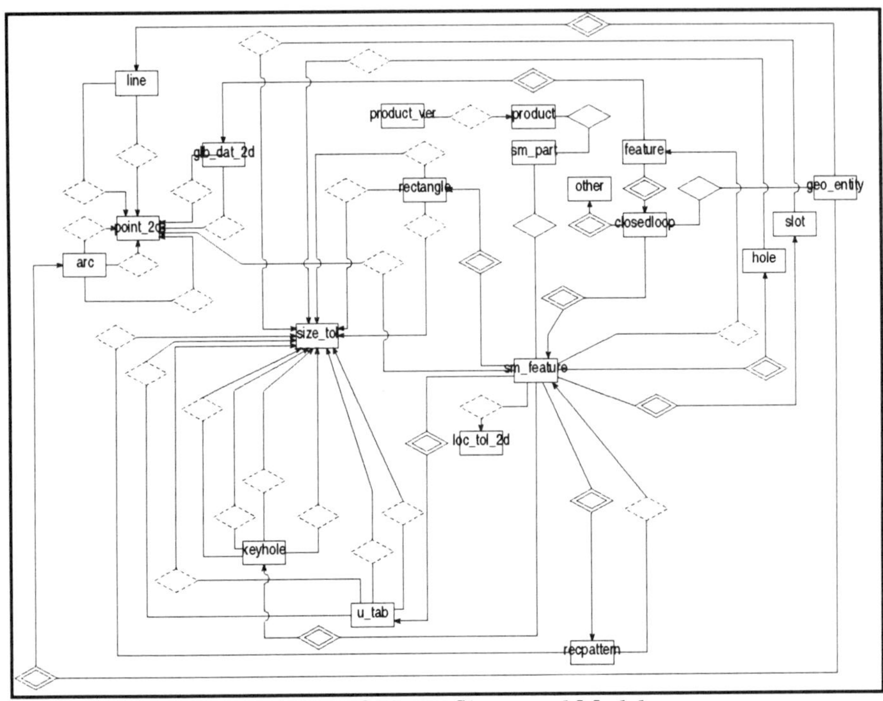

Fig. 4.6. OER for Sheetmetal Model

4.5. INFORMATION INTEGRATION USING META-MODELS

In sum, a compact meta-model solution is provided in this chapter. The basis of this solution, the TSER approach, is designed to be simplistic while accomplishing the necessary requirements of a meta-model method. At present, the TSER approach supports rule-based systems, object-oriented models, Entity-Relationship models, relational systems, CODASYL systems, and flat file systems in both concepts and methods; its software implementation includes automatic paradigm translations for EXPRESS and SQL and metadatabase creation capabilities for MicroVAX using Rdb and RS6000 using ORACLE. Its overall ontology is compatible with the spirit of the IRDS standards. New results from the ongoing research are expected to include further development of paradigm translations for particular models, database systems, and CASE tools. Development of a reference model with economical evaluation capability to guide integration modeling is an extension to the meta-model system. The Windows 3.1 version of the TSER software is made available - see the Free CASE Tool page of the book.

As a final remark, we might mention three contributions of this work to enterprise integration and modeling: the concept of meta-models, a complete model of its implementation using a metadatabase, and a tested modeling environment for supporting the needs of meta-modeling in an enterprise. Furthermore, the compactness of TSER, as evidenced in its implementation, is a significant advantage compared to other methods for models integration (See Chapter 10 for more discussion on this subject).

Acknowledgment

This chapter is based on a paper written by the author and three colleagues: Mr. Yicheng Tao and Drs. M'hamed Bouziane and Gilbert Babin. The paper is entitled "Paradigm Translation in Integrating Manufacturing Information Using a Meta-Model: The TSER Approach," *Information Systems Engineering*, Vol. 1, No. 3, 1993, pp 325-352. Particular recognitions include that, Mr. Tao developed the paradigm translation algorithm RM1 in section 4.4, with the help of Dr. Babin, and Dr. Bouziane developed the rulebase model described in section 4.3.3.

5

THE METADATABASE MODEL

The enterprise modeling method in chapter 4 provides enterprise metadata for information integration; thus an enterprise information manager (EIM) turning these metadata into action is readily in line to be developed. The metadatabase model develops such an EIM. In particular, it provides an organic architecture using ubiquitous enterprise metadata to facilitate dynamic alignment, as discussed in chapter 1. The details of the model are provided in the ensuing chapters while a technical overview is presented below.

5.1 THE BASIC CONCEPT OF THE METADATABASE MODEL

From the technical perspective, why can't the enterprise integration problem be sufficed with the available database results? What kind of a new model do we need? The answer to both questions is: Enterprise information management in significant organizations is characterized with multiple data and knowledge systems operating over wide-area networks whose hallmark is their defiance of traditional control models; in particular, they do not abide by any single standard, are not amenable to centralized administration, and cannot be comprehensively modeled for the entire enterprise once and for all. A prime case would be a modern manufacturing enterprise, where a single factory could easily include over a thousand databases running at a scale of over a million transactions a day. The complexity is overwhelming; in addition to such well-known issues of heterogeneous databases as interoperability and distributed updates, this environment also faces rapid changes in its underlying (data and knowledge) technology, business processes, and applications. Thus, the unpleasant reality of legacy systems and heterogeneity can hardly be expected to fade away over time as new standards are being brought in, since not only today's standards will become tomorrow's legacies, but also new cutting edge technologies will always emerge ahead of the standards that tend to require a long time to develop and take effect.

Succinctly this problem has a few unique technical imperatives:

Wide-area. The concept of enterprise naturally lends itself to an extended information model where customers, suppliers, and dealers are an integral part of the enterprise, just as the organization itself. Thus, the scope of interoperability must be explicitly and expressly anchored in wide-area or even global networks, as opposed to the LAN orientation of virtually all other models in the field.

Scalability. The total enterprise information integration environment must allow incremental development and be expandable, such that the integration can start with a small part of the enterprise and gradually extend to the rest (even to other organizations) over time, without losing operational continuity and structural integrity.

Adaptability. Systems that use either standard or non-standard technologies as well as new and legacy systems, can be incorporated into the integrated environment in a seamless way without causing any disruption to any existing system. Integration is not a one-shot accomplishment, but evolutionary.

Parallelism. The multiple systems must be able to operate concurrently while achieving synergism for the enterprise, without requiring global serialization or similar synchronization mechanisms imposed on any instance-level transactions.

Autonomy. Local systems in the integration need to have the flexibility to be designed, constructed, and administered independently by the local management alone, without having to conform, nor later convert, to a global schema.

An interesting observation of the above requirements is the revelation that they are fundamentally identical to the classical concept of data independence using the three-schema architecture; the difference is the "primitive," or primary concern, in each: At the (single-site) database level, the primary concern is multiple applications processing (shared) data instances; while at the enterprise level the primitive is multiple (database and knowledge-based) systems processing applications. Consider the fact that systems are modeled and hence substantiated with metadata, then it is evident that the enterprise-level problem can be formulated as a metadata problem whose conceptual complexity, in metadata terms, is similar to the traditional database-level problem. Therefore, in the spirit of data independence for scalable, adaptable, parallel, and autonomous applications against a database, we refer to the enterprise-level requirements of wide-area, scalable, adaptable, parallel, and autonomous databases against a globally integrated environment (called metadatabase) as **metadata independence**.

With this property, application systems and models will be viewed, operated, modified, added, or deleted against the EIM without uncontrollable repercussions on the rest of the environment. The search for a solution to the enterprise information management problem is, it follows, focused on transforming the data problem into a metadata problem and bringing the proven model of databases to the enterprise level, thereby effecting a **metadata independent architecture** to simplify the complexity. The key idea is to concentrate the EIM on metadata management rather than the virtually intractable task of managing directly the data instances (the above manufacture that incurs millions of data instance transactions would most likely incur only hundreds or at most thousands of changes of models and rules, and hence orders of magnitude less transactions in metadata). The management of data instances, on the other hand, can be coordinated with distributed, embedded metadata at the local database level by the local databases. The result is the metadatabase model.

The next question is, ofcourse, how to develop such an architecture. Traditionally, database researchers all cherished three principles: the use of a (global) data model, the reliance on an integrated schema, and the enforcement of global serialization. This tradition has been carried on throughout the myriad efforts in developing distributed databases, federated databases, and multidatabases, and is still dominating in many of the latest endeavors; all of which are primarily limited to local-area network environments. Although a great deal of progress has been accomplished in the past decade on, e.g., interoperability, local autonomy, and open system architecture, a great deal more still remains to be accomplished, which centers especially around the issues of concurrent processing and architecture adaptability. Other aspects of metadata independence mentioned above are also based on these two technical issues. The metadatabase solution to this problem, therefore, entails three basic elements addressing these issues and transforming the three database principles into an enterprise-level design to achieve metadata independence:

(1) **An enterprise information model:** this model globally represents all local data models and their contextual knowledge in the enterprise with a metadata-independent structure which, when put online, allows all local models and other metadata contained in it to be added, deleted, or modified through ordinary metadata transactions (as opposed to a fixed global data model);

(2) **An online (independent, but sharable) metadatabase:** this metadatabase implements the enterprise information model, and comprises a scalable, distributed hierarchy of super-, peer-, or sub-metadatabases for any scope of integration in a (WAN-expandable) client-server manner (as opposed to schema integration); and

(3) **A concurrent architecture for execution:** this architecture (including its execution model) supports concurrent processing of local systems with localized distributed control knowledge at local systems (as opposed to global serialization); in fact, it is knowledge-based and reconfigurable through the metadatabases.

These three basic elements are joined into the metadatabase-supported scalable integration hierarchy. While most of other database research in the field today is concerned mainly with technologies which are based either on single-system or on LAN environments and considers integration as an accomplishment at and for a fixed point in time, the metadatabase model provides a unique solution for the enterprise integration problem that responds to the challenge of dynamic alignment over time. We claim, without proof at this moment, that the model minimizes the global traffic and maximizes the global performance. Its computational complexity can be shown as O(N) in the number of sites.

Immediately based on the metadatabase model, an extension into user interface using the Visual Information Universe paradigm is also achieved. The objective is to develop necessary information technology supporting the kind of ubiquitous user interface that enterprises need to do things like employee empowerment and corporate-wide networking. Multimedia and virtual reality technologies are included in this information visualization technology. The basic design of the metadatabase model is overviewed next.

5.2 THE BASIC DESIGN

The metadatabase model as discussed above, realizes the unique solution approach that converts the integration problem from one that deals directly with data instances to one that controls through metadata, and thereby provides metadata independence for multiple systems. This approach effects concurrent processing and architecture adaptability through the following portfolio of results.

5.2.1 The Basic Model: A Metadatabase-Supported, Rule-Oriented Concurrent Architecture

The concurrent architecture that effects the third element in the above metadatabase solution is depicted in Figure 5.1. A detailed discussion of its development and execution methodsis found in Chapter 9.

The metadatabase itself (a rigorously constructed collection of enterprise metadata) provides an integrated enterprise model for the multiple information systems, their databases, and the interactions among the different systems; i.e. the information contents and their contextual knowledge. The metadatabase approach (1) uses the enterprise model to assist end-users performing global queries free of both technical details and a hierarchy of integrated schemata; (2) distributes the contextual knowledge to empower these local systems to update data and communicate with each other without central database control; and (3) incorporates legacy, new or changed local models into its generic structure of metadata to support evolution without system redesign or recompilation. The shells in the concurrent architecture, therefore, implements the distributed (localized) knowledge which, in turn, is managed by the metadatabase. The shells are designed in a rule-based manner that can be implemented using the local programming environment, i.e., can be created either automatically by the metadatabase, or directly by the local system registering with the metadatabase. The shells interact with the local systems in which they reside to "empower", and also interact with the underlying network system to perform the necessary information flow and configuration tasks that the local system (along the network system) do not. The metadatabase will leave these shells to operate on their own (as a part of the local environment) and will intervene only when the control knowledge they embed needs to be updated. Therefore, the existence of the metadatabase effects adaptability and re-configurability to these shells and hence to the global architecture. This dynamic management of the architecture is lacking in previous technologies, where an architecture (shells or agents or other similar designs) is created once and stay unchanged globally for ever.

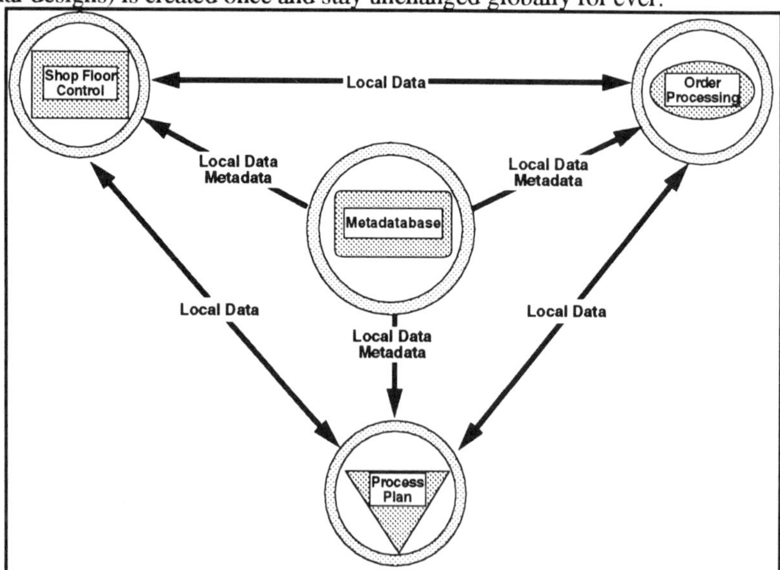

Fig. 5.1. The Concurrent Architecture Using a Metadatabase

5.2.2. The Metadatabase Structure: GIRD Model

The metadatabase itself employs a generic meta-structure, the Global Information Resource Dictionary (GIRD) model shown in Figure 5.2 (see chapter 7 for detailed discussion.), to abstract the enterprise metadata resources (i.e., models) into an enterprise schema. As such, each and every local model is represented (but not duplicated, nor removed) into the metadatabase as ordinary metadata instances (rows or "tuples") populating the structure. The metadata independence at the model integration level is achieved since any change in enterprise models would involve only ordinary metadata transactions similar to the usual relational processing, and do not require any change to the structure itself, nor reloading/recompilation. The structure itself, as well as the representation of local models, is developed according to the Two-Stage Entity Relationship (TSER) method, which serves for this purpose as a meta-model (see chapter 4 for details). TSER provides at the first, functional stage two basic representation constructs: SUBJECT (similar to objects in object-oriented paradigm) and CONTEXT (rule-based description of process and other contextual knowledge). At the second, structural stage, ENTITY (characterized with singular keys) and RELATIONSHIP (characterized with composite keys) plus two more types of associations signifying special integrity rules (functional and mandatory) are defined. All these constructs, combined with hardware and software classes of metadata, are included in the GIRD model and give rise to a generic enterprise schema that does not change from application to application, nor from one technology to another.

5.2.3 The Meta-Model System

The integration of enterprise functions must deal with the full scope of paradigm translation problem facing business, manufacturing and engineering design databases pertaining to the enterprise. Therefore, the notion of using a meta-model to anchor these paradigm translations is featured in the metadatabase model. Furthermore, the metadatabase itself needs to be modeled, created, and put online for the EIM purpose. To bring all these concepts into prominence, the stand-alone metadatabase is referred to as a meta-model system.

The meta-model system spans three levels:

(1) At the modeling (or metadata) level, the meta-model is a neutral paradigm serving as the common representation method that all paradigms are translated into. TSER is embedded to provide a compact solution to this need

(2) At the models integration (or metadata management) level, the meta-model is a generic metadata schema abstracting and structuring all models into an integrated enterprise metadatabase (see figure 5.2).

(3) At the information management (or data instances) level, the meta-model is the integrated enterprise model contained in the metadatabase that supports all metadata applications for enterprise functional systems(see figure 5.3).

The GIRD model and the meta-model system together provide a design for the first element, an enterprise information model, called for by the metadatabase solution. They also pave the way for the second element, the online metadatabase.

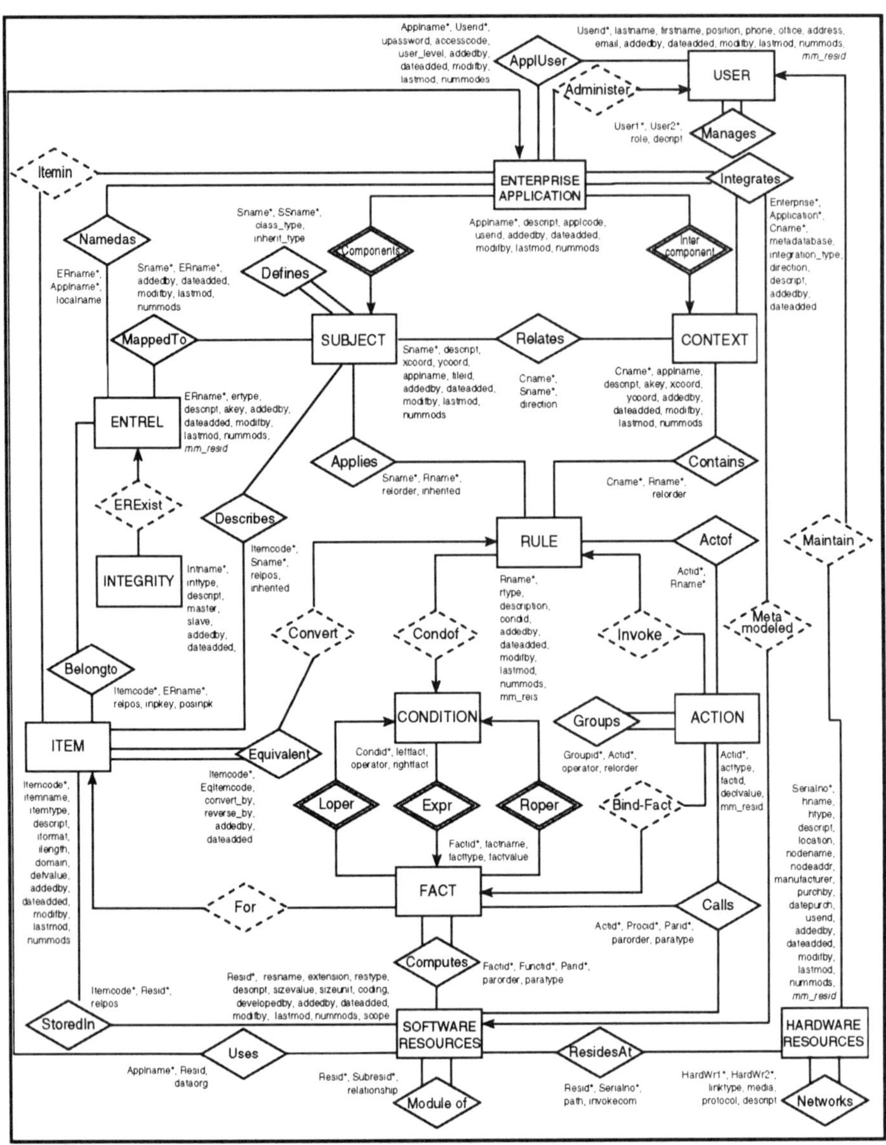

Figure 5.2. The GIRD Model

5.2.4 The Metadatabase-Supported Scalable Integration Hierarchy

In large-scale systems, the metadatabase can be distributed in a recursive manner and constitutes a hierarchy of nodes, illustrated in Figure 5.4, where, for simplicity, only three levels are shown. At the leaf, several of the application systems are represented in a sub- or mini-metadatabase. This mini-metadatabase then can be represented in the main metadatabase system such that the mini-metadatabase becomes the gateway to the application systems it represents. There can, of course, be as many levels of sub-/mini-metadatabases as needed, and at each level additional metadatabases can be added laterally for horizontal expansion. The real significance of this hierarchy, however, is not its top-down construction, which is the predicament of virtually all other integration models; but rather its ability to effect bottom-up, incremental development and expansion — i.e., scalable integration: the higher level nodes can be constructed from the ones immediately below it. A key element in this bottom-up, scale-up approach is the GIRD meta-model discussed above. This structure allows new application models to be incorporated into a metadatabase without disrupting the current systems. Another key element is the basic architecture in Section 5.2.1, which is operationalized with new software engineering design, the Rule-Oriented Programming Environment (ROPE) presented in the next section. To be precise, the shell-based concurrent architecture shown in Figure 5.1 should be super-imposed on the hierarchy depicted in Figure 5.4; i.e., every node has a ROPE shell to interoperate it with the rest of the environment. The adaptability and re-configurability of the concurrent architecture are also availed to the scalable hierarchy.

Thus, large scale, overwhelming integration environments can be achieved gradually, by first developing individual nodes in client (application systems) - server (metadatabase) type of clusters and then integrate them in a grand clustering of such clusters. In a similar way, the main metadatabase can be incorporated into a super or inter-enterprise metadatabase and become a mini-metadatabase of the latter. This concept is illustrated through the scalable architecture in Figure 5.4. Both the clusters of metadatabases and the clusters of application systems at the leaf nodes are managed by the same metadatabase in a recursive manner.

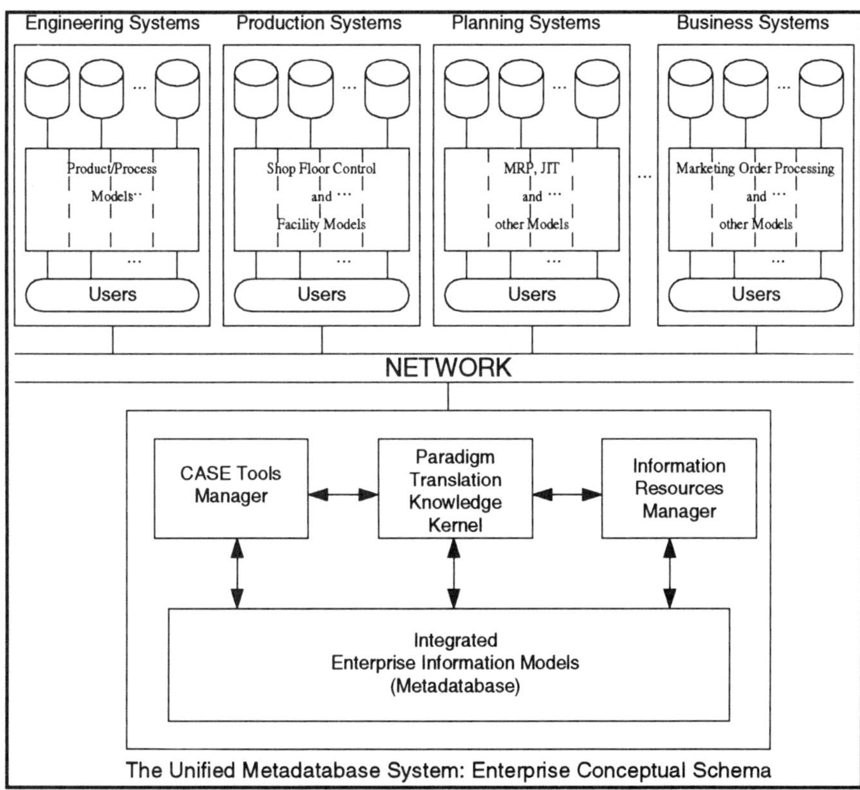

Fig. 5.3. Enterprise Information Integration Using a Metamodel

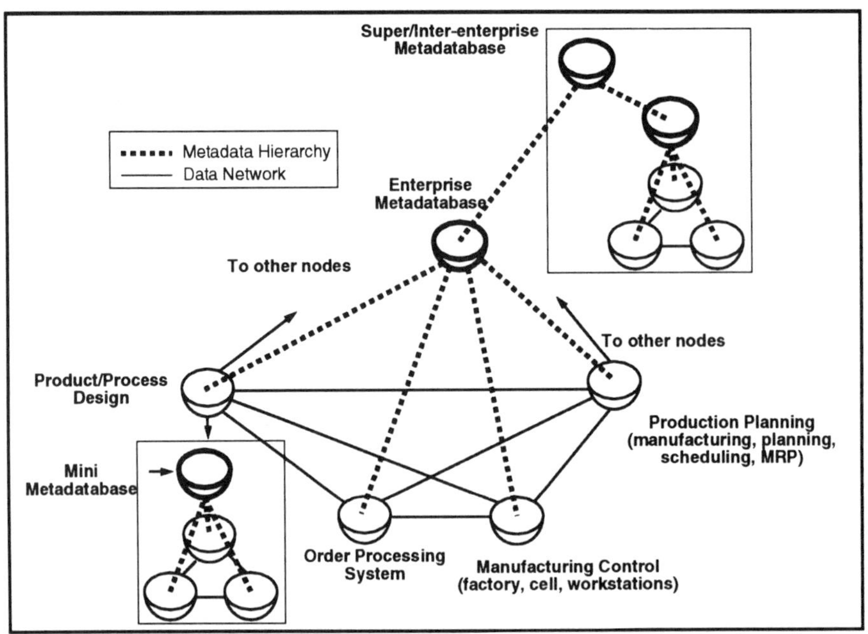

Fig. 5.4. Scalable Enterprise Integrated Through Distributed Metadatabase System

5.2.5 ROPE: The Execution Model for the Architecture

The ROPE method develops the shell technology needed for the adaptive and scalable architecture of multiple systems (see Figure 5.1). defines: (1) how the rules are stored in the local shells (representation and format used); (2) how the rules are processed, distributed, and managed, (3) how each shell interacts with its corresponding application system; (4) how the different shells interact with each other; and (5) how the shells are designed (i.e., their architecture). Furthermore, the ROPE approach prescribes three principles: (1) rules representing processing logic are seperated from the program code by placing them in a distinct rulebase section for easy modifiability; (2) communications among shells are conducted through a message system; and (3) the rule processing and the message system are implemented into local environments and combined into the shells. As such, the local shells are invisible to the users, but control the "external" behavior of the local systems. These elements are detailed in Chapter 9.

5.2.6 The Model-Assisted Global Query System

Another basic task of EIM is to allow enerprise users retrieving information from anywhere in the (extended) enterprise without having to possess involved technical knowledge concerning what, where, and how to retrieve the information. The metadatabase is itself an online repository of knowledge that can assist the enterprise users achieve this purpose. Thus, a model (enterprise metadata) - assisted method is developed for this task. The basic logic of the model-assisted global query approach proceeds as follows: First, all classes of enterprise metadata are specified and structured through a metadata representation method. This metadata structure (abstraction) then serves as the basis for organizing and implementing enterprise information models into an on-line and shared metadatabase facilitating all tasks of information integration. As such, the functional views, processes, data models, business rules and other knowledge concerning the global query operation are readily available to both the users and the system through the metadatabase. Therefore, on-line assistance on query formulation and processing becomes a feasible and fully characterized concept. Specific methods based on this knowledge can be defined and developed in terms of metadata requirements and utilized in each major task of the problem. The details are provided in Chapter 8.

5.2.7 The Metadatabase Management System

A complete management system is developed for the metadatabase towards satisfying the requirements of the second element, an online metadatabase, of the solution discussed above in Section 5.1 (the system is signified as the center shell in Figure 5.1). The major elements of this system are depicted in Figure 5.5. It performs three major tasks: (1) management of the metadatabase itself, including metadata queries, analyses, and rulebase processing ; (2) formulation and processing of global queries, utilizing the metadatabase to provide online intelligent support to users; and (3) generation of data management rules as well as operating rules and interfacing with ROPE for event-based information flows and data management. The elements performing these tasks are self explanatory in the Figure.

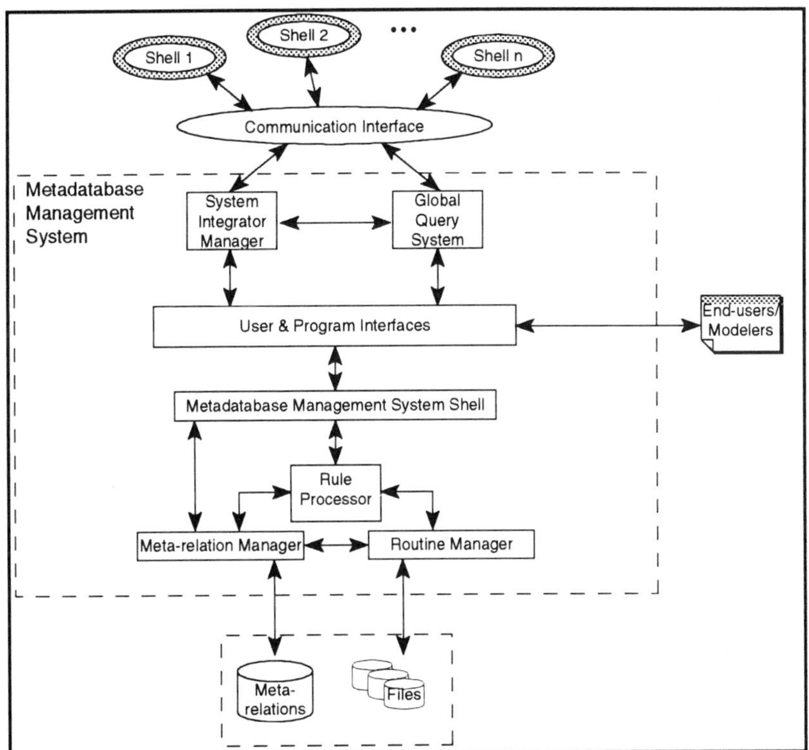

Fig. 5.5. The Metadatabase Management Shell Architecture

5.2.8 The Visual Information Universe Model

One key area that has not received adequate attention - or more accurately, has not been sufficiently understood - is the next generation user-interface for enterprise information management. The metadatabase model does not prescribe a new user interface element, but does describe a novel approach to developing this next generation technology beyond the present concept of GUI (graphical user interface) and VR (virtual reality). It should feature a new paradigm of information visualization with metaphors suitable for cyberspace ideas and applications; should possess contextual knowledge of the underlying information resources to assist end users acquire and assemble any pieces of information desired from everywhere needed; and should, thereby, effect a virtual environment for information access over networks where the user "fly" freely and query globally with little or no prior technical knowledge about the system. The new concept will be exemplified as the Visual Information Universe (VIU) model using the new Globe metaphor (representing information resources), some basic VR tools (for direct spatial manipulation), and a metadatabase. The VIU model will be further connected with network protocols and interfaces such as Mosaic and Netscape to support electronic commerce over the Internet as well as the information management needs in distributed enterprises. Chapter 11 develops these ideas in detail.

Using the metadatabase for the sources of contextual knowledge as well as the object of visualization, the overall architecture of the VIU model is depicted in Figure 5.6 below.

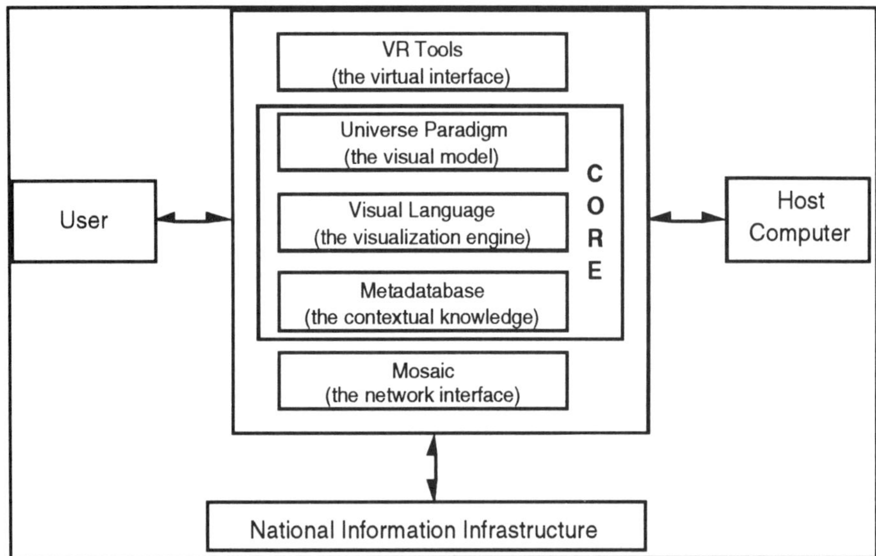

Fig. 5.6. VIU Architecture for Ubiquitous Interface Over Network

Together, the above elements constitute a solution responding to the information integration needs discussed in chapter 1. The metadatabase encompasses all four types of enterprise metadata, which is in turn used to provide ubiquitous support for the organic architecture effecting dynamic alignments throughout the extended enterprise.

5.3 POSSIBLE IMPLEMENTATIONS

The metadatabase model can be implemented in a variety of ways. It can, of course, be developed as a stand-alone technology using its own proprietary designs; but it can also be mapped completely onto existing technologies and develop only the elements that are missing presently. A combination of both strategies might work well in actuality. To illustrate this point, an implementation solution is illustrated in figure 5.7 for the industrial scenario discussed in section 1.2 of chapter 1. It incorporates a metadatabase to serve as an EIM on top of two conventional types of information management. The two conventional capabilities are:

(1) Information Object Storage and Management - a collection of information stored as objects on optical discs, magnetic disks and magnetic tape. Examples of objects include raster images of pre CAD engineering and manufacturing drawings and text material like old typewritten copy which were produced by means that do not lend themselves to digital representation. In addition, standalone technologies such as CAD drawings and dedicated application systems continue to provide their own services.

(2) Information Warehouse which contains selected shareable information stored as data in an appropriate database. Examples include CAD system data files, analysis data, vector drawing files and the like to provide work flow management (file transfer) and certain pre-determined global quries.

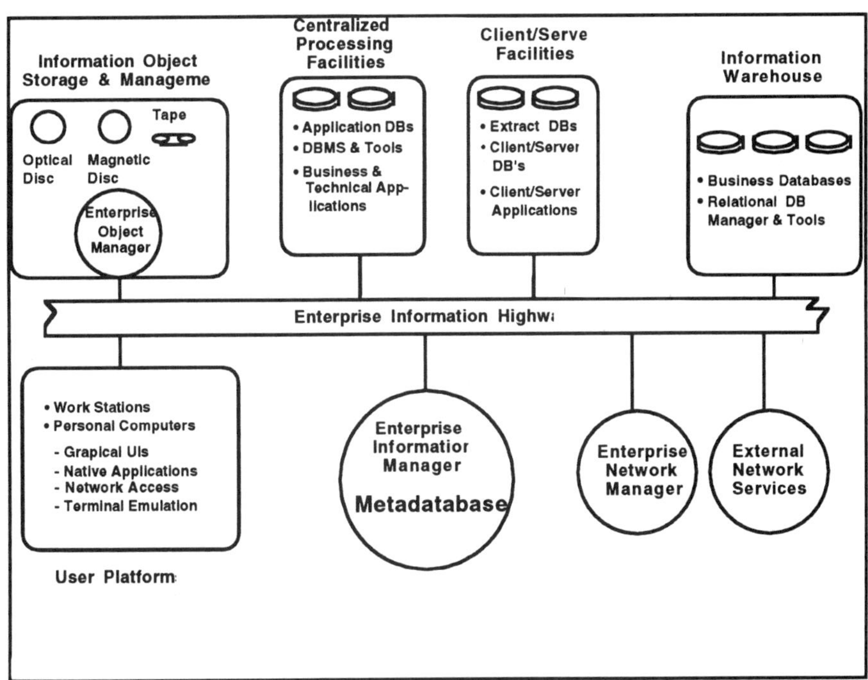

Fig. 5.7. Preliminary Solution

The metadatabase is then added as an EIM to provide additional functionalities required. Each of the conventional resources contains appropriate tools and management software to allow retrieval and in some cases editing of appropriate information provided the user has detailed knowledge of the location and content of the information. The new EIM, therefore, provides integration to these these resources at all three levels of functionality (file transfer, global query, and information management). The use of metadata will free the users from much of the need to possess detailed technical knowledge and the concurrent architecture will allow global query and management of changes to information resources. The file transfer will continue to be performed mainly by the information warehouses, just like local use of the resources will continue to be the responsibility of local applications.

The resultant Enterprise Information Management system can also include new visual information system (i.e., VIU) to make it possible for all designated users to have access to all of the information over an enterprise information highway. When this highway is connected to the Internet and global networks, dynamic alignment of resources throughout a globally extended enterprise is supported.

The metadatabase model has been prototyped at Rensselaer. It is being developed into a product for some corporations. We review below the development effort at Rensselaer for this technology.

Tnformation integration project is being approached in a manner that reflects the entire scope of required technology, from information modeling methodology to integration theory (Figure 5.8). First, an enterprise information modeling method satisfying the unique requirements of information integration has been developed. This method combines user's information *subjects* with their *contextual* knowledge and globally consolidates them into normalized *entities* and *relationships*. As such, it encompasses the process-oriented functional modeling (e.g., IDEF and Data Flow Diagram) and data-oriented semantic modeling (e.g., Object-oriented and Entity-relationship) in a way that automates the mapping from high-level conceptual models to logical systems designs while connecting data with knowledge. It also provides linkages and translations with commonly used models such as CODASYL, relational, and object-oriented systems Therefore, the meta-model system in Section 5.2.3 is developed.

A new repository model was then originated to extend prior government and industry results. These results tended to focus only on data dictionary and software design functions, whereas the new repository model includes substantial knowledge about the interaction of data. Since the structure is based on the information modeling method, it is generic and largely independent of particular applications. The GIRD model in Section 5.2.2 is developed. Through the use of this new repository model as a knowledge base, advanced global query capabilities have been provided to end users and programmers. First, the users are assisted with the on-line knowledge, thus both query formulation and processing can be performed directly in terms of information models with which they are familiar, without either requiring detailed technical knowledge of the local systems, nor relying on integrated schemata which tend to impose changes on local systems (the methods in Section 5.2.6). Similarly, using the metadatabase for managing concurrent systems, methods (the methods inSection 5.2.5) have been developed to make heterogeneous application databases work together concurrently and synergistically, without necessitating a central computer to control them directly. The MDBMS in Section 5.2.7 is developed. The metadatabase-driven concurrent architecture in Section 5.2.1 is verified. The scalable hierarchy in Section 5.2.4 is ready to be verified on this basis. A Visual Information Universe consisting of globes of interpreted enterprise information resources for all phases of information management is developed to test its usefulness for global query applications. This result consolidates the ideas in Section 5.2.8.

Finally, the research also develops a theory of integration and economical evaluation for integration (using IT) to guide the planning, analysis and design of integrated systems for enterprise information management. The theory provides an information requirements model containing fundamental elements of production and their data classes and knowledge classes needed to achieve parallel interactions among decision processes. It is being further extended to provide microeconomical assessment of systems through the concept of transaction costs and utility. All of these results contribute to a prototype metadatabase as an EIM.

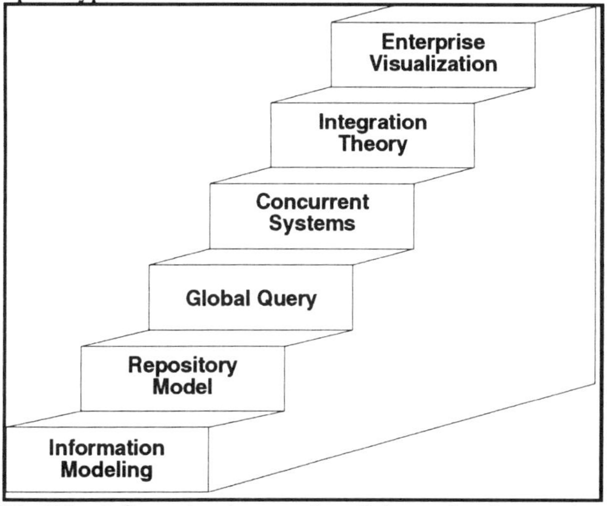

Enterprise Visualization
Integration Theory
Concurrent Systems
Global Query
Repository Model
Information Modeling

Fig.5.8. A Stepwise Approach to Information Integration

The ongoing effort is continued on developing distributed metadatabase, economical evaluation methods, strategic information planning, and vizualization. The industrial and government sponsors of the metadatabase research are found in the Preface of this book.

Acknowledgement

Mr. Alan Rubenstein created Figure 5.8 based on input from Mr. John Manthorp, formerly of GE.

6
DEMONSTRATION OF A METADATABASE

A metadatabase prototype based on the basic elements described in chapter 5 has been developed to verify the metadatabase model and illustrate the concepts. The prototype supports enterprise information management at all three levels (file transfer, global query, and data and knowledge management), plus the management of information model resources themselves. A detailed description of the operation of the system is provided in this chapter, which in essence is a simulated demonstration. Some advanced functionalities such as adaptability and scalability are also shown in Section 9.4 of Chapter 9. A viable EIM is, therefore, presented.

6.1 THE METADATABASE PROTOTYPE

6.1.1 Properties

An enterprise information manager (EIM) should provide access to the organization's information resources and will use this information to assist in designing, implementing and controlling the enterprise. This information includes an enterprise information model describing the data resources of the local subsystems and their control strategy and tactics in the form of rules. The information model also includes knowledge about the dynamics of information transfer such as what and how information is shared among local systems and under what circumstances it is used. The metadatabase prototype is aimed at effecting such an EIM at Rensselaer's Computer-Integrated Manufacturing Program (June 1986 - June 1992) and the Adaptive Integrated Manufacturing Enterprise (AIME) Program (June 1992 - June 1995) and has been successfully demonstrated to industrial sponsors including Alcoa, Digital, GE, GM, IBM, and Samsung.

Compared to previous results in databases, the metadatabase prototype offers some salient properties. In particular, virtually all previous efforts employ as a cornerstone of its approach the traditional Von Neumann model of synchronization, which integrates schemata and serializes transaction across local systems under a central administrator. Consequently, there are fundamental limitations imposed by the architectures of these systems. These limitations place restrictions on local autonomy because of the complexity of serialization, and system evolution because of the need to re-compile or even re-design major elements of the global system when changes are made.

The Rensselaer metadatabase architecture, on the other hand, allows concurrent, automatic update of all databases in a distributed environment through shells which accommodate the rules for information interaction. A new correctness criterion focusing on event/usage consistency is developed and employed, as opposed to the conventional instances consistency. The shell concept of the metadatabase system makes it possible for information transfer among local systems to occur without requiring that each transaction be routed through the central metadatabase, thus minimizing the load on the information communication systems. Also, this new approach minimizes concerns about software and hardware issues with regard to performance, since the metadatabase system becomes, in effect, an exception management system.

Thus, there are three advanced distributed information system concepts which we have implemented in Rensselaer's metadatabase: (1) combination of information about enterprise data with knowledge about how this data is used to assist users and systems, (2) the capability to automatically update several remote databases simultaneously when a local database is updated, and (3) the design to allow changes to the configuration and membership of the local system in the global integration. Furthermore, the system has accomplished a new, much-needed goal: the ability to extend over LAN, WAN, and global networks to support dynamic alignment of systems (accommodating existing systems, changing local systems/shells, and adding new systems, all without requiring redesign or recompilation of the integration system).

6.1.2 The Structure

The metadatabase system (Figure 6.1) can be viewed as comprising the metadatabase itself, the Metadatabase Management System (MDBMS), the Information Base Modeling System (IBMS) and the Rule-Oriented Programming Environment (ROPE) which operationalizes the concurrent architecture.

Metadatabase

The metadatabase is a repository of information about the structure and functions of the enterprise's multiple local application programs, their functional and information models, their databases, their interactions, and the information dynamics of the enterprise. The metadatabase is structured according to a unified metadata representation method. Since this method is generic, so does the metadatabase structure. Therefore, new information models or changes to existing ones can be incorporated into the metadatabase through ordinary metadata transactions, without triggering redesign or recompilation. This is both a basic class of metadata independence and a foundation to truly open systems architecture.

Metadatabase Management System (MDBMS)

The metadatabase management system is the user interface to the metadatabase and the processor which makes it possible to create, maintain and utilize the information in the metadatabase for enterprise information management. MDBMS consists three basic elements: systems integrator, global query manager, and metadata manager. The metadata manager, in turn, features a rulebase processor, a routine manager, and a meta-relation manager.

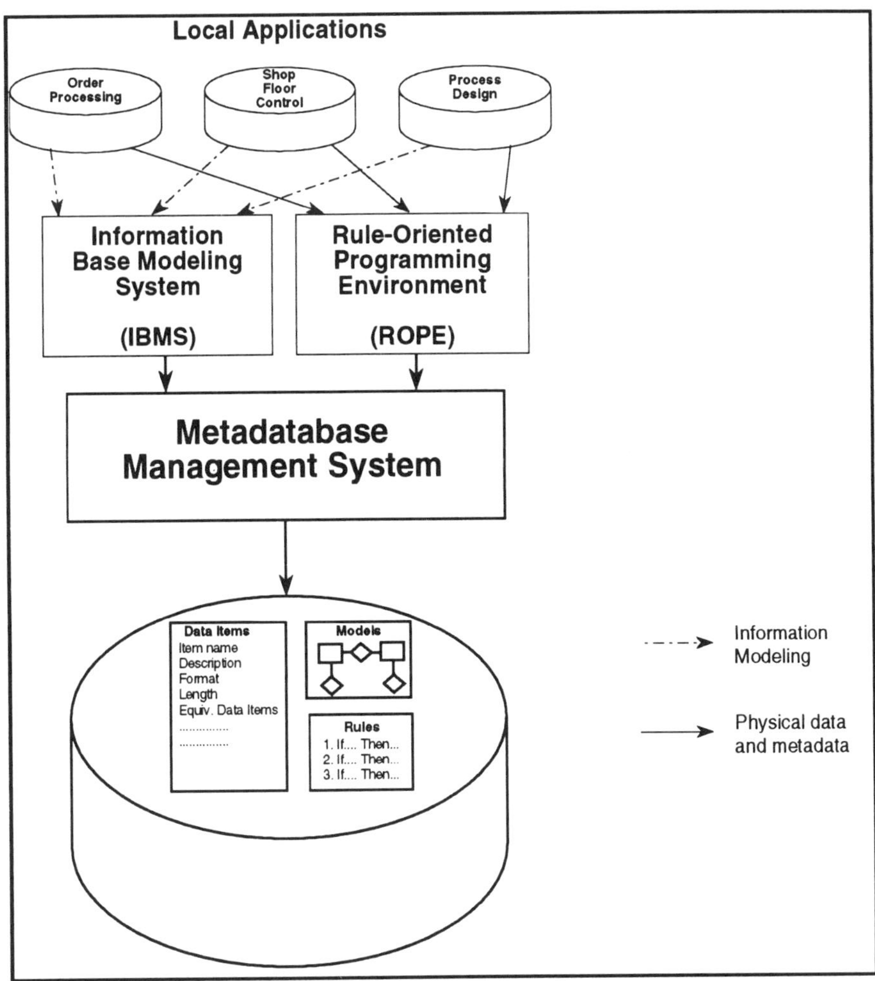

Fig. 6.1. The Metadatabase System

The metadatabase management system has been implemented on two platforms: a micro VAX platform using Digital's Rdb as the database engine for the metadatabase version using the IBM AIX RS/6000 workstation and Oracle DBMS to provide a multi-platform and distributed metadatabase environment. To facilitate user and program interactions with the metadatabase, a shell has been developed in the C language. Currently, enterprise users interact via a menu (in the VAX version) or an X-Windows/Motif® (in the AIX version) interface, while other systems interact through a metadatabase query language application program interface (API).

Information Base Modeling System (IBMS)

The Information Base Modeling System is a computer-aided software engineering tool implementing the TSER method that assists users in designing an enterprise information system and creating a consolidated dictionary of information resources. The dictionary is the source of metadata in an automated environment, while metadata could also be provided to the metadatabase directly. Individual applications can be created using IBMS, or mapped into the global model through

IBMS; but otherwise, IBMS is not required by MDBMS. To facilitate usability, however, model translators have been developed to reverse-engineer EXPRESS (PDES/STEP) products schemata into the information model, as well as to create Oracle and Rdb (both are commercial relational database management systems) schemata. A version of IBMS running on PC/Windows is available to the public (see the Web home page announcement at the beginning of the book, and Chapter 3).

Rule-Oriented Programming Environment (ROPE)

Rule-Oriented Programming Environment is a software environment which makes it possible to implement the knowledge about information interactions among the several subsystems. It is a layer between the Metadatabase Management System and the local application systems. It creates, maintains, and manages the distributed rule-based shells of the concurrent architecture according to (the changes to) the metadatabase. Furthermore, ROPE also monitors local systems behavior and effect communications among them. Thus, it essentially masks the local systems from global users and provides a logically uniform behavior of the multiple systems as a whole without intervening local operations. Major elements of ROPE include: (1) a rules distribution algorithm that optimally allocates global rules (contained in the metadatabase) into local shells; (2) a shell definitional language that creates (and changes) the architecture and localized rule-bases; (3) a shell manipulation language which employs a message protocol to perform inter-shell communications, i.e. rule-base inference (chaining), and other data and rules processing tasks of the shell. The shell architecture is discussed next.

The Concurrent Shell Architecture

The basic structure of the entire metadatabase environment is characterized with a concurrent architecture depicted in Figure 5.1 of Chapter 5. Each of the local subsystems and the metadatabase system has a software shell around it (see Figure 9.7 of Chapter 9) designed according to ROPE. The shells are responsible for monitoring events that are significant for the enterprise, for executing the rules assigned to it and for communicating with other shells. Shells can be written for each local application without disturbing the existing local system code. Figure 5.1 illustrates the flow of metadata through the shells to and from the metadatabase system and the flow of actual data among the local applications. This way, local systems interact directly with each other in parallel according to their own localized rulebase shells, while the metadatabase controls, and only controls, these local shells. Local autonomy, open systems architecture, and global adaptiveness are accomplished.

The Metadatabase-Integrated Enterprise

In large-scale systems, the metadatabase system can be distributed as illustrated in Figure 5.5 of Chapter 5. In the Rensselaer CIM environment, several of the application programs can be represented in a mini-metadatabase. This mini-metadatabase then can be represented in the main metadatabase system such that the mini-metadatabase becomes the gateway to the application programs it represents. The total model shown in Figure 6.2 signifies the expansibility of the metadatabase prototype, where the minimetadatabase handles in-process inspection and a product design system using the ROSE DBMS (a product of STEP Tools, Inc.).

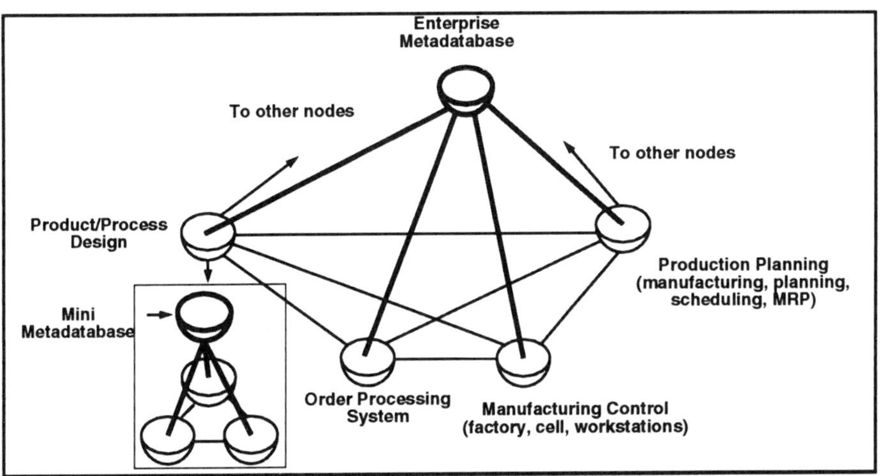

Fig. 6.2. Extensions Toward a Distributed Metadatabase System

6.2 METADATABASE SYSTEM FUNCTIONALITY

The following discussion is intended to assist in developing an understanding of the core functionality of the metadatabase system. For the purpose of this discussion, the Rensselaer CIM facility consists of three application systems; the Process Planning System, the Shop Floor Control System and the Order Processing System. The core functionality is defined in three modes: passive, semi-active and active modes.

The three operational modes of the metadatabase serve different users for different purposes. The passive mode is mainly useful to a programmer or analyst who can easily access and make use of the information in the metadatabase to facilitate maintenance of existing information systems or to develop new information systems. The semi-active mode is useful to a manufacturing user such as a production supervisor who needs to know the status of a manufacturing entity such as a manufacturing order without knowing on which information system(s) the information resides. If information is in more than one system, the metadatabase has the capability to join the results. This replaces the current technique of calling up a number of people in the organization, getting their untimely input and integrating the data manually.

The active mode provides the facility for automatic movement of information from one information system to others under defined conditions called rules. This provides an integration control for the enterprise. The rules are specified by the management according to the degree of automatic control desired.

In order to illustrate the unique functionality of each mode, a different scenario is appropriate for each of the modes of operation. In the passive mode, the metadatabase system acts as a repository of information about the information in each of the several application systems. The metadatabase can be perused to get information about the location and design of data resources in the enterprise, about commonly shared data items, about the functional and information models of the applications or about the control knowledge. This information can be used, for instance, by a systems analyst who is developing a new application to be integrated into the enterprise. The individual application systems communicate with their own databases, and the metadatabase management system communicates with the metadata in the metadatabase. In the passive mode, the metadatabase and the individual application systems do not have to be connected.

In the semi-active and active modes, the metadatabase management system can interact with the applications to provide global query and systems integration functionality. Semi-active mode functionality is implemented with a global query system that can obtain data from the application systems through the information stored in the metadatabase. The metadatabase management system can generate queries to the individual databases and join the responses when the required information is in several different application databases. The global query system has the capability of on-line assistance for query formulation.

The active mode has the metadatabase management system communicate with the metadatabase and with the individual applications in the enterprise through the shells, which are represented as circles around the applications and the metadatabase system. The shells are built on top of the individual applications so that the applications themselves do not have to be modified to operate with the metadatabase system. A shell is also built around the metadatabase system to coordinate with the shells around the applications. In the active mode, when a local update is made, the rules incorporated in the shells control the updating of other local databases either through the local data and metadata commands or through the shell-to-shell local data commands.

To illustrate these capabilities, the prototype environment is comprised of several heterogeneous application systems: engineering design (object-oriented ROSE database using STEP/EXPRESS on IBM RS6000), process planning (dbaseIII+ on PC), shop floor control (Oracle on PC), order processing project management (both use Oracle on IBM RS6000 using AIX library, C and Oracle.

6.3 DETAILED PRESENTATION OF THE THREE MODES

6.3.1. Passive Mode

We now take a closer look at the three operational modes of the metadatabase system. Both the menu-driven version (based on the Digital platform) and the X-Window version (on the IBM platform) are used to generate sample screens for illustration. The logic is identical for both versions. Several screens built into the prototype will be used to illustrate the scope and functionality of the different modes. Figure 6.4 provides an overview of the system, in which we can see part of the metadatabase management system menu tree. The main menu corresponds to the five elements at the top level. MANAGE THE METADATABASE and PERFORM METADATA QUERY are used in the passive mode. MODEL LOCAL SYSTEMS is used to input information into the system. ACCESS LOCAL SYSTEMS is the Global Query System and MANAGE SYSTEM INTEGRATOR provides the facilities for Active Mode Operations in coordination with the Rule Oriented Programming Environment.

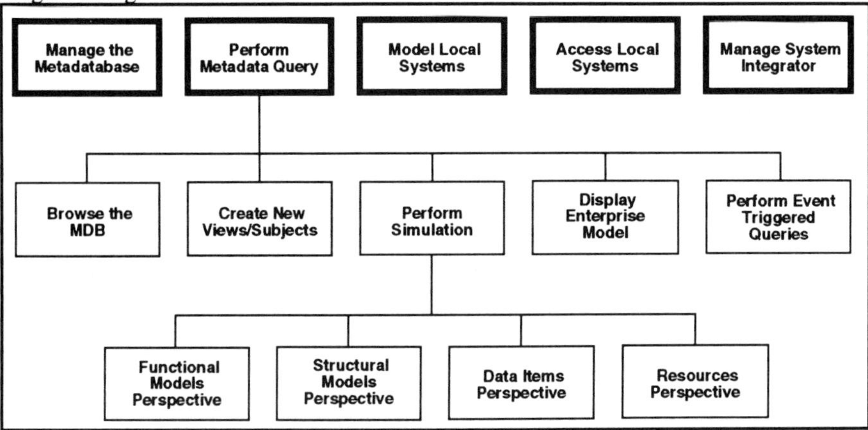

Fig. 6.3. Partial MDBSS Menu Tree

We will first examine the passive mode functionality. The example shows a typical path taken by an analyst who is about to modify the Shop Floor Control Application or who is planning to develop a new application. In either case, the analyst needs to know what information resources and requirements are currently available that can be or have to be consolidated into the new effort.
To do this we will select PERFORM METADATA QUERY and choose PERFORM SIMULATION from the next level, then DATA ITEMS PERSPECTIVE (Figure 6.3).

The screen presented in Figure 6.4 displays individual data items represented in the metadatabase and allows the user to select the data items to be studied. Item #55 in the list, PART_ID from application Shop Floor Control, is selected. Some detailed information about the data item PART_ID is given in Figure 6.5. In this screen, for instance, its description and format are shown.

Figure 6.6 illustrates other information resources in the enterprise that are related to "part". Note that the same object "part" has three different names and two implementation formats. They all are recognized by the metadatabase and presented to the user as three equivalent forms. The information resources displayed here include rules, files, and database tables. This list of resources is derived from the knowledge about the enterprise model included in the metadatabase. The analyst will use this information to review the possible ways of incorporating "part" into the new design, or assess the impact of changing the data item PART_ID.

******* LIST OF THE ITEMS IN THE METADATABASE ****** *

NO.	ITEM NAME	DESCRIPTION
45	NUM_SCRAPPED	NUMBER OF SCRAPPED WORK ORDERS
46	OD_STATUS	CUSTOMER ORDER STATUS
47	OI_STATUS	ORDER ITEM STATUS
48	OPDESC	OPERATION DESCRIPTION
49	OPID	OPERATION IDENTIFIER
50	ORDER_ID	CUSTOMER ORDER IDENTIFICATION NUMBER
51	PARTDESC	PART DESCRIPTION
52	PARTID	PART IDENTIFICATION IN PROCESS_PLAN SYSTEM
53	PARTREV	PART REVISION
54	PART_ID	PART IDENTIFICATION IN ORDER ENTRY SYSTEM
55	PART_ID	PART IDENTIFICATION IN SHOP_FLOOR SYSTEM
56	PART_ID_ASSEM	ASSEMBLY PART IDENTIFIER
57	PART_ID_COMP	COMPONENT PART IDENTIFIER
58	PLANDATE	PLAN CREATION DATE
59	PLANNER	PLANNER NAME

<PRESS RETURN KEY TO CONTINUE>

*****PLEASE ENTER ITEM NAME/NUMBER, (OR
– TYPE (L) TO LIST ALL THE ITEMS
KNOWN TO THE METADATABASE.
– TYPE (Q) TO QUIT THIS QUERY) : 55

Fig. 6.4. Data Item Selection

****** ITEM DEFINITION METADATA ******

-- Item Code : ITEM_64

-- Item Name : PART_ID

-- Description: PART IDENTIFICATION IN SHOP_FLOOR SYSTEM

-- Format : CHARACTER

<PRESS RETURN KEY TO CONTINUE>

Fig. 6.5. Data Item Metadata

```
***** Any Changes to this Item may affect :

  – Application(s) :
    --- PROCESS_PLAN
    --- ORDER_ENTRY
    --- SHOP_FLOOR

  – Database Tables :
    --- PARTREV              — PART
    --- BILL_MAT             — ORDER_ITEM
    --- WORK_ORDER           — PARTS_AVAIL

  – Rules :
    --- SFCRULE_11           — SFCRULE_16
    --- SFCRULE_17           — SFCRULE_12
    --- SFCRULE_13           — SFCRULE_3

  – Data Files :
    --- PARTS_AVAIL
    --- WORK_ORDER

  – Equivalent Data Items :
      Data-Item Name       Format           Application System
      --------------       ------           ------------------
      PART_ID              CHARACTER(5)     SHOP_FLOOR
      PART_ID              CHARACTER(5)     ORDER_ENTRY
      PART_ID_COMP         CHARACTER(5)     SHOP_FLOOR
      PART_ID_ASSEM        CHARACTER(5)     SHOP_FLOOR
      PARTID               CHARACTER(10)    PROCESS_PLAN

                    <PRESS RETURN KEY TO CONTINUE>
```

Fig. 6.6. Metadata Related to a Data Item

6.3.2. Semi-Active Mode

Recall that in the active and semi-active modes the metadatabase management system communicates with the individual applications in the enterprise. The interface circles around the individual applications are called shells and are built on top of the applications. This is so that the applications themselves do not have to be modified to operate with the metadatabase system. A shell is also built around the metadatabase system to manage the shells around the applications.

In the semi-active mode, the interaction between the metadatabase management system and the local systems consists of queries for local data and responses to the queries. The semi-active mode has been implemented with a Global Query System that can obtain data from the application systems by using information stored in the metadatabase. The metadatabase management system can generate queries to the individual databases and join the responses when the required information comes from several different application databases. The Global Query System has the capability of on-line assistance for query formulation.

To illustrate the semi-active mode operation for technical details of the model, methods, and techniques developed for this mode of operation, we look at how the Global Query System deals with a query which requires the retrieving of data from three distributed application systems. The sample query is:
"Find the Customer Order, PartID, Part Description, Quantity and Quantity Completed for Jane Doe's Customer Order which has a desired date of 10/25/95."
While it is possible to write out this query with an appropriate syntax, the Global Query user interface can be used to specify the data items required for the query and thus have the appropriate queries generated automatically.

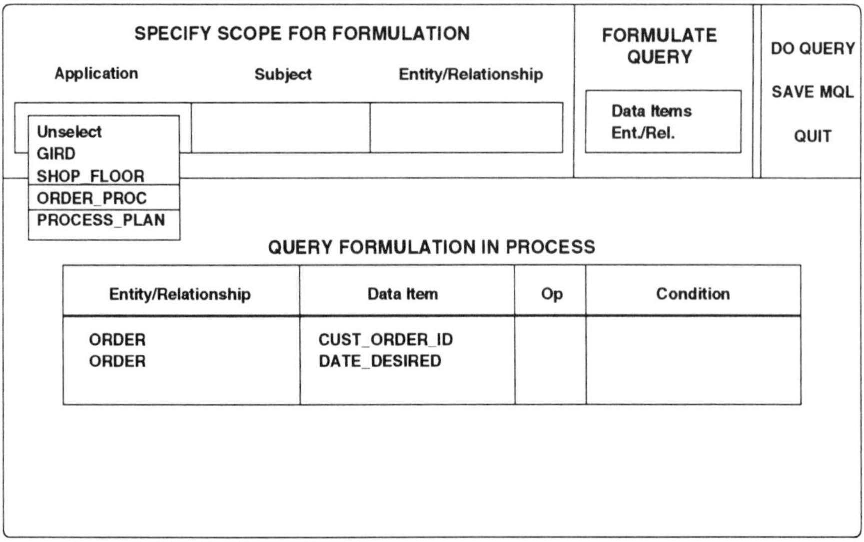

SPECIFY SCOPE FOR FORMULATION

Application Subject Entity/Relationship

Unselect
GIRD
SHOP_FLOOR
ORDER_PROC
PROCESS_PLAN

FORMULATE QUERY

Data Items
Ent./Rel.

DO QUERY
SAVE MQL
QUIT

QUERY FORMULATION IN PROCESS

Entity/Relationship	Data Item	Op	Condition
ORDER	CUST_ORDER_ID		
ORDER	DATE_DESIRED		

Fig. 6.7. Global Query System Interface

The user interface provides pop-up menus whose items are generated dynamically from the contents of the metadatabase (Figure 6.7). The user needs only to choose the appropriate data items in order to formulate the query. Prior to the formulation, and throughout the formulation, the scope of data items from which to choose can be narrowed as desired. Notice that the initial pop-up menu shown here allows for selecting a particular application, say Order Processing. The scope may also be set, using a pull-down menu, to a particular subject within the application, and similarly an entity or relationship within the subject may be set.

The data items that we select will appear on the bottom half of the screen. These data items may later be deleted or may have conditions placed on them. Figure 6.8 illustrates a path through the data items that could be followed to generate the sample query. This figure does not depict the user interface but rather shows how related tables are traversed to identify the various data items.

We choose first the table ORDER, and select the two data items that have been darkened in the diagram. CUSTOMER_ORDER_ID and DATE_DESIRED are selected since they are both data items needed to answer the query or needed for a condition in the query. Notice that DATE_DESIRED with a value of "10/25/95" is a condition in the query. When we have selected all data items that are needed from a table, a pop-up menu allows us to select a related table that could provide further data items that we need.

For this query, we choose CUSTOMER, which is related to ORDER due to the common field CUSTOMER_ID. We select the data item CUSTOMER_NAME since it is a condition in the query that customer name be "Jane Doe". We then return back to the related table ORDER to find more related tables.

We choose the related table WORK ORDER, which has moved us from the Order Processing system to the Shop Floor Control system. The two tables are related by virtue of the field ORDER_ID, which is equivalent to the field

CUSTOMER_ORDER_ID. In this database, the Order ID in Shop Floor does not actually have the same value as the Customer Order ID in Order Processing, although there is a correspondence between them, so that when tables from these two applications are joined later, the Global Query System will have to use conversion rules from the Metadatabase to do the join. We select the data items PART_ID, WORK ORDER QUANTITY (WO_QUAN), and NUMBER_COMPLETED.

Again moving to a related table, we choose PART, which is in the Process Planning system. This is related due to the equivalent field PARTID. We select the data item PART DESCRIPTION.

Now we have specified all data items for our query. We move to the bottom half of our user interface and attach conditions on CUSTOMER_NAME and DATE_DESIRED. Since this terminates our query, we indicate so by selecting the DO QUERY button on the upper right corner of the screen (Figure 6.7). Then, after waiting for requests over the network to be satisfied and then joined together, we have the answer to our query (Figure 6.9).

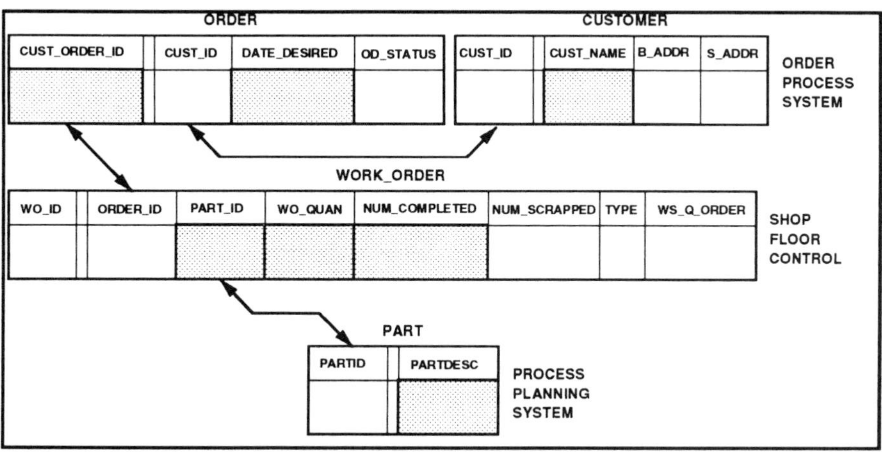

Fig. 6.8. Query Formulation

CUST_ NAME	DATE_ DESIRED	CUST_ ORDER_ ID	PART_ ID	WO_ QUAN	PART_ DESC	NUM_ COMPLETD
Jane Doe	10/25/95	18790_25	PZ57	5	Burr Puzzle	3
Jane Doe	10/25/95	18790_25	B	1	Burr Puzzle	0

Fig. 6.9. Query Answer

6.3.3. Active Mode

The Active Mode is the level of Metadatabase functionality where systems integration takes place. The approach is unique in that enterprise metadata, especially contextual knowledge is incorporated in the form of rules to control the systems' information interactions. The following are details and examples of how the metadatabase system achieves this.

Many integration efforts focus on integrating systems at the data-level; that is, determining what pieces of data are used at what systems and writing the code to move shared data between applications. If the task is to transfer information between a Shop Floor Control System and an Order Processing System, many programmers would choose to obtain the requirements from each and hardcode the data extraction and upload between these systems (Figure 6.10a). In this sense, regardless of the actual technology used - be it information warehouse or CORBA-based APIs, the configuration (of integration) is fixed.

The metadatabase approach incorporates the control logic through a model based methodology. Instead of hard-coding the data links between systems, knowledge of information interaction is derived from the model, and rules are generated for moving information (Figure 6.10b). This rule based architecture is adaptive since a change in the model can automatically change the rules. The process in a nutshell is described below:

The defined operating rules are first incorporated into the metadatabase according to the schema utilizing either IBMS or registering with the metadatabase management system. Once the rules have been incorporated into the metadatabase, automatic determination of how the rules should be distributed among the local and metadatabase shells is conducted and then the rules are distributed into local shells using ROPE. Any changes to these globally defined operating rules will be similarly mapped to changes to local rules and propagated through ROPE to update the shells and, thereby, their behaviors, since the rules route the communication path and content.

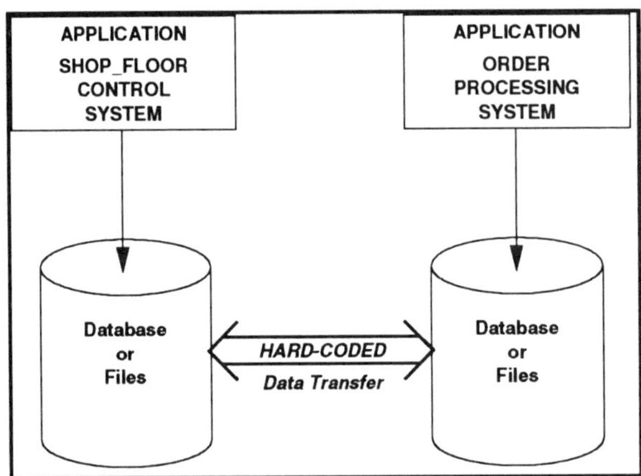

Fig. 6.10 (a). Traditional Approach to System Integration

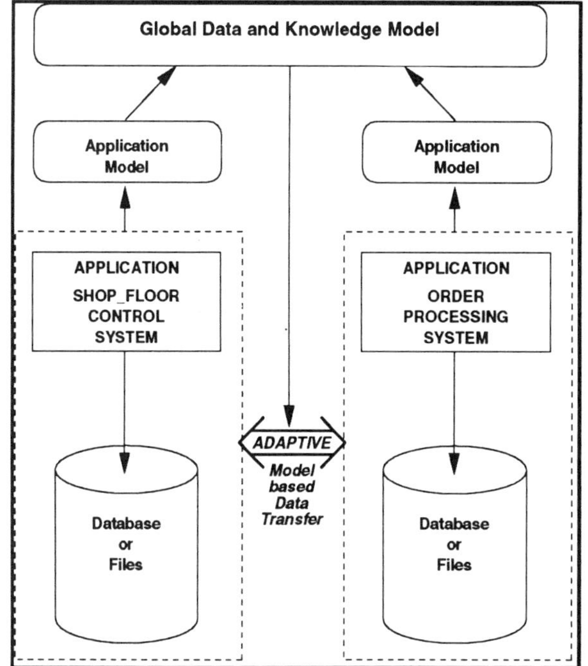

Fig. 6.10 (b). Metadatabase Approach to System Integration

The active mode component of the metadatabase architecture includes facilities to: (1) generate data integration rules from models, (2) model operational rules from users, (3) implement rules automatically, and (4) manage the modification of existing rules.

The prototype system will demonstrate these functions with examples. First we will generate data integration rules from models. Beginning with the Metadatabase Management System main menu (Figure 6.3), we select MANAGE SYSTEM INTEGRATOR for the management of the global control rules. In order to view the global control rules, a local application system, Shop Floor Control System is selected.

We then get to the GLOBAL DATA MANAGEMENT MENU FOR APPLICATION : SHOP_FLOOR (Figure 6.11). The active-mode menu shows three groups of selections. The first set, DATA MANAGEMENT REPORTS provides a description of the data management rules. The second set, DATA MANAGEMENT RULE PROCESSING FACILITY presents the data management rules in a rule format appropriate to local information system managers. The third set, PROCESS GLOBAL RULES distributes the global data management rules to the local systems.

The first two categories of selections are further broken down into three classes of data management rules. These three classes of rules represent : (1) common data items, which are globally shared data elements of the same name and type, (2) equivalent data items, which are globally shared data elements that have different names or types, but that have the same meaning, and (3) integrity constraints, which are direct relationships between pieces of data among systems. Classifying them in this manner allows for convenient management of these rules. In our tour of the active mode functions, only one representative example will be viewed.

```
************************************************************
   GLOBAL DATA MANAGEMENT MENU FOR APPLICATION : SHOP_FLOOR
************************************************************
DATA MANAGEMENT REPORTS:
   1. View Common Data Items
   2. View Equivalent Data Items
   3. View Integrity Constraints
DATA MANAGEMENT RULE PROCESSING FACILITY:
   4. Generate Rules for Common Data Items
   5. Generate Rules for Equivalent Data Items
   6. Generate Rules for Integrity Constraints
PROCESS GLOBAL RULES:
   7. Implement Rules to Local System Shells

   P. Exit to Previous Menu

 **** Please enter your selection:
```

Fig. 6.11. Active Mode Facility Main Menu

To show the generation of a Data Integration Rule, we will go into the Active Mode Main Menu and pick GENERATE RULES FOR EQUIVALENT DATA ITEMS (Figure 6.12). Shown in Figure 6.13 is the rule representation of equivalent data ORDER_ID and CUSTOMER_ORDER_ID involving Shop Floor Control and Order Processing System respectively. This rule is derived from the knowledge embedded in the model. This rule will be implemented locally at the Shop Floor site. The rule itself states that if the value of ORDER_ID in Shop Floor is updated, then the value of CUSTOMER_ORDER_ID in the Order Processing System must also be updated. The local system shells will be able to process these equivalent data rules and propagate the generated updates to distributed systems. This demonstration illustrates the generation of data management rules that integrate systems. These rules were derived from a model of how the systems interact with each other.

The systems integration approach also accommodates user defined operational rules, as is described in the second component of the Active Metadatabase: MODEL OPERATIONAL RULES FROM USERS.

This component is accessed in the Metadatabase Management System Main Menu by selecting MODEL APPLICATION SYSTEMS (Figure 6.4).

```
*****************************************************************
   GLOBAL DATA EQUIVALENCE FOR APPLICATION : SHOP_FLOOR
*****************************************************************

IF
     The data item "ORDER_ID" involved in the
     entities/relationships ( WORK_ORDER )
     in application [ SHOP_FLOOR ] is updated

THEN
     The data item "CUST_ORDER_ID" involved in all
     entities/relationships ( ORDER_ITEM ORDER )
     in application [ ORDER_PROCESSING ] must be updated.
```

Fig. 6.12. Global Data Equivalence Rule

By loading part of the CIM model as displayed on the left side of the screen, rules can be entered in the INPUT KNOWLEDGE WINDOW (Figure 6.13). As an example, the rule entered will update the status of all orders in the Order Processing System, for all the completed work orders in the Shop Floor Control System at 2:00 PM. The rule is defined by giving the rule a name, description, and type, and by typing the rule in the form of a "if-then" statement.

This is the second class of rules that the metadatabase architecture supports. These two classes of rules (model generated and user defined) are dynamically distributed and implemented at each location of the application systems. The distribution of the rules to the local systems is under the control of the Active Mode Facility.

To implement these rules, we choose IMPLEMENT RULES TO LOCAL SYSTEM SHELLS from the Active Mode Facility Main Menu (Figure 6.11). This will extract the data management rules for each local application system and send them over a network to the local operating shells from which they will be automatically put into effect. The rules are managed centrally at the Metadatabase level and are propagated to local system shells (metadata), shown as the shaded ring around each application system. At this point, each application shell will monitor the data elements based upon these data integration rules for changes and initiate appropriate updates to other application systems.

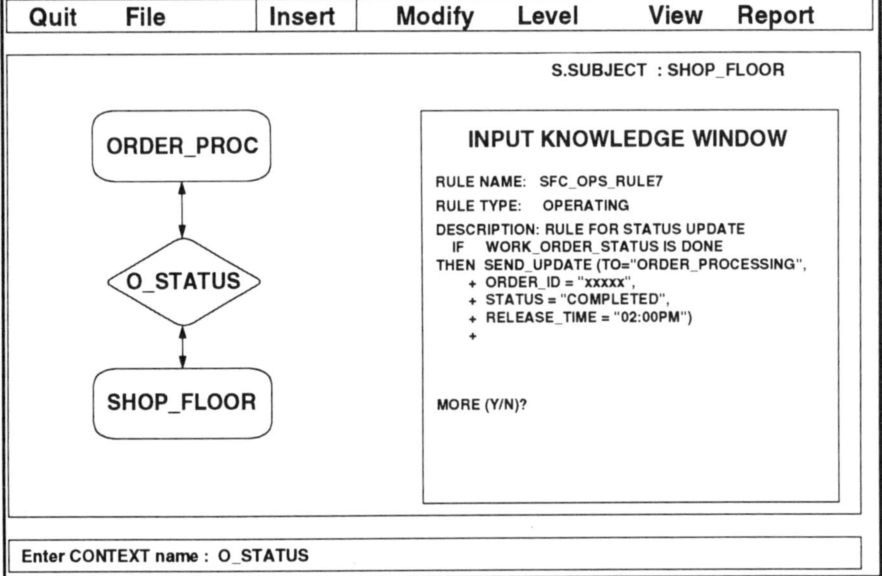

Fig. 6.13. Knowledge Input Window

It is important to note that the rules we refer to are responsible for linking systems together, as in our user defined rule for sending order status from Shop Floor to Order Processing System at a predetermined time. In Figure 6.14, we see that at 2:00 PM, the information flow from Shop Floor to Order Processing contains needed information on order status. Furthermore, no centralized data manager is involved in this integration strategy, which leads us to be able to have many such interactions operating simultaneously.

Lastly, the active mode provides facilities to manage these rules. The management function includes the ability to manage the modification of existing rules in the metadatabase, and dynamically propagate them for update in the local system shells.

Whenever a rule is edited through the Rule Management Facility, the facility will automatically send this revised rule to all the affected local systems and update the local rulebase shells.

A final scenario illustrating the active mode capability is shown in Figures 6.15a-6.15c. A project management engineer interacts with the metadatabase to enter control rules and assemble information from all applications involved. These figures show three steps in the scenario and are self-explanatory.

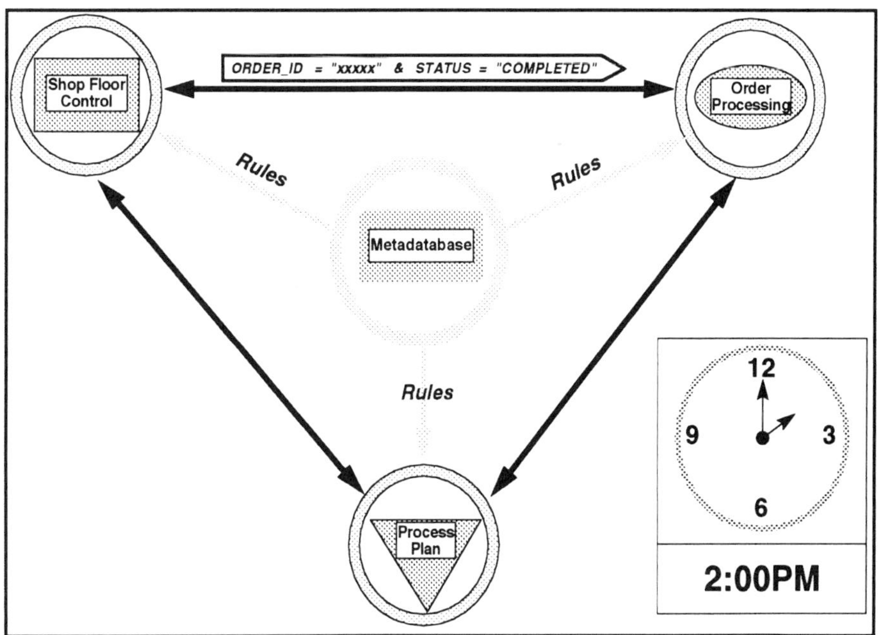

Fig. 6.14. Operational Rule Execution

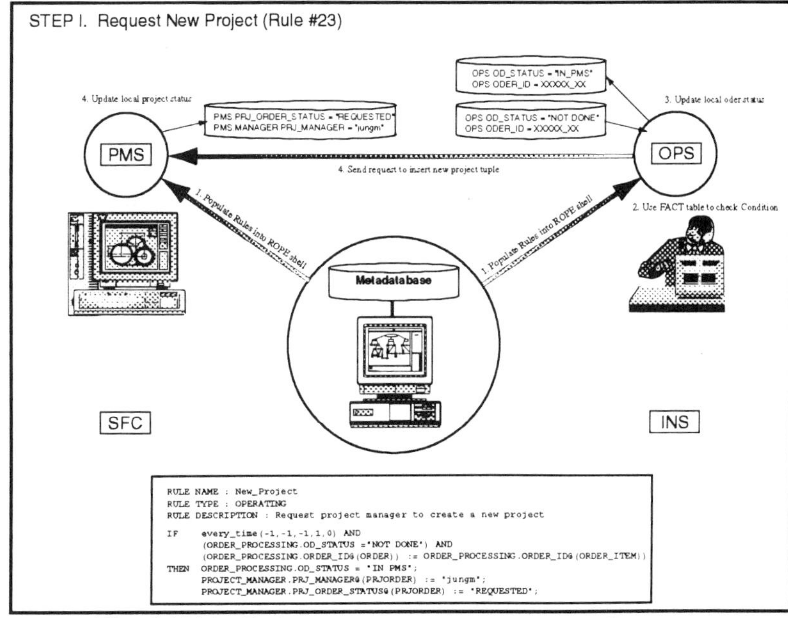

Fig. 6.15(a). Project management system - step 1

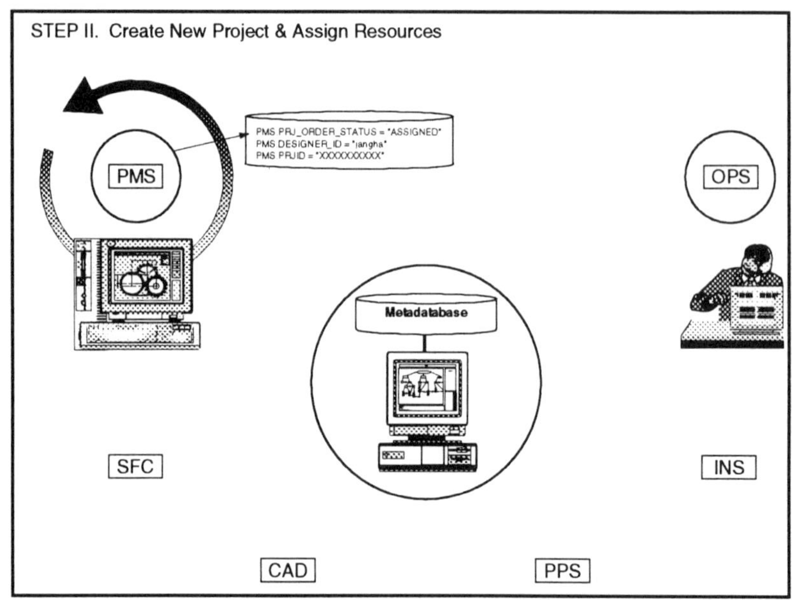

Fig. 6.15(b). Project management system - step 2

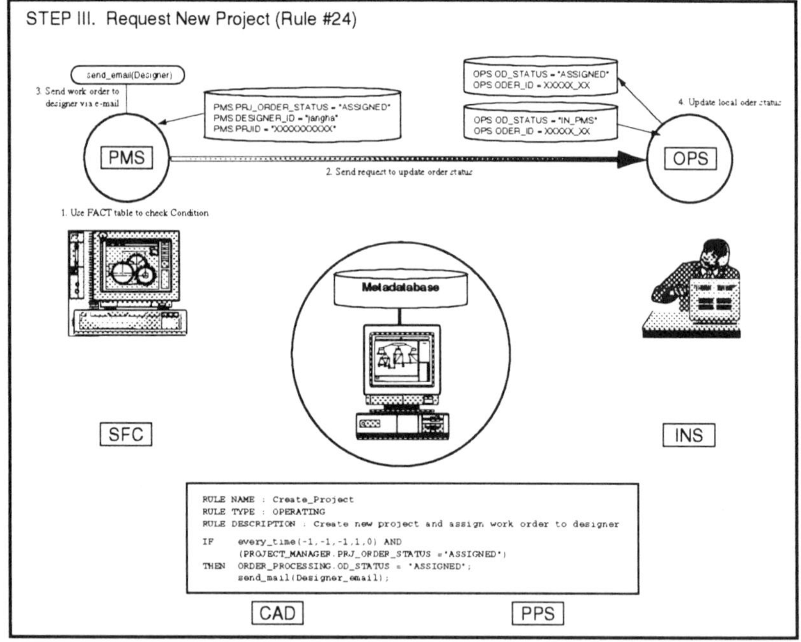

Fig. 6.15(c). Project management system - step 3

6.4 CONCLUSIONS

Recall that the metadatabase includes information about both data and knowledge, and this unique property enables an analyst to perform a simulation and other advanced analysis and modeling tasks, as in the above examples. The use of metadata, as managed in the passive mode, enables the semi-active and active modes of operation. More specifically, it provides the active mode with the information to perform data updates without central control. The semi-active mode illustrates one of the key Metadatabase concepts: the combination of data and of knowledge in the form of rules. Data models in the Metadatabase are referenced in generating the global queries, and rules are employed as necessary for the joining of data from tables in different applications. The active mode relates the two basic metadatabase concepts: the combining of data and knowledge for information exchanges in a CIM system, and the automation of updates in a distributed system without employing central database management. Both of these concepts are unique to the Metadatabase system and have been illustrated through examples from our demonstration system.

Finally, the complete model provides an important capability -- i.e., open systems architecture -- through the metadatabase residing at the global level. The metadatabase incorporates old, new, or changed local system models into its generic and integrated structure, and then implements, updates and manages the distributed shells accordingly. This capability is a new, fundamental breakthrough in the field. By virtue of the prototype, the metadatabase model is empirically verified to the extent of the core functionality demonstrated in this chapter.

Acknowledgment

This chapter is based on a paper written by the author and several colleagues: Gilbert Babin, M'hamed Bouziane, Waiman Cheung, Laurie Rattner, Alan Rubenstein, and Lester Yee. Drs. Babin, Bouziane and Yee created the prototype with the help of Dr. Rattner, and Mr. Rubenstein contributed to the development of the text of the paper. The paper is entitled "The Metadatabase Approach to Integrating and Managing Manufacturing Information Systems", *J. of Intelligent Manufacturing*, 1994, pp 333-349. In addition, the project management scenario is created by Mr. Myung-Joon Jung and Mr. Jangha Cho.

7

THE ENTERPRISE SCHEMA

All four types of enterprise metadata discussed in chapter 1 are integrated in the metadatabase; which itself is constructed as an independent database to support the organic architecture of EIM. Therefore, the metadatabase calls for a schema for itself - the schema of the enterprise metadata. A particular metadata representation method is developed to facilitate this task and is referred to as the Global Information Resources Dictionary (GIRD) model. With this design, the generic concept of a metadatabase is made particular to provide certain unique functionalities critical to an EIM. Based on the GIRD model, the metadatabase is also capable of serving as the global schema for the enterprise integrating multiple databases. A global schema designed this way possesses unique properties and advantages over the traditional designs of muti-databases, which all rely on schema integration methods that are connective in nature rather than fusing and hence are difficult to evolve.

7.1 THE GLOBAL INFORMATION RESOURCES DICTIONARY (GIRD)

The GIRD model is constructed as the logical design for a stand-alone (passive mode) metadatabase, which, in turn, is the first phase in the development of an active metadatabase that implements the knowledge (see Chapter 6) to directly facilitate the integration of local systems. Therefore, the GIRD model is developed not only to support passive metadata applications, but also to effect functionalities needed in global query processing or system interactions.

7.1.1 Overview of the GIRD Model

The GIRD model is represented according to the TSER approach described in Section 2 above. As such, TSER is used in two planes. First, it is used to describe each application system within the enterprise, and therefore, each such system has an SER and an OER model (e.g., the example in Section 2.2). These models constitute the major contents of the metadatabase. Secondly, however, TSER is used to abstract the metadatabase contents into a generic metadata model: the GIRD model. Thus there are both an SER and an OER model for the metadatabase itself; together they constitute the GIRD model. By using these two planes, a definitive structure consisting of five layers is determined, thereby achieving a desirable form of self-descriptiveness.

As a preview, Figure 7.1 shows the five layers of the GIRD modeling concept. The TSER constructs are used recursively at each layer to achieve both typing and self-description for metadata management. This structure is essentially generic and deterministic, since it is derived directly from the TSER model itself. Nonetheless, a part of the GIRD structure (i.e., Resources-View of the GIRD/SER and its corresponding HARDWARE RESOURCE and SOFTWARE RESOURCE of the GIRD/OER) is extensible in the sense that it may be changed to accommodate other views or requirements of particular industries or functions.

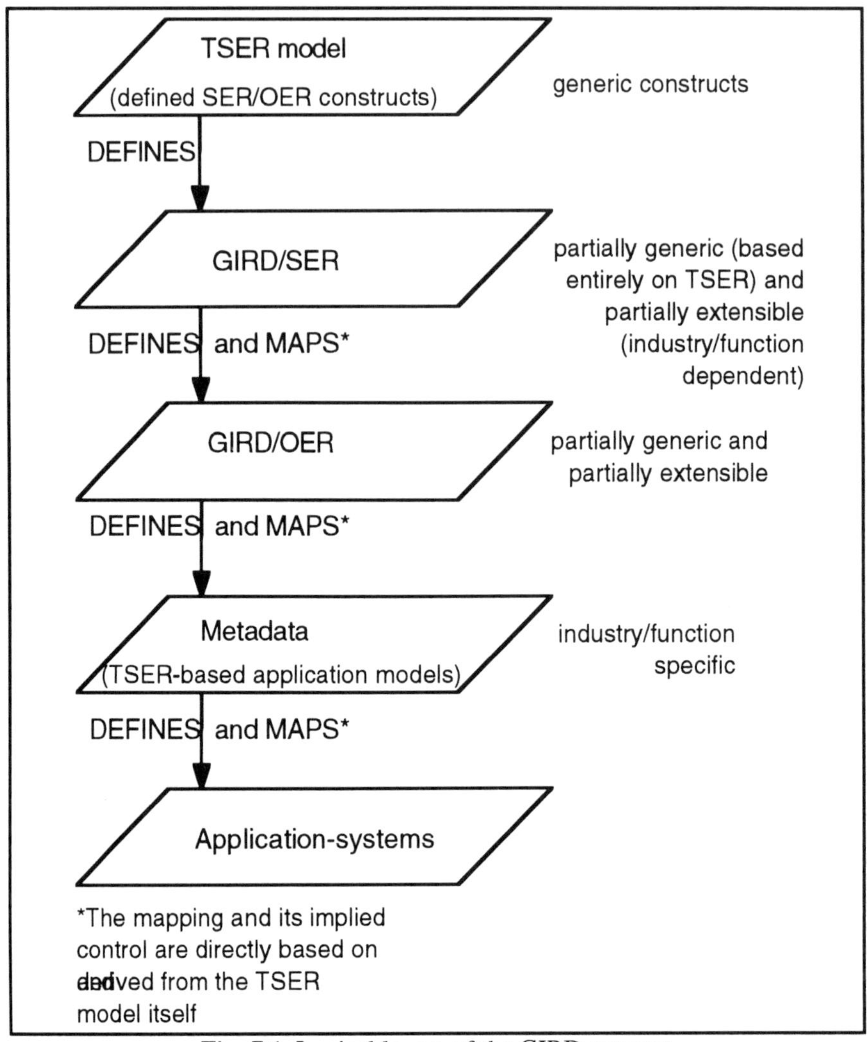

Fig. 7.1. Logical layers of the GIRD concept

Any such changes would result in a slightly different GIRD structure, but nevertheless, a structure that should be able to retain all of the design properties so long as the same process is used as described in this section. For clarity, we shall refer to the TSER constructs that are used to represent metadata in the GIRD layers as *meta*constructs; e.g., metasubject, metacontext, metaentity, metarelationship, and metaattribute, respectively.

7.1.2 The GIRD/SER Layer

The contents of this layer are depicted in Figure 7.2. These contents are derived directly from the general modeling process discussed in chapter 4.

As depicted in this figure, an enterprise can be viewed as a number of application systems encompassing users and organizational requirements (view 1). Since each system is represented by an SER model, another view of the enterprise is the set of SER models describing semantics, contextual knowledge and processes (view 2). Similarly, since each such SER is mapped to a corresponding OER data-structure model, the enterprise may be viewed as a set of OER models that are integrated into one global OER to define the data resources and their logic structures (view 3). Each of these three views is essentially a category of metadata determined entirely from the model constructs themselves, which in turn represent the general stages in the systems analysis and design process. These categories, along with a fourth one representing the implementation of information resources using hardware and software resources in the enterprise, constitute an SER-level schema for the metadata. Each category is modeled as a metasubject in Figure 7.2. The only metasubject that is not rooted in the model itself is Resources-View, which, however, is arguably always implied in an information model.

In sum, the information resources are represented at the SER level using four metasubjects (Application-View, Functional-View, Structural-View, and Resources-View) and five metacontexts specifying the interactions among the metasubjects. The metaattributes of these metasubjects comprise information resources determined from three sources: the literature (e.g., IRDS schema), target modeling paradigms (i.e., relational, object-oriented, and TSER), and empirical studies (viz., manufacturing). The functional modeling logic and rules are contained in the metacontext, "**Represented By**"; metacontext "**Map**"stores the mapping algorithms (i.e., dependency theory and heuristic rules) that produce data structure (OER) models from SERs. The contents of both these metacontexts are stored in files using routines and programs; in the future, their knowledge will be modeled explicitly. The metacontext "**Directory**"contains the knowledge about where OER files are stored. The remaining "**Use & Maintain**"metacontext specifies security and maintenance knowledge.

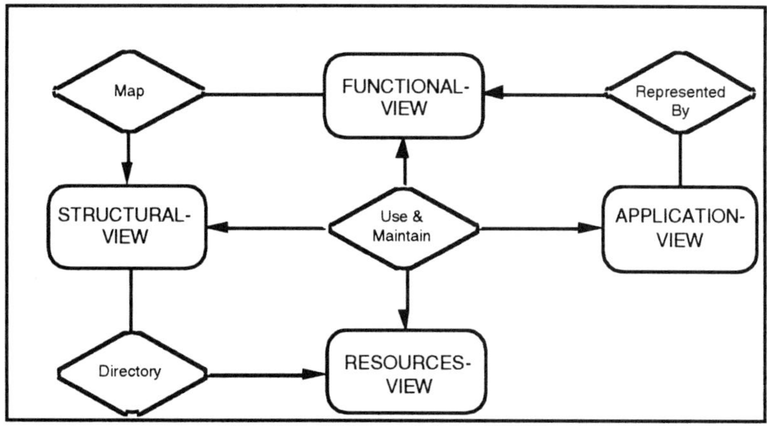

Fig. 7.2. SER model for GIRD

7.1.3 The GIRD/OER Layer

The TSER methodology is then applied to further develop the GIRD model. Each metasubject is first mapped to its OER submodel, and then the submodels are consolidated into an OER model — this model is the integrated representation for the global metadatabase. This representation, in turn, is mapped to a schema design in a target software environment for implementation as an enhanced database by itself. Because the TSER methodology is employed, the submodel data structures (and therefore those in the consolidated GIRD OER) are in at least third normal form.

All the submodels are consolidated using the TSER rules In consolidating the GIRD submodels, four metaOEs have been merged: **APPLICATION** (occurs in all four submodels); **SUBJECT** (occurs in Functional-View and Structural-View submodels); **ITEM** (occurs in "**FUNCTIONAL-VIEW**," "**STRUCTURAL-VIEW**," and Resources-View submodels); and finally, **PROGRAM** (in the Functional-View submodel) was merged with **SOFTWARE RESOURCE** (in the Resources-View submodel). Further, after consolidating identical constructs, metaFRs are created to represent referential integrity constraints across submodels. In this case, it is the metaFR **HardMaintain** between **USER** and **HARDWARE-RESOURCES**. Figure 7.3 shows the consolidated model, with the complete description of all metaentities and -relationships given below. Metaattributes provide documentaton and audit trail information for the metaentities and -relationships; they are also defined below. Since the design is based entirely on the logic of the TSER model for organizing metadata, it self-describes the modeling concepts and provides the global semantics. For example, the model shows that **APPLICATION** includes **SUBJECT** and **CONTEXT** which are consolidated into ENTITY and RELATIONSHIP plus two more types of associations signifying special integrity rules. These constructs are defined in terms of two common primitives, data **ITEM** (with equivalence definitions) and **RULE**, where the latter is further represented by **CONDITION** and **ACTION**, and then relates to **ITEM** through **FACT**. Associating constructs such as expressions and left-/right-operands for **CONDITION** are also defined along the way. All these constructs, combined with **HARDWARE** and **SOFTWARE** classes of metadata that show implementation models, are corresponded in the GIRD model.

Meta-Entities

KEY: **CONSTRUCT NAME**(Primary key, attribute[1],...attribute[n])

1. **ACTION** (Actid, acttype, factid, addedby, dateadded, modifby, lastmod, nummods)
2. **APPLICATION** (Applname, descript, addedby, dateadded, modifby, lastmod, nummods, userid)
3. **CONDITION** (Condid, leftfact, operator, rightfact, addedby, dateadded, modifby, lastmod, nummods)
4. **CONTEXT** (Cname, applname, descript, xcoord, ycoord, addedby, dateadded, modifby, lastmod, nummods)
5. **ENT-REL** (ERname, ertype, descript, akey, addedby, dateadded, modifby, lastmod, nummods)

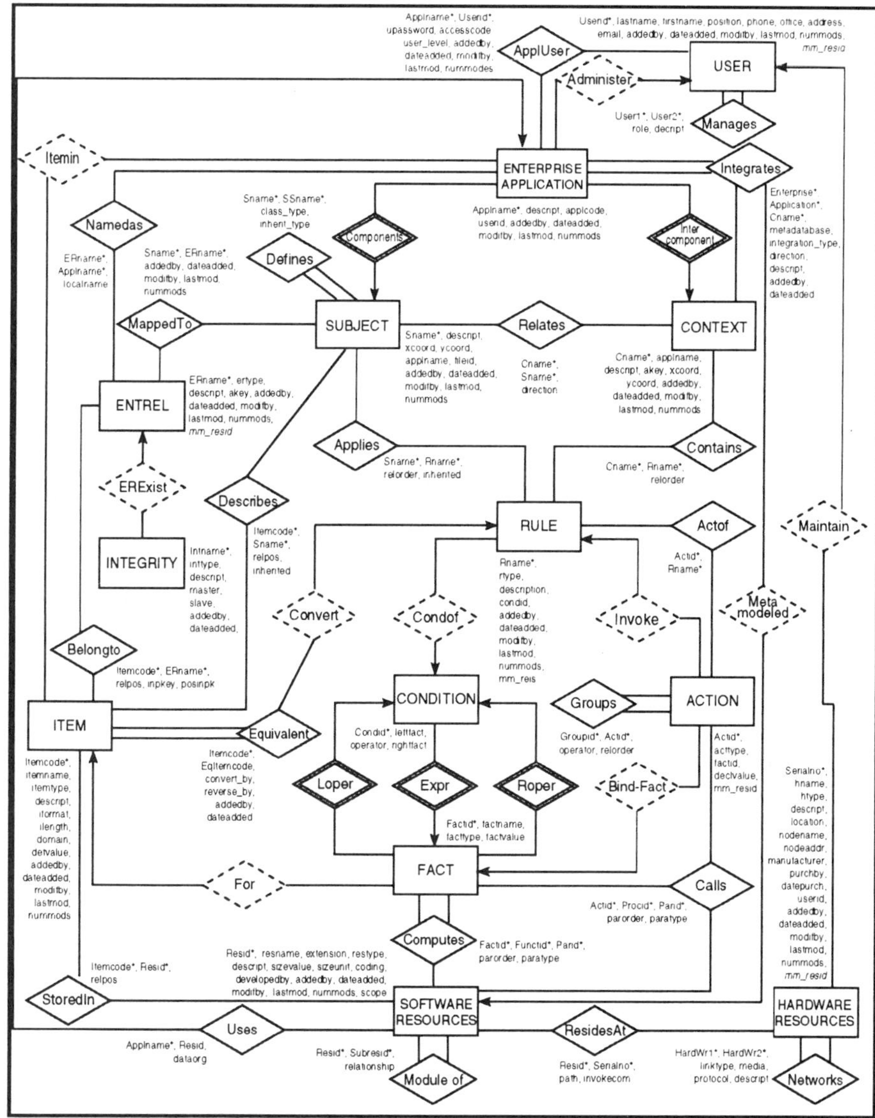

Fig. 7.3. OER model: global information resources dictionary (GIRD)

6. **FACT**(<u>Factid</u>, factname, facttype, factvalue)
7. **HARDWARE RESOURCE** (<u>Serialno</u>, hname, htype, descript, location, nodename, nodeaddr, manufacturer, purchby, datepurch, addedby, dateadded, modifby, lastmod, nummods, userid)
8. **INTEGRITY** (<u>Intname</u>, inttype, descript, master, slave, addedby, dateadded, modifby, lastmod, nummods)
9. **ITEM** (<u>Itemcode</u>, itemname, itemtype, descript, format, length, domain, defvalue, addedby, dateadded, modifby, lastmod, nummods, applname)
10. **PROGRAM**(<u>Functid</u>, ...) *Note: This meta-entity is consolidated in **SOFTWARE RESOURCES**.*

11. **RULE** (Rname, rtype, descript, condid, addedby, dateadded, modifby, lastmod, nummods)
12. **SOFTWARE RESOURCE** (Resid, resname, extension, restype, descript, sizevalue, sizeunit, coding, developedby, addedby, dateadded, modifby, lastmod, nummods)
13. **SUBJECT** (Sname, descript, xcoord, ycoord, addedby, dateadded, modifby, lastmod, nummods, supersname, applname, fileid)
14. **USER** (Userid, username, class, position, phone, office, address, addedby, dateadded, modifby, lastmod, nummods)

Meta-Plural Relationships (PRs)

1. **ActOf** (Actid, Rname, relorder, addedby, dateadded, modifby, lastmod, nummods)
2. **Applies** (Sname, Rname, relorder)
3. **ApplUser** (Applname, Userid, password, accesscode, addedby, dateadded, modifby, lastmod, nummods)
4. **BelongTo** (Itemcode,ERname, relpos, inpkey, posinpk)
5. **Calls** (Actid, Procid, Parid, parorder)
6. **Computes** (Factid, Functid,Parid, parorder)
7. **Contains** (Cname, Rname, relorder, addedby, dateadded, modifby, lastmod, nummods)
8. **Describes** (Itemcode, Sname, relpos)
9. **Equivalent** (Itemcode, EqItemcode, rname, addedby, dateadded)
10. **MappedTo** (Sname, ERname, addedby, dateadded, modifby, lastmod, nummods)
11. **ModuleOf** (Resid, Subresid, relationship)
12. **NamedAs** (ERname,Applname, localname)
13. **Relates** (Cname, Sname, direction)
14. **ResidesAt** (Resid, Serialno, path, invokecom, addedby, dateadded, modifby, lastmod, nummods)
15. **StoredIn** (Itemcode, Resid, relpos)
16. **Uses** (Applname, Resid, dataorg, addedby, dateadded, modifby, lastmod, nummods)

Meta-Mandatory Relationships (MRs)

1. **Component** (APPLICATION, SUBJECT)
   Role APPLICATION = owner
   Role SUBJECT = owned
2. **ComposedOf** (SUBJECT1, SUBJECT2)
   Role SUBJECT1 = owner (i.e; the superclass)
   Role SUBJECT2 = owned (i.e; the subclass)
3. **Express** (CONDITION, FACT)
   Role CONDITION = owner
   Role FACT = owned
4. **InterComponent** (APPLICATION, CONTEXT)
   Role APPLICATION = owner
   Role CONTEXT = owned
5. **LtOperand** (FACT, CONDITION)

Role FACT = owner
Role CONDITION = owned

6. **RtOperand** (FACT, CONDITION)
   Role FACT = owner
   Role CONDITION = owned

Meta-Functional Relationships (FRs)

1. **ApplMaintain** (APPLICATION, USER)
   Role APPLICATION = determinant
   Role USER = determined
2. **BindFact** (ACTION, FACT)
   Role ACTION = determinant
   Role FACT = determined
3. **CondOf** (RULE, CONDITION)
   Role RULE = determinant
   Role CONDITION = determined
4. **Convert** (Equivalent, RULE)
   Role Equivalent = determinant
   Role RULE = determined
5. **ERExist** (INTEGRITY, ENT-REL)
   Role INTEGRITY = determinant
   Role ENT-REL = determined
6. **For** (FACT, ITEM)
   Role FACT = determinant
   Role ITEM = determined
7. **HardMaintain** (HARDWARE RESOURCE, USER)
   Role HARDWARE RESOURCE = determinant
   Role USER = determined
8. **ItemIn** (ITEM, APPLICATION)
   Role ITEM = determinant
   Role APPLICATION = determined
9. **SubjectIn** (SUBJECT, SOFTWARE RESOURCE)
   Role SUBJECT = determinant
   Role SOFTWARE RESOURCE = determined

Definition of Meta-attributes

KEY (for meta-attribute name):
attribute - (lower case) non-key field in meta-relations
Attribute - (upper/lower case) key field in meta-relations
Attribute - (underlined upper/lower case) both key and non-key field in meta-relations

Meta-attribute Name	**Description**
accesscode	An attribute of the meta-PR ApplUser that identifies a user's authorized data access level; e.g., Read (R), Write (W), Execute (E), Delete (D).
Actid	Unique identifier (primary key) for meta-entity ACTION.

acttype	Class of consequences of the production rule. Ex. Takes on a value of 0 if result of rule is binding of a fact or a value of 1 for a procedure call.
addedby	Name/initials of a modeler or information administrator who entered the meta-entity or relationship into the GIRD. Provides for an audit trail.
address	Home address of a user. Attribute of meta-entity USER.
akey	Alternative primary-key(s) for an ENT-REL base relation.
Applname	Unique name (primary key) for an application.
class	Classification scheme for end-users; can serve to control priveledges and data access.
Cname	Unique name (primary key) for the meta-entity CONTEXT.
coding	The type of physical representation of a software sesource; e.g., Pascal or LISP for program code; or ASCII, VSAM, or ISAM for data files.
Condid	Unique identifier (primary key) for meta-entity CONDITION. Also an attribute of meta-entity RULE.
dataorg	Indicates how the data is organized in an application in meta-PR USES.
dateadded	Date that instance of meta-entity or meta-relationship was added to GIRD.
datepurch	Date on which a hardware resource was purchased/acquired.
defvalue	Default value, if any, for a meta-entity ITEM.
descript	Description of all defined meta-entities and meta-relationships.
developedby	The name of the firm or person who developed a software resource.
direction	Indiates how the link (data flows) between a CONTEXT and SUBJECT is directed graphically. (i.e.; 1 = toward SUBJECT; 2 = toward CONTEXT; 3 = bidirectional; nil = none) Attribute of meta-PR Relates.
domain	The set of values that can be assigned to a data item (meta-entity ITEM).

EqItemcode	Synonym for Itemcode in meta-PR Equivalent.
ERname	Unique name (primary key) for meta-entity ENT-REL.
ertype	The type of ENT-REL; takes on a value of "OE" or "PR" corresponding to operational entity and plural relationship respectively.
extension	The file-name extension (if any) for a software resource.
Factid	Unique system-generated identifier (primary key) for meta-entity FACT. Also, an attribute of meta-entity ACTION.
Factname	Attribute of a fact that is either an Itemcode or an expression (Condid).
facttype	Attribute of a fact that indicates how the value of the fact is to be assigned: 0 if the fact value is to be retrieved from a local database, 1 if it is the result of an expression evaluation, and 2 if it is computed by a function call.
factvalue	The calculated or referenced value, or a constant, that binds a fact during the rule inferencing process.
fileid	Attribute of meta-entity SUBJECT. Synonym for Resid.
format	The data item representation type. Attribute of meta-entity ITEM. Examples: Character (C), Integer (I), Real (R), BCD (B), EPCDIC (E), etc.
Functid	Synonym of Resid; identifies the function to be called for binding a fact. Key field in meta-PR Computes.
hname	Model number or name of a hardware resource.
htype	The type of hardware. Attribute of meta-entity HARDWARE RESOURCE. Examples: line-printer, mainframe, mini-, micro-computer, harddisk, etc.
inpkey	A flag (boolean value) indicating whether or not a data item is part of the primary key of ENT-REL. Attribute of meta-PR BelongTo.
Intname	Unique name (primary key) for an integrity constraint.
inttype	The type of integrity constraint, either "FR" or "MR" corresponding to functional relationship or mandatory relationship respectively.

invokecom	The command to invoke a software resource on a hardware resource. Attribute of meta-PR ResidesAt.
Itemcode	Unique system-generated identifier (primary key) for a data element (meta-entity ITEM).
Itemname	The name of a data item in meta-entity ITEM.
itemtype	An attribute of meta-entity ITEM to indicate whether the data item is "persistent" (exists in at least in one local DB) or is generated at runtime.
lastmod	Date of last modification of GIRD meta-entities and meta-relationships.
leftfact	Synonym of Factid and represents the left operand of an expression.
length	The length of a data item. May refer to length in character positions or bytes depending upon implementation.
localname	Attribute of meta-PR NamedAs.
location	Physical location for meta-entity HARDWARE RESOURCE.
manufacturer	The manufacturer of a hardware resource.
master	An attribute of meta-entity INTEGRITY which, in the case of an FRtype, plays the role of determinant; and in the case of an MRtype, plays the role of owner.
modifby	Identifier (name or initials) of an individual who last modified an instance of a given meta-relation.
nodeaddress	Network address for a hardware resource.
nodename	Network "node" name for a hardware resource.
nummods	Number of modifications to a meta-entity. This attribute is in all meta-entities and most meta-PRs.
office	Office location or address of meta-entity USER.
operator	The logical operator in antecedant of a production rule. This includes the set of arithmetic and set operators.
Parid	Synonym of Factid which represents a parameter of a function in meta-PR Calls.
parorder	The relative position of the parameter in a function/procedure parameter list .

path	Path to top level directory in which an software resurce resides on a hardware resource.
password	The password to an application in meta-PR ApplUser.
phone	Business telephone number of a user.
posinpkey	The relative position of a data item field in the primary key of ENT-REL.
position	Organizational position of the user; e.g., president, DBA, data-entry clerk.
Procid	Synonym of Resid, it identifies the procedure to be called for a rule action.
purchby	Identifier of individual resposible for the purchase of the hardware resource.
relationship	The relationship among software resources; in meta-PR ModuleOf.
relorder	Relative order (sequence) of a rule within a SUBJECT or CONTEXT — or of a condition in a rule.
relpos	Relative position of a data item in meta-entity ENT-REL.
Resid	A unique identifier (primary key) for meta-entity SOFTWARE RESOURCE
resname	Title/name of a software resource.
restype	Software resource type; e.g., program, data file, network, document.
rightfact	Synonym of Factid and represents the right side operand of an expression.
Rname	Unique name (primary key) for meta-entity RULE.
rtype	The type of rule; e.g., Modeling (M), Operating (O), Production (P), etc.
Serialno	The unique identifier (primary key) for meta-entity HARDWARE RESOURCE.
Sizeunit	The unit of measure for describing storage of a software resource; e.g., KBytes, blocks, cylinders, pages, etc.

Sizevalue	Quantity of units of storage for a specified software resource (expressed in sizeunits).
slave	An attribute of meta-entity INTEGRITY which, in the case of an FRtype, plays the role of determined; and in the case of an MRtype, plays the role of owned.
Sname	Unique name (primary key) of meta-entity SUBJECT.
Subresid	A synonym for Resid. .Key field in meta-PR ModuleOf.
supersname	The upper-level (if any) subject name for meta-entity SUBJECT.
Userid	Unique identifer (primary key) for meta-entity USER.
username	Full name of a user in meta-entity USER.
xcoord	X-coordinate of the graphical representation of a SUBJECT or CONTEXT.
y coord	Y-coordinate of the graphical representation of a SUBJECT or CONTEXT.

7.1.4 Summary

Based on the above discussions, several salient characteristics and design properties of the GIRD model are summarized below (see also Figure 7.3).

(1) A hierarchy of models (as represented by the four metasubjects) corresponding to the usual life cycle of systems analysis and design are covered and stored in a structured way.
(2) Three basic dimensions of data representations found in representative data models are included; namely, dependency theory-based relations, integrity constraints, and data abstraction hierarchy.
(3) By virtue of intra-subject rules (encapsulation), inter-subject rules grouped into contexts, and digraphs (flows), the knowledge representation encompasses both static and dynamic dimensions of the major classes of knowledge required for information integration.
(4) The classes of metadata are unified to the extent of the GIRD/OER model that connects all its elements through two interrelated primitives: data items and predicate logic (in the form of production rules).
(5) The GIRD model achieves a fundamental level of capacity for both representing some heterogeneity and facilitating information integration (through e.g., equivalence knowledge).
(6) Integration of heterogeneous data models is achieved purely at a logical level (i.e., via the enterprise information model) and implemented by virtue of links represented in the GIRD model, thus it does not require physical integration of local schemata.

(7) The basic structure of GIRD is rooted in TSER and derived directly from the modeling logic; therefore, it is self-descriptive (in the sense of recursive definition) up to the TSER definition itself.

(8) When TSER is employed for information modeling, and therefore provides metadata for populating the GIRD structure, the modeling process is reversible; i.e., the original functional and structural models can be reproduced directly and completely from the metadatabase.

We might stress that, although the GIRD model is developed using TSER, it can be implemented without having to use TSER as the modeling methodology. The structure, definition, and conventions of GIRD become independent after its development is completed. The next section provides details on how this model can be implemented in a typical environment.

7.2 GIRD IMPLEMENTATION: A METADATABASE

Basically, the GIRD model (see Figure 7.3) calls for four classes of computing capabilities to operate fully: (1) metarelation processing to implement all metaentities and -relationships (e.g., basic relational technology), (2) rule processing to fire the rules represented in the model (e.g., the rule-based techniques), (3) integrity control to enforce the links among metarelations (e.g., data management shells), and (4) routine management to execute the programs and function calls (e.g., system programming modules). These capabilities require common techniques that are readily available from the software industry. Further, it should be pointed out that rule processing and routine management are not required for a passive metadatabase where rules are simply stored for querying and are not fired. Storage and display of rules can be done in the same manner as metarelations.

Therefore, there can be a number of practical strategies for metadatabase implementation in a typical enterprise; the choice depends mainly on the usual criteria of cost-benefits and efficiency vs effectiveness. A simple approach is to employ as the engine a database management system that provides extended relational capabilities, runs under an operating systems with sufficient file management functions, and interfaces with rule-based languages or their equivalent. Although custom-designed software shells would still be needed to put these components together and to provide a user interface, the effort will, at most, amount to a moderate software engineering endeavor.

A somewhat designated approach using custom architecture and software was adopted to develop the metadatabase prototype at Rensselaer. This strategy takes advantage of TSER and the particular computing environments at hand. This implementation is detailed below.

The metadatabase system is presently implemented using a relational database management system (RDBMS). At the core is the populated GIRD model; i.e., the passive metadatabase. The entire metadatabase schema and most of the metadata are managed using the RDBMS according to the GIRD model, while routines and other software resources are managed through the operating system of the compiling system chosen. The metadatabase schema includes both data structures and integrity rules.

The schema design is derived entirely from the GIRD/OER model according to TSER definitions. To facilitate this effort, however, a custom tool was used for the Rensselaer prototype. This tool, Information Base Modeling System (IBMS), is a CASE implementation for TSER. A schema generator that maps the GIRD model into an implementation system is included in IBMS. The metadatabase prototype was populated with metadata from the information model created with IBMS. The same logic, however, can be performed without using IBMS.

Access to the metadatabase is through its management shell (Metadatabase Management System - MDBMS) built on the RDBMS and C. For metadatabase users, MDBMS would be the only interface needed; IBMS would be invoked mainly for tasks that involve modeling (e.g., creating or evolving the enterprise information system). In addition, this management system is designed to provide rulebase processing capabilities as well as to support metadata applications. Users such as systems analysis and design professionals can query against the metadatabase for rnterprise information models. These models may be used or reused as the basis for new developments; "what-if" type of analyses can also be performed on this basis to assess the impact of proposed changes (or growths) to existing models.

Once the appropriate base relations have been created, view and functional model information (from the SER) and application schema information (from the OER) are entered into the system using appropriate data definitional statements. The mapping algorithms for this process have also been automated. After the creation of an SER model and corresponding OER model for a given application system, a set of data definitional statements are generated to input these classes of metadata into the corresponding GIRD relations.

As an example, consider a metadatabase that is created for a CIM system described by the CIM SER model in Section 3.5 of Chapter 3. The OER model of the example is given by the core model in Section 10.3.3 of Chapter 10. When both SER and OER models are populated into the metadatabase, the metarelation **APPLICATION** contains four rows, or instances (see Table 7.1) corresponding respectively to the four application systems in Figure 3.5. The metarelation **SUBJECT** (table 7.2) contains all leaf level subjects in Figures 3.6 and 3.7 since the SER model involves only pure decomposition and has no inheritance hierarchy. In the event that a hierarchy of subjects needs to be stored in the metadatabase, super-subjects would also be included, with their inheritance relationships represented in **Define** metarelation. Some other metarelations are also shown in tables 7.3 - 7.10. A key property to note here is the important fact that application information models are always integrated (fused) into and through the GIRD model. The metarelation **Equivalent** maintains the global correspondences among data items from heterogeneous model at all time with computational ease. When a new model is added to a previously integrated global model (i.e., the contents of the metadatabase), only the new subjects, contexts, rules, items, entities, and all their associations need to be entered into the metadatabase as new rows. With the specification of equivalence to any one of the previous items in the **Equivalent** metarelation, the equivalence of an item to all items established previously is automatically established. The rest of the global model stays the same. There is no need for ad hoc, unwieldy modifications or additions of new global calibration on to the existing global schema (like all other technologies must do) since the GIRD model provides the global semantics and the action of being stored into it is the calibration.

Table 7.1 The Metarelation APPLICATION for the CIM Example [APPLICATION]

APPLNAME	DESCRIPT	APPLCODE	USERID	ADDEDBY	DATEADDED ...
SHOP_FLOOR	SHOP FLOOR CONTROLLER	sfc	LESTER	LY006	3/1/1990
PROCESS_PLAN	PROCESS PLANNING	pps	LESTER	LY006	11/1/1989
ORDER_PROCESSING	ORDER PROCESSING	ops	LESTER	LY006	11/17/1990
SHEETMENTALOBJECTS	SHEETMENTALOBJECTS	pdb	LESTER	LY006	11/17/1990

Table 7.5 The Metarelation SUBJECT for the CIM Example [SUBJECT]

SNAME	DESCRIPT	XCOORD	YCOORD	APPLNAME	FILEID	ADDEDBY ...
SHOP_FLOOR	SHOP FLOOR CONTROLLER	54	33	SHOP_FLOOR	NL007	3/1/1990
OPERATOR	INSTRUCTIONS FOR THE OPERATOR	26	9	SHOP_FLOOR	WC002	4/19/1990
PROCESS_PLAN	PROCESS PLANNING	12	25	PROCESS_PLAN	JK008	11/1/1989
MATERIAL	MATERIAL CHARACTERISTICS	26	1	PROCESS_PLAN	WC002	4/30/1990
ORDER_ PROCESSING	ORDER ENTRY AND TRACKING SYSTEM	40	25	ORDER_ PROCESSING	MB001	11/17/1990
CUSTOMER	CUSTOMERS INFORMATION	26	1	ORDER_ PROCESSING	WC002	8/21/1990
SHEETMETAL OBJECTS	SHEETMETAL OBJECTS	12	9	SHEETMETAL OBJECTS	JK008	11/1/1990
FEATURE		110	81	SHEETMETAL OBJECTS	NL007	12/15/1990

Table 7.2 The Metarelation ENTREL for the CIM Example [ENTREL]

ERNAME	ERTYPE	DESCRIPT	AKEY	ADDEDBY	DATEADDED ...
SEQUENCE	OE			WC002	4/19/1990
PART	OE		((ITEM_11)(ITEM_12)(ITEM_173)(ITEM_54)(ITEM_100))	WC002	4/19/1990
PAGE	OE			WC002	4/19/1990
LINE	OE			WC002	4/19/1990
WK_STATION	OE			WC002	4/19/1990

Table 7.3 The Metarelation ITEM for the CIM Example [ITEM]

ITEM CODE	ITEM NAME	ITEM TYPE	DESCRIPT	IFORMAT	ILENGTH	PRECISION	DOMAIN	APPL NAME	ADDEDBY	DATE ADDED ...
ITEM_1	WS_ ID	0	WORK STATION IDENTIFIER	CHARACTER	4	-1	WS_ID	SHOP_ FLOOR	LR005	4/19/1990
ITEM_2	WS_ NAME	0	WORK STATION NAME	CHARACTER	10	-1	WS_ NAME	SHOP_ FLOOR	LR005	4/19/1990
ITEM_3	WO_ID	0	WORK ORDER IDENTIFIER	CHARACTER	9	-1	WO_ID	SHOP_ FLOOR	LR005	4/19/1990
ITEM_4	SEQ_ ID	0	SEQUENCE IDENTIFIER	CHARACTER	4	-1	SE_QID	SHOP_ FLOOR	LR005	4/19/1990
ITEM_5	PART_ ID	0	PART IDENTIFIER	CHARACTER	5	-1	PART_ID	SHOP_ FLOOR	LR005	4/19/1990

Table 7.4 The Metarelation RULE for the CIM Example [RULE]

RNAME	RTYPE	DESCRIPT	CONDID	NUMB	ADDEDBY	DATEADDED ...
OR_RULE_2	CONVERSION	CONVERT ORDER ID FFROM OPS TO SFC		0	WC002	02/10/1991
OR_RULE_1	CONVERSION	CONVERT ORDER ID FROM SFC TO OPS		0	WC002	02/10/1991
PREPARE_SFC_R5	OPERATING	PREPARE SFC IF ROUTING IS READY	COND_4	1	GSER	8/4/1993
ASSIGN_QUANITY_R7	OPERATING	COPY OPS.QUANTITY TO SFC.WO_QUAN	COND_7	1	GSER	8/4/1993
ASSEMBLED_STATUS_R8	OPERATING	CHANGE OI_STATUS INTO ASSEMBLED	COND_11	1	GSER	8/4/1993

Table 7.6 The Metarelation BELONGTO for the CIM Example [BELONGTO]

ITEMCODE	ERNAME	RELPOS	INPKEY	POSINPK
ITEM_4	SEQUENCE	1	1	1
ITEM_5	PART	1	1	1
ITEM_56	PART	2	0	0
ITEM_99	PART	3	0	0
ITEM_24	LINE	1	1	1
ITEM_1	WK_STATION	1	1	1

Table 7.7 The Metarelation CONTAINS for the CIM Example [CONTAINS]

CNAME	RNAME	RELORDER
SFC_OPS	PREPARE_SFC_R5	1
SFC_OPS	ASSIGN_QUANITY_R7	2
OPS_PPS	PREPARE_NEW_PLAN_R1	1
OPS_PPS	SKIP_P_PLAN_R2	2
PDB_PPS	DESIGN_REVISION_R4	1
NSP_SFC	HOLD_WO_STATUS_R13	1
OPS_SFC_PP	PREPARE_SFC_R6	1
OPS_SFC_PP	P_PLAN_REVISION_R13	2
PDB_OPS	R15	1
PDB_OPS	R154	2

Table 7.8 The Metarelation DESCRIBES for the CIM Example [DESCRIBES]

ITEMCODE	SNAME	RELPOS	INHERITED
ITEM_4	OPERATOR	1	0
ITEM_11	BILL_MAT	1	0
TEM_1	INVENTORY	1	0
TEM_1	WK_ORDER	1	0
ITEM_29	WK_ORDER	20	0
ITEM_1	WK_STATION	1	0
ITEM_2	WK_STATION	2	0
ITEM_30	MATERIAL	1	0

Table 7.9 The Metarelation RELATES for the CIM Example [RELATES]

CNAME	SNAME	DIRECTION
ALLOCATED	BILL_MAT	2
USED_BY	WK_ORDER	2
ALLOCATE_MATL	MAT_INFO	3
QUEUED_AT	WK_ORDER	2
LOCATED_AT	MAT_INFO	2
INSTRUCTS	MAT_INFO	1

Table 7.10 The Metarelation MAPPEDTO for the CIM Example [MAPPEDTO]

SNAME	ERNAME	ADDEDBY	DATEADDED...
OPERATOR	SEQUENCE	WC002	4/19/1990
WK_ORDER	SEQUENCE	WC002	4/19/1990
OPERATOR	PART	WC002	4/19/1990
INVENTORY	PART	WC002	4/19/1990
OPERATOR	PAGE	WC002	4/19/1990
OPERATOR	LINE	WC002	4/19/1990
INVENTORY	WK_STATION	WC002	4/19/1990
WK_STATION	WK_STATION	WC002	4/19/1990

7.3 UNIQUE PROPERTIES OF THE GIRD MODEL

7.3.1 The Metadatabase As an Information Resources Dictionary

The GIRD and the traditional repositories such as IRDS models differ at a fundamental level; i.e., the scope and use of metadata as discussed in chapter 1. In sum, GIRD (1) aims to facilitate information integration for functional synergy of the enterprise as opposed to managing software resources per se, (2) accommodates adaptable, scalable and heterogeneous systems, and (3) supports all four types of enterprise metadata including knowledge.

Some technical points are discussed herein. The Global Information Resources Dictionary model extends the concept of metadata to encompass subjects and contexts including events and the rules that trigger such events in both the enterprise and the metadatabase itself - e.g. the knowledge which dictates how, when, and why the information is passed between the mover and operator workstations.

An analytical benefit of the metadatabase using GIRD model is that as a **system**, the metadatabase is modeled and the model is stored within itself. The modeling of the metadatabase produced SER and OER models which were stored as instances of a system within the implemented metadatabase system. In fact, as depicted in Figure 7.1, the GIRD model entails five layers in its logic — layers that are independent of industry or application functions. Each layer is definitively structured for its own contents and linked with other layers through mapping algorithms that are derived directly from the modeling constructs. Controls are also provided by virtue of the types and definitions of these TSER constructs. This is a class of strong self-descriptiveness unique to the GIRD model. As a result, the self-description permits comprehensive yet concise control of metadata and also allows a user to query about the underlying GIRD model itself. In contrast, the four layer structure of other repository systems anchor less in its underlying model or logic than in applications. Therefore, it does not allow for stable and generic self-description

The TSER methodology (functional modeling, structural modeling, and metadata modeling) provides the GIRD model the necessary structures to fully represent modeling hierarchies. The three levels of modeling (views, structural models, and physical implementation models) are represented through the metaentities **SUBJECT** and **CONTEXT**, **ENT-REL** , and **SOFTWARE RESOURCES**, respectively. In addition, since the GIRD model employs the TSER approach for modeling application systems (i.e., the metadata layer in Figure 7.1), the metaentities **SUBJECT** and **CONTEXT** actually contain a hierarchy of semantic models for the enterprise information system.

Although the majority of associations of data in implemented systems can be considered to be binary relationships, data modeling capabilities for advanced and future systems require them to be more flexible in handling complex data. Increasing use of complex data-structures such as geometric data, however, requires n-ary relationships be supported in a global data dictionary. N-ary relationships are supported within the GIRD model by the **ENT-REL** metaentity.

The unique inclusion of knowledge in the GIRD model is comprised of contextual rules for application models, integrity constraints applied to the modeling structure, and classification knowledge over data. For complex models or ones with control information, the GIRD model metaentities **CONTEXT**, **RULE**, **CONDITION**, and **ACTION** provide for such knowledge representation. Combining these metaentities with **SUBJECT**, **ENT-REL**, and the capability of n-ary structures creates appropriate provisions for representing object-oriented models. For instance, objects would be represented by SUBJECTs with their transaction knowledge corresponding to intra-subject rules. CONTEXTs would be created when inter-subject rules are present. Inheritance constraints would be interpreted into OER integrity rules. These results are all supported in the above structure.

To address the need for thesaurus capabilities, especially in a multi-information systems environment, the GIRD model provides for global equivalence among data items that represent the same logical objects -- but that happen to be implemented differently. This property, which is important for heterogeneous database systems, was developed in the GIRD model via a meta-PR called **Equivalent**. Instances of this metaPR have two attributes in their composite primary key and a non-key attribute pointing to a rule for translation. The key appears as **Itemcode** and **EqItemcode** corresponding to a pair of system generated **ITEM** identifiers. The **Rname** attribute references the data translation rules, if any, for data interchange. Finally, the addition of a control shell and an inference engine on top of the GIRD gives it the capability of becoming an intelligent, active metadatabase. These added features serve to manage data and knowledge within complex enterprises with greater efficiency and effectiveness.

7.3.2 The metadatabase as the Global/Enterprise Schema

The metadatabase also provides the global enterprise schema needed for managing the multiple systems in the integrated enterprise. Different from other EIM technology, however, this global schema is itself a database that has a stable global semantic structure abstracting all enterprise metadata and managing them just like a database. All other multi-database systems lack such a metamodel and can only connect schemas (so-called schema integration) into an ad hoc hierarchy that is hard to globally reconcile and adapt (also see Section 7.2).

In particular, the GIRD model in Figure 7.3 shows the types of abstraction (e.g., all subjects from local data models are represented as instances into the **SUBJECT** metaentity; their attributes, **ITEM**, and so on). Furthermore, all categories of metadata are constructed in an integrated manner amenable for implementation using primarily relational technology (i.e., each type can be mapped to and implemented as a base table). Thus, even though the local databases can be of a variety of classes, from relational to object-oriented and flat files, the metadatabase itself is always of a uniform environment. An object hierarchy defined in EXPRESS for a local engineering database would, for example, be represented as a set of subject tuples and a set of (data) item tuples, along with a few other sets of metadata tuples for inheritance/integrity, equivalence, rules and so on for incorporation into the metadatabase. As such, each and every local model is represented and integrated (but not duplicated, nor removed) into the metadatabase as ordinary metadata tuples populating the structure. When a subject's attributes are recorded generically and globally in the **ITEM** metaentity separate from the **SUBJECT**, with their associations recorded as such, the global representation of local models is virtually infinitely extensible without losing structural integrity; yet structural limitations are precisely a common problem with traditional canonical data representations. Therefore **metadata independence** at the model integration level is achieved since any change in enterprise models (which are simply metadata instances) would involve only ordinary metadata transactions similar to the usual relational processing, and does not require any change to the structure itself, nor reloading/recompilation. The term metadata independence is phrased in the same philosophy as the well-known data independence concept (see Section 2.3.1 of Chapter 2).

For the purpose of providing a global schema for the EIM, the GIRD model gives the metadatabase certain unique properties that distinguish it from previous IT. They are summarized below:

(1) The GIRD model can be implemented in the same manner as a regular schema using a relational DBMS, where the TSER constructs of the model provide design specifications.

(2) Local information models (represented in the metadatabase as tuples) can be added, deleted, or modified without causing the metadatabase to restructure nor recompile.

(3) All meta-relations in the GIRD model (e.g., **APPLICATIONS, SUBJECT, DEFINE, CONTEXT, RULE, ITEM, Equivalent,** and **BelongTo**) are normalized. Thus, they can be managed and processed as a (relational) database implementing the model.

(4) Contextual knowledge is represented in terms of relations as well. A particular class is the equivalence between data items. For instance, the fact that 5/31/94 in the American format of date is equivalent to the European 31/5/94 is

established through **ITEM** and **Equivalent**, with the attendant conversion rules and routines represented through **RULE**.

(5) The required metadata as discussed in Chapter 1 are all included in the GIRD model. Thus, Figure 7.3 shows the high-level semantics of the metadatabase.

(6) In addition to effect a full-fledge metadata management facility, the metadatabase also simplifies the mapping requirements. Since all local databases map directly with the metadatabase rather than among themselves, the complexity is O(N) as opposed to $O(N^2)$.

(7) The usual concern of semantics loss during local-global mapping is also kept to a minimum since the mapping is based on metadata constructs as opposed to relying on data structures. While the latter tends to be arbitrary and rigid, the former can be accomplished through rigorous (reverse) modeling at the time when the local databases are represented into the metadatabase.

(8) The modeling and creation of metadatabase follow exactly the tradition of data and knowledge systems analysis and design. Full discussions of a particular methodology and its CASE implementation can be found in Chapter 4.

(9) The metadata independence nature of the architecture supports naturally scalability in terms of adding new systems; while its implementation using a regular DBMS assures scaling up in software engineering. When a new model (application system) is added to the metadatabase environment for integration with other systems, the administator needs only to know this new model. Once reverse-engineered or registered, the metadatabase automatically fuse it into the rest of the global schema.

Acknowledgment

The GIRD model is originally published in a paper written by the author and three colleagues: Drs. M'hamed Bouziane, Laurie Rattner, and Lester Yee. The paper is entitled, "Information Resources Management in Heterogeneous, Distributed Environments: A Metadatabase Approach," *IEEE Transactions on Software Engineering*, Vol. 17, No. 6, 1991, pp. 604-625. Dr. Bouziane developed the detailed design of the GIRD model along with Drs. Rattner and Yee. Since then, the model has been updated slightly to support multimedia resources, rulebases, and distributed metadatabases; the latest result is reported in this chapter. Drs. Gilbert Babin and Waiman Cheung, Mr. Jangha Cho, and Mr. Yicheng Tao have contributed to these revisions in addition to the original authors.

8

THE GLOBAL QUERY SYSTEM

This chapter is co-authored with **Waiman Cheung**, Ph.D.
Lecturer, Chinese University of Hong Kong.

The enterprise metadata are a potent source of knowledge that users can tap into to facilitate their interaction with the information environment. The metadatabase is, hence, put to action to serve as the online intelligence for all three levels of enterprise information management tasks discussed in Chapter 1. The Global Query level (which implies the file transfer level, too) functionality of the metadatabase (as the EIM) is developed in this chapter.

8.1 MODEL ASSISTED GLOBAL QUERY

A key requirement of an EIM for information integration is what might be called the "on-line intelligence and assistance" capabilities of the integrated systems for supporting enterprise users' (varying) needs in retrieving information at a global level from the multiple local systems, which may frequently change their operating rules as well as contents. Numerous research and commercial systems have evolved over the past decade towards providing these capabilities for single-site or multiple-site databases. However, a rigorous formulation of this requirement for expressly the global query needs of multiple systems has not been provided previously; nor has such a technology.

8.1.1 The Need for Metadata Support

Metadata has been increasingly recognized as a key element in global query systems. The questions raised here are, how much and what metadata should a global query system process in order to effect on-line intelligence and assistance capabilities, and what architecture can manage and utilize the metadata to suffice these capabilities?

To illustrate the significance of these envisioned capabilities, we consider below some basic tasks required of a global query system in a heterogeneous, distributed environment . A typical global query operation involves two steps; namely, global query formulation and global query processing. In the first step, the user's requests are articulated and represented in a way that the global query system understands. The query formulation is done primarily through the user interface of the system. In the second step, accomplished by the system internally, queries are sent to appropriate local systems to retrieve pertinent information and reassembled for the users.

Towards query formulation, on-line intelligence enables the user interface to provide assistance in the articulation as well as allow for high-level, intuitive representation of queries. Specifically, for the **articulation** of queries, the system would utilize its knowledge on the enterprise information resources (which are metadata; including information models, implementation models and business and operating rules -- see Section 8. for a formal description) to alleviate semantic ambiguity, facilitate logical analysis, and enhance adaptive construction during the formulation of queries. Similarly, the **representation** itself could accommodate heterogeneity in local models across the enterprise through, e.g., the knowledge on enterprise SUBJECTs and the equivalence of data items among different local systems without having to impose a single, fixed "integrated schema" on all databases.

In addition to supporting high-level and non-syntax-based queries for enterprise users, the system would also handle all context-based interpretations and dynamic mappings between the globally formulated query and the locally implemented file structures or database schemata. Assisted with these capabilities, the second step - global query processing - would be accomplished in the following fashion:

(1) query optimization: the global query is first optimally decomposed into local queries taking into account both semantics and performance;

(2) query translation: the local queries are then encoded in their respective data manipulation languages;

(3) query execution: the encoded local queries get dispatched to and processed at their respective systems; and finally

(4) result integration: results from local systems are assembled to answer the global query.

Each of these processing steps makes use of metadata as well. For instance, local database schemata, directory and network information, and the contextual knowledge of data are required for query optimization; local DBMS information for query translation; operating rules on information flows for query execution; and knowledge on equivalent objects, incompatibility and data conversion for result integration.

Without the assistance from sufficient on-line knowledge in the form of metadata, all of the remaining information required, as mentioned above, for both query formulation and processing would have to be provided by the users or application programs, such as the case in pervious systems regardless of the interfacing designs used. The problem of lacking on-line metadata support is especially acute for multiple systems, where researchers have increasingly emphasized the use of enterprise metadata. A basic reason is the significant differences in the CONTEXTs in which data are utilized, on top of the complexities in varying data semantics (models), data manipulation languages, and data structures among local systems. Either the users or the global system itself must abridge these differences for each query before the information can be shared. Since enterprise users generally do not possess the expertise in database technology, nor the technical knowledge about the local systems, they cannot truly benefit from a global query system which does not possess sufficient metadata to provide on-line intelligence and assistance. The notion of enterprise metadata is concerned with all metadata pertaining to the above SUBJECTs and CONTEXTs.

8.1.2 User Interface for Query Formulation

User interface techniques are important to global query systems. Techniques such as windows, icons, menus, graphics, visualization and other forms of non-textual formalisms free the typical non-programmer user from having to learn sophisticated programming languages. Therefore, graphical user interface (GUI) technologies have been employed together with cognition-theoretic interface design principles and guidelines to facilitate database query tasks. The results have improved significantly the commercially available database query systems, especially those emerging in the '90s (e.g., GUI add-ons to SQL for a few relational systems). Notwithstanding, these latest products still do not support users with on-line metadata on enterprise models (especially contextual knowledge of data) required for global query system in heterogeneous environments. Users are still charged with the responsibility of furnishing many of the technical information mentioned above. Moreover, since these systems do not offer an on-line global model separate from the schemata, which are fixed, their user interfaces tend to be hard to change or to customize, as the underlying systems or the users change.

The same observations are largely applicable to the so-called natural language interfaces. In principle, any systems that use natural languages should not require the users to learn the artificialities of correct command formats or modes of interaction. Unfortunately, few systems (even research systems) have successfully achieved this goal, due mainly to insufficient results in linguistics and artificial intelligence to support this class of user interface. However, even in the ideal case, a natural language interface would not be able to assist on the query formulation itself for the same reasons as GUI faces: It does not provide users with such knowledge as the local and global data resources, dictionary and directory knowledge, and business rules about the enterprise; all of which are needed before a user interface could ever support non-technical user in a "natural" mode of query formulation.

Addressing the need of providing metadata to users, database browsers have been developed to help end users to look through the contents of a particular database. Most of these database interfaces are limited to browsing the data instances and support only single-site and single-tuple queries; moreover, few look beyond the simple database schema per se, which does not include other types of enterprise metadata [20, 39, 52, 55, 58, 59]. They, ironically, provide interesting evidence supporting the thesis that enterprise metadata can lead to a new breakthrough for the problem.

8.1.3 Integrated Schema for Global Query

Enterprise metadata as discussed above are complex in their own right. Thus, it is natural to expect an architecture devoted to them for the above stated tasks. Is the conventional integrated schema technology sufficient?

A key issue concerning expressly multiple systems is how to reconcile and consolidate the various views and representation methods across the enterprise and yet still retain local differences for autonomy and flexibility. Most previous efforts employ a solution strategy emphasizing the development of global architectures based on a schema integration approach. Although an integrated schema is a facility of metadata, its hard-coded nature, i.e., a fixed hierarchy of definitions that cannot be easily changed, globally re-defined, or integrated tends to contradict or even nullify some of the basic promises of true local autonomy, such as openness and adaptiveness. Moreover, additional enterprise metadata beyond the integrated schema are needed to facilitate the representation of global views and the management of query transactions among local databases. Therefore, these efforts have by contradiction shown an even bigger role for enterprise metadata, that is, minimizing the reliance on some fixed, hard-coded global schemata or controller to effect information integration.

A conclusion from the above discussion is evident: the man-machine interface of global query systems require a combination of technology, cognition and knowledge. The one dimension that has long been neglected is "knowledge," which should be put on-line to provide intelligent assistance to users. We submit that enterprise metadata holds a key for effecting this dimension; that is, knowledge through enterprise metadata is elevated and explicitly formulated to play the central role in the new metadatabase approach to solving the global query problem. Since enterprise metadata are essentially information models, this approach is referred to as the **model-based global query system**.

Specifically, the approach provides a conceptual model to formulate the fundamental needs for enterprise metadata in general terms, which other systems can adopt, with or without the metadatabase. It then offers an execution model featuring a direct method of using model traversal to assist end users and a new high-level language in terms of global model constructs. Automatic derivation of required metadata which the users do not provide is a key element in this approach; thus new methods such as rule-based consistency checking and message-based search for shortest solution path are developed for the execution model.

8.2 THE CONCEPTUAL MODEL

The basic logic of the model-assisted global query approach proceeds as follows: First, all classes of enterprise metadata are specified and structured through a metadata representation method. This metadata structure (abstraction) then serves as the basis for organizing and implementing enterprise information models into an on-line and shared metadatabase facilitating all tasks of information integration. As such, the functional views, processes, data models, business rules and other knowledge concerning the global query operation are readily available to both the users and the system through the metadatabase. Therefore, on-line assistance on query formulation and processing becomes a feasible and fully characterized concept. Specific methods based on this knowledge can be defined and developed in terms of metadata requirements and utilized in each major task of the problem.

8.2.1 The Goals

The target of the Model-assisted (used interchangeable with metadatabase-assisted) Global Query System (MGQS) is delineated in the goals below; which will later be used as the criteria for comparing the MGQS with the existing technologies.

1 Information sharing: achieve information sharing in heterogeneous, distributed, and autonomous environments by means of global queries.
2. Sub-system transparency: support a global model of the whole system and hide local implementations from the users.
3. Local autonomy: maintain local control of its own applications and allow (potentially) for local differences. In addition, it also implies that integration of local systems should not necessitate major conversions or merging of the existing systems.
4. Interoperability: accommodate local heterogeneities while resolving conflicts in data equivalency, different data models and different data manipulation languages.
5 Open system architecture: support the flexibility and adaptability for incorporating new application systems or updating the old ones without imposing major recompilation of reconstruction efforts.
6. Direct query formulation: provide sufficient enterprise metadata to facilitate the articulation and representation of global query using directly the information models via non-command user interface (or minimum-syntax query language for program interface). The user or programmer is not responsible to providing the technical details of the local systems.
7. On-line assistance: use enterprise metadata (including business rules and other contextual knowledge) and knowledge processing capability to assist on difficult tasks for both query formulation and processing. These tasks include, but are not limited to, model traversal and semantic check in direct query formulation, derivation of implied data items and operating rules in query, context-based joint path optimization, and data equivalence in the assembly of local results.

8.2.2 The Definitive Model for Metadata Requirements

We first formally characterize the role of metadatabase as on-line knowledge for global Query operation. This characterization starts with a technical analysis of the major global query tasks and their basic metadata requirements.

A global query operation algorithm

Let GQ denotes a global query characterized by a set of attributes/data items (A) that are involved in the query operation; a set of persistent, stored data objects (D) from which all the attributes are drawn; and an expression <C> that specifies the retrieval conditions. Expression <C> consists of sub-expression for selection conditions <SC> and join conditions <JC>. Finally, all data items, objects, and expressions are subject to specification in terms of systems metadata <M>. These metadata, may be either supplied by the user or provided by the global query system, must satisfy a minimum scope required by each particular query. Specifically,
GQ = (A, D, <C> | <M>) where

$A = A^u \cup A^s$ with $A^u \neq \emptyset$,

$D = D^u \cup D^s$ with $D \neq \emptyset$ and $D^u \cap D^s = \emptyset$,
<C> ::= [<SC> | <JC> | <SC> AND <JC>],
<M> ::= {<M^u>} $\cup$ {<M^s>}.

The additional data subsets are explained below:

A^u: This represents the set of data attributes selected by the user. It includes both the items requested directly for retrieval and the items indicated in the selection conditions. A global query must have at least one data item in A^u.

A^s: The system may determine that additional data items are also needed or implied in the query, and hence fill in some data attribute (the set A^s) for the purpose of query processing.

D^u: The user could also specify the set of data object(s) D^u which contain the selected item(s) (i.e., the set A^u).

D^s: Since D^u may not contain all items in A^u, therefore the system will again determine the remaining data objects (D^s) which are involved in the global query operation.

<M^u>: This is the user-supplied metadata; which represents the technical knowledge that the user must possess about the enterprise information models and multiple systems in order to represent and sufficiently specify a query.

<M^s>: This is the system-supplied enterprise metadata. The set of <M^s> is the complement of {<M^u>} with respect to the minimum metadata requirements for a particular query.

The global query operation can be described as a process consisting of the following steps:

Step 1: Global query formulation

Since the user is not necessarily required to specify all of the technical details (the remaining ones will be filled in by the query system automatically), the result of the formulation is likely to be an incomplete global query IGQ defined as:
IGQ = (A^u, [D^u], [<SC>] | [<M>]) where the data objects D^u and selection conditions <SC> may or may be required. For example, a global query: "Find part ID and quantity completed for Jane Doe's order which has a desired date of 5/10/91" could imply the following sets in the formulation step:

A^u = {PARTID, NUM_COMPLETED, CUST_NAME, DATE_DESIRED}
D^u = {WORK_ORDER, CUSTOMER}
<SC> = CUST_NAME="Jane Doe" AND DATE_DESIRED = "5/10/91"
<M> = the exact names and syntax used to specify the elements of A^u, D^u, and <SC>.

A direct approach for end user global query formulation may be employed to formulate the above query via model traversal where the user has the choice of picking as few as only some data items in A^u, or as many as other information she/he wants to include.

Model traversal

Model traversal is a direct approach whereby users gain the enterprise metadata and utilize them to articulate the query directly in terms of information models. The technical details and semantics of the heterogeneous systems are provided interactively and may be iteratively. The user will, for example, "pick" the data items and objects directly from the models as opposed to "enter" their names to the query. Every step along the way, on-line assistance is provided to the user to traverse as well as pick. Some common semantic errors due to syntax-based translation or interpretation of information models in conventional "indirect" approaches are avoided, as the user sees and deals directly with the comprehensive and unequivocal system models. The purpose is to allow the user formulate a global query while traversing the information models.

The specific traversal method is designed according to the characteristics of the model constructs and logical associations among the information models stored in the metadatabase.

The following is a basic model traversal process:

Repeat (for each visit)

Step1.1 Traverse to the data object identified at the ith visit (d_i) and select the data item(s) (a_i) from d_i for retrieval.

Metadata required: names of the applications, functional views, data constructs, attributes and their associations (i.e., the global data model).

Step1.2 Specify selection condition(s) <SC> that will be imposed on a selected data item(s).

Metadata required: formats, domains and operating constraints of the data items

Step1.3 Resolve semantic ambiguity.

Metadata required: semantic constraints such as functional dependencies and business rules that describe the intended use of the data.

Until no more intended data attributes (i.e., all elements of A^u are specified) $A^u = \bigcup_i (a_i^u)$ and $D^u = \bigcup_i (d_i^u)$.

Step 2: Join conditions determination

A global query may involve multiple data objects that are stored in one or more local systems. Normally, the user has to explicitly specify the equi-join conditions between these data objects for a complete global query. The specification would require detailed understanding of the information model. To relieve the user of this burden, the system with on-line metadatabase can perform this job through an automatic join condition determination algorithm using enterprise metadata, as follows:

Step2.1 Determine the set of data objects, O*k* which contain all the user selected attributes, Au and their equivalent data items.
This step establishes the maximum space of data objects that the query involves.

metadata required: associations between the entities/relationships and their data items, and data equivalence information.

Step2.2 Determine a minimum set of data objects (Omin) that contain all $au_k \in$ Au and Du $\subseteq$ Omin.

Step2.3 Identify the shortest path (SP_{min}) which connects all data objects $d_m \in O_{min}$.

metadata required: associations between the entities and relationships (global data model).

Step2.4 Insert join conditions for every connected pair of data objects in D.
The results of step 2 for the earlier example would be:

A^s = {ORDER_ID CUST_ID CUST_ORDER_ID}
D^s = {ORDER}
<JC> = ORDER_ID = CUST_ORDER_ID AND
ORDER.CUST_ID = CUSTOMER.CUST_ID

Step 3: Global query processing

A formulated global query GQ = (A, D, <C>) is decomposed into a set of local queries $\{LQ_i\}$ where i indicates the local system. The decomposition is based on the physical whereabouts of the intended data. Each local query LQ_i is pertaining to one and only one local system.

$LQ_i = (LA_i, LF_i, <LC_i>)$ where

LI_i is a set of local items with $\bigcup_i(LA_i) = A$,

LF_i is a set of local files/base relations/record types/objects, and,

$<LC_i>$ is a condition expression concerning only the data item(s) that is contained in the local system *i*.

Step3.1 Determine all data files which contain $a_j \in A$

metadata required: data equivalence, physical storage such as files, relation tables, and their data items (implementation models).

Step3.2 Determine a minimum set of data files (F_{min}) from which the query system retrieves data items (A).

Step3.3 Formulate local query LQ_i for local system $_i$, such that
a) $\forall(lf_i)\ (lf_i \in LF_i) \wedge (lf_i \in F_{min})$,
b) $\forall(la_i)\ \exists(lf_i)\ (la_i \in LA_i) \wedge (lf_i$ contains $la_i)$
c) all items involved in <LC_i> are elements of LA_i.
metadata required: physical storage methods such as files, relation tables, and their data items.

Step3.4 Preserve global join conditions <GJC> such that
<GJC> ::= <j_condition> [AND < j_condition>]
<j_condition> ::= item1 = item2
where item1 and item2 belong to two different systems.
metadata required: same as Step3.3.

Suppose, two local systems, shop floor control and order entry system, were involved in the query in the previous example, then two local queries would result from this step:

LQ_{SFC}:
li_{SFC} = {PART_ID NUM_COMPLETED ORDER_ID}
lf_{SFC} = {WORK_ORDER}
<LC_{SFC}> ::= (*no condition*)

LQ_{OES}:
li_{OES} = {CUST_NAME CUST_ID DATA_DESIRED ORDER_ID}
lf_{OES} = {ORDER CUSTOMER}
<LC_{OES}> ::= CUST_NAME = "Jane Doe" AND
DATE_DESIRED = "5/10/91" AND
ORDER.CUST_ID = CUSTOMER.CUST_ID

<GJC> ::= WORK_ORDER.ORDER_ID = ORDER.ORDER_ID

Step 4: Local query generation

A language generator is needed for each distinctive data manipulation language used in the enterprise. A local query is generated using the local language for each LQ. For the earlier example, the query language LQSFC generated for the shop floor is in Oracle/SQL:

```
SELECT      WORK_ORDER.ORDER_ID, '|',
            WORK_ORDER.PART_ID, '|',
            WORK_ORDER.NUM_COMPLETED, '|'
FROM  WORK_ORDER;
```

The query language LQOES generated for the shop floor is in Rdb/Rdo:

```
invoke database filename OES$DIR:OES
FOR A IN ORDER
      CROSS B IN CUSTOMER
            WITH A.DATE_DESIRED = "5/10/91"
            AND B.CUST_NAME = "JANE DOE"
      PRINT "@",
            A.CUST_ID ,"|",
            A.CUST_ORDER_ID ,"|",
```

```
                A.DATE_DESIRED ,"|",
                B.CUST_NAME ,"|"
END_FOR
```

metadata required: implementation models: local DBMS, local DML, and access path, and security metadata: user's access authority and password.

Step 5: Query execution

A local query, LQ must be sent via the network to the destination for processing by the local database, and then the result will be sent back.

Step 5.1 A message is produced for each local query generated from step 4 containing destination, priority and other metadata, in addition to the LQ.

Step 5.2 These messages are transmitted to the appropriate local system by a network administrator/monitor.

Step 5.3 At the local system shell, message is received by the network administration/monitor and dispatched to the database management system where the local query is executed.

Step 5.4 Local result is sent for Result Integration by the network administration/monitor as a message.

Note: The above description assumes a networking system using the message methods and possessing local as well as global administration monitoring capabilities. These assumptions are consistent with virtually all network protocols such as TCP/IP, MAP, and TOP.

metadata required: For a minimum network, the metadata requirements can be satisfied by the previous steps. For more advanced systems, metadata such as priority and alternate sources can be used for flows management and optimization.

Step 6: Result integration

The results of local queries (LQ's) must be interpreted and assembled according to the global join conditions (<GJC>) in Step3.4. Logically equivalent data items may be implemented differently in terms of format, scale, and encoding in different local systems. In our example, ORDER_ID in WORK_ORDER and CUST_ORDER_ID in ORDER are encoded differently for local processing purposes. Therefore, data conversions must be performed on one or both of them before the results from these two systems can be joined and presented to the user.

metadata required: data equivalence, contextual knowledge: conversion rules, operation rules.

A minimum model for on-line knowledge

The minimum metadata requirements identified above are organized into a definitive model as follows to characterize the knowledge needed for the global query operation.

<u>Definition</u>: Enterprise metadata gives rise to the knowledge required in global query formulation and processing for both end-users and application programs.

<u>Knowledge for global query formulation</u>

- Global data model: a logical model representing the data resources of the enterprise. Specifically, the (names of) applications or functions, data constructs and their relationships are needed for model traversal; format and domains of the data items are used for selection condition(s) specification; functional dependencies are for integrity checking of the selection conditions, and primary keys, and foreign keys are for implicit join conditions determination.

- Data equivalence: the knowledge needed in most steps to convert as well as identity/clarify multiple data definitions; including typing, semantic (interpretation of) presentation, and scale.

- Contextual knowledge: business rules describing the intended use of the data and the needs of the user, also used for ambiguity checking of the selection conditions.

<u>Knowledge for global query optimization and decomposition</u>

- Data equivalence.

- Implementation models: physical storage methods of the logical data items, including the size of the files or relation tables and the like used for query optimization and decomposition.

<u>Knowledge for global query generation</u>

- Implementation models: metadata about local data language environments and access paths, used to determine the language generators to use and the heading of a query program.

- Security metadata: users' access privileges, used to determine whether the retrieval requests are legitimate and the passwords are used for obtaining access permission.

Knowledge for results integration

- Data equivalence

- Contextual knowledge: conversion rules and operating rules needed for resolving conflicting data definitions and computing derived data items.

The Conceptual Model

The above analysis, while applies to the global query problem in general, also defines the overall algorithm and the minimum contents of the metadatabase for the model-assisted global query approach. Thus, a defining characteristic of the MGQS approach is: $\{<M^S>\} = \{<M>\}$; i.e., the system provides all of the metadata required.

The methods that are required to implement this approach are discussed next.

8.3 THE EXECUTION MODEL

The metadatabase discussed in chapter 7 anchors the design of the execution model. Since there are a number of ways to implement the conceptual model using the metadatabase, we focus on two examples that highlight the power of this model-assisted approach.

8.3.1 Model Traversal

Two basic methods are employed for model traversal: vertical and horizontal (Figure 8.1). The vertical method specifies the traversal depth cutting across application systems, functional models, structural models, and data items. The horizontal method, on the other hand, traverses the global model from an entity/relationship (ER) to others in a network manner.

The user could page through the global model according to the logical associations between these modeling constructs. Depending on the user's experience with the information models, the traversal could be very pinpointing (specifying the exact constructs containing the data items needed) or very general (browsing through a list of data items with little precise specification or through only the applications), or anything in between. The different entry points shown in Figure 8.1 indicate how a user might choose to perceive and approach the global model. It is interesting to point out that the instances shown in Figure 8.1 would be stored as instances of the metasructure in the metadatabase, and the system would generate the equivalent GUI of Figure 8.1 by deriving these instances directly from the metadatabase. The traversal mode does not assume nor impose any a priori syntax other than the semantics of the constructs used. Thus, the semantics of a query formulated this way is specified completely through the selection of the constructs, their metadata instances, and particular data values.

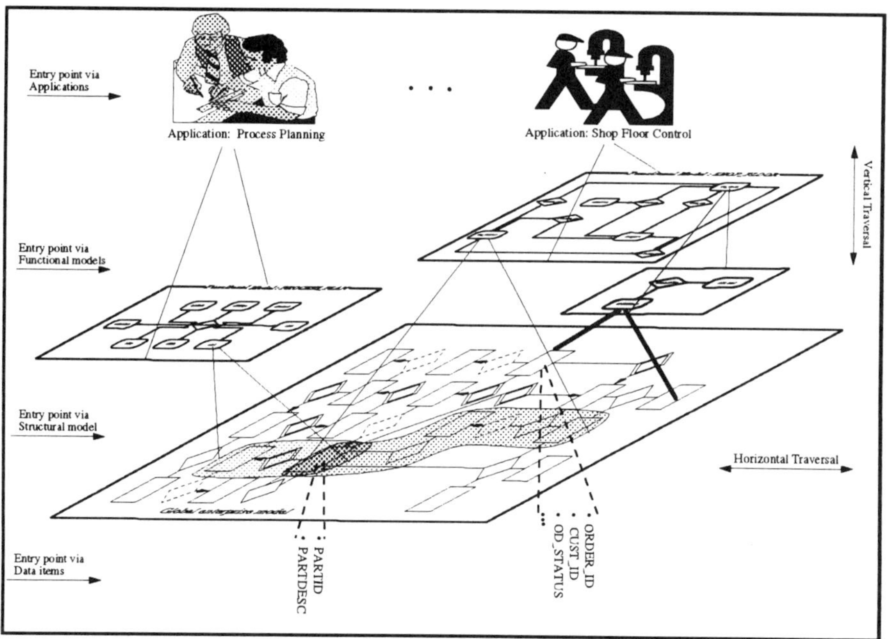

Fig. 8.1. Model traversal methods

8.3.2 Rule-Base Conversion

Another example of online intelligence is the rule-based capability for converting formats between heterogeneous but equivalent data items, automatically. The function find_convert_rules(itemA, itemB) searches the equivalent table of the metadatabase for the conversion rule(s) (Figure 8.2) that could convert the value of itemA (valueA) into the format of itemB. As an example in Figure 8.3 find_convert_rules(itemA, itemB) returns two rules (i.e., rule2 and rule4), which will first convert the value of itemA to itemC format (using rule2) then to itemB format (using rule4). The function returns "NULL" if no conversion is needed for comparing itemA and itemB. The function covnert_item() triggers the rule processor which will search and fire the actions of the conversion rules. Both functions are part of the software resources in the metadatabase.

In the whole, the CIM facility at Rensselaer provides an environment with a reasonable complexity to test the prototype MGQS and the model-assistance concept. All major objectives (i.e., information sharing, local system autonomy, and model assistance) of the MGQS are achieved and proven to be feasible with the prototype system. Most of the envisioned functionalities (with the exception of ambiguity checking and derived item querying) are implemented. In addition, the data conversion capability has demonstrated a use of the contextual knowledge and rule processor for providing on-line intelligence. This same method can be applied to the function of ambiguity checking and derived data querying.

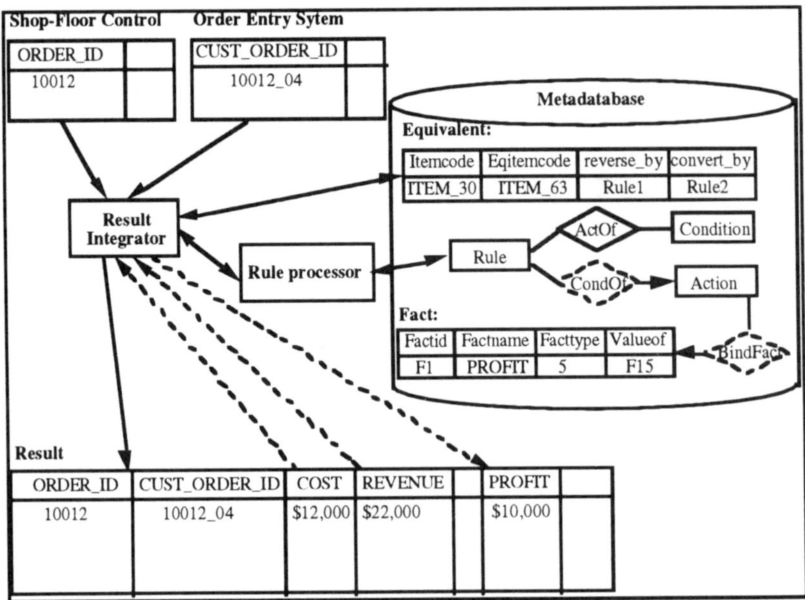

Fig. 8.2. Data conversion and derivation through rule-base approach

Equivalent table:

Itemcode	Eqitemcode	reverse_by	convert_by
itemA	itemC	Rule1	Rule2
itemB	itemC	Rule4	Rule3

Fig. 8.3. Equivalent table

There are, however, the needs to investigate the performance issues especially when run-time data conversion and other rule operations are involved. The empirical study did not provide sufficient observations to draw scientific conclusions from. Nonetheless, the preliminary results do not appear to suggest theses operations as bottleneck. One reason might be the fact that data conversion in MGQS is performed at local nodes in a truly distributed manner by local systems using concurrently the common global representations as the target. Most other rules are processed in a similar concurrent design using the metadatabase's distributed shells for local systems.

8.4 ANALYSIS

The MGQS approach is compared with previous results with respect to the objectives of information sharing in heterogeneous distributed environments.

8.4.1 Metadata Modeling vs. Schema Integration

A key element in conventional distributed databases is schema integration. All databases are logically structured and controlled under a single integrated schema in a homogeneous environment . The user would be able to share information across all databases as if there were only one classical centralized database. Therefore, local transparency and conflict resolution are achieved through enforcing an integrated schema under a single data model. The primary problem with this approach, however, is lack of local system autonomy and adaptability.

To illustrate, consider the following example involving three systems. In this example SNO and SID are two synonyms of the same logical attribute (one in data object SUPPLY of database PJ at site A and the other in data object SUPPLIER of database S at side B). Further, PNO in PART at site C and the PNO in SUPPLY are structured differently with different domains CODE1 and CODE2, respectively. The integrated schema could be developed as shown in Figure 8.4 (assuming a relational system). In the integrated schema, the conflicting definitions are reconciled by changing attribute name SID to SNO in SUPPLIER and the value domains of PNO in both SUPPLY and PART to type integer. The local systems will recompile and reload so as to implement the changes according to the integrated schema.

```
CREATE TABLE PROJECT (
    JNO  INTEGER,
    J_LOC  CHAR(40));
CREATE TABLE SUPPLY (
    SNO  INTEGER,
    PNO  INTEGER,
    JNO  INTEGER);

CREATE TABLE PART(
    PNO  INTEGER,
    PNAME  CHAR(20),
    LENGTH  REAL);
CREATE TABLESUPPLIER (
    SNO  INTEGER,
    S_LOC CHAR(4O));
```

Fig. 8.4. Integrated schema for the example using DDBMS approach

Figure 8.5 shows the global model that MGQS would employ for this example. Note that each data item in the global model is assigned with a unique item code For instance, the two PNO's in PART and SUPPLY are logically the same attributes with the same name but reside in different local systems, and hence they have different item codes. However, the attribute JNO in the database PJ is only a single data item since, albeit shared by both SUPPLY and PROJECT, it is the same attribute with the same name in the same system, therefore they have the same item code. The fact that PNO in PART and SUPPLY are coded differently is represented as a tuple in **Equivalent** along with the conversion rules Rule1 and Rule2. Synonyms SID and SNO are also reflected in **Equivalent.** Therefore, no change is required of the local systems using this method while any names could be used by users in any systems to address the attributes and obtain globally consolidated results. The same process is utilized to effect equivalent with respect to types, semantic formats (e.g., dates) and user-dependent presentation. Note that the process does not require an integrated global schema. Concerning adaptability such as modifying, adding or deleting (local) models, any such changes to the enterprise models can be simply handled as metadata transactions against the metadatabase. without affecting its schema (the GIRD model). This, as mentioned in section 3.1, is the significance of metadata independence. Most of previous results, some of which avail the similar local system autonomy as discussed in the above example, do not satisfy metadata independence.

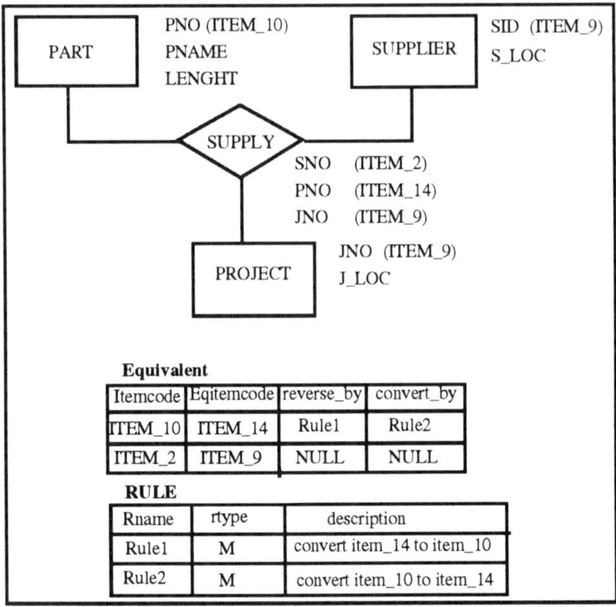

Equivalent

Itemcode	Eqitemcode	reverse_by	convert_by
ITEM_10	ITEM_14	Rule1	Rule2
ITEM_2	ITEM_9	NULL	NULL

RULE

Rname	rtype	description
Rule1	M	convert item_14 to item_10
Rule2	M	convert item_10 to item_14

Fig. 8.5. Global model for the example using the MGQS

8.4.2 Conceptual Evaluation of the MGQS Approach

The model-assisted global query approach provides several important functionalities for sharing information in heterogeneous distributed environments. Based on the discussions in the above sections, these properties are categorized into five areas, as discussed below.

Maintain local system autonomy using the metadatabase

As mentioned above, MGQS employs on the metadatabase for identifying and resolving the heterogeneities among these systems. Instead of imposing an integrated schema over all the local systems, the metadatabase approach allows the local systems to keep their environments insulated for their own as well as to control their own data definitions and everything else. The metadatabase and local systems are completely independent bubbles whose operations do not rely, nor infringe, on each other; unlike the integrated schema environments. The functional model, structural model, implementation model and the associations among these models of each local system are independently represented, consolidated, and stored in the metadatabase. Thus, their manipulation and management are as easy as any ordinary data in a database.

Allow direct and visual query formulation from enterprise metadata

A global query is formulated by selecting the data constructs while browsing the global enterprise information models. Regardless of the entry point chosen, the user will eventually lead to the needed data constructs by paging through the global model without noticing the boundary of local systems. This is a high level of direct manipulation (of information objects) that researchers have advocated for cognitive user interface. The constructs used (see Figure 2) are clearly compatible with graphical representation and hence supports immediately visual methods for query formulation.

Provide on-line intelligence and assistance for challenging tasks such as semantics, path selection, and result integration

MGQS provides on-line knowledge to facilitate both global query formulation and processing. During query formulation, the pertinent information contents and semantics of the heterogeneous systems are either provided interactively to the user, or MGQS utilizes them to automate certain tasks for the user (see sections 2 and 3). The on-line knowledge provided to the global query processing is transparent to the user. They include the automatic decomposition and optimization of global query and the recognition and conversion of equivalent data resources across local systems. Combined, the approach provides a broad range of metadata support covering the entirely of the definition discussed in Section 2.2. They are sufficient for certain difficult tasks, including semantics, path selection for query optimization, and result integration using data equivalence knowledge (see above comparisons). Since the metadatabase contains both enterprise knowledge resources and data models, its extent of metadata is unique, and capable of providing significant on-line intelligence and assistance.

Include rule-based knowledge processing for extensibility

MGQS acquires contextual knowledge from the knowledge model of the metadatabase to provide on-line intelligence for the global query operation. Two representative examples of contextual knowledge are business rules which describe the intended use of data and operating rules which facilitate decision processes across systems. Global queries involving derived items is another example on the use of contextual knowledge. A rule base model and an inference engine are part of the metadatabase system. New rules concerning MGQS can be relatively easily incorporated into its architecture and execution model.

Achieve open system architecture through metadata independence

The MGQS approach provides an open system architecture which is flexible for adding, deleting, or modifying a local system in the integrated enterprise. The property is referred as metadata independence in Section 3.1. For instance, to remove the shop floor control system from the CIM enterprise in section 5, no change is required of the MGQS. The metadata pertaining to the shop floor system will be removed from the metadatabase through ordinary transactions (i.e., deleting tuples from the meta-relations). Accepting a new sub-system to the integrated enterprise requires primarily modeling effort, which is no more than those required by conventional approaches. However, the addition of this new model to the existing global model is merely a matter of performing, again, ordinary metadatabase addition transactions. A documentation of this modeling process is provided.

In conclusion, the MGQS approach contributes a direct method to end user query formulation through on-line assistance using metadata. It allows the user to articulate directly in terms of information models with which they are familiar. The pertinent information contents and data semantics of the heterogeneous multiple systems are provided interactively to the user, thereby further alleviating the technical complexities and semantic ambiguity during formulation. In a similar manner, some technical support is also afforded, including diagnosis and feedback of query formulation according to the business rules and other contextual knowledge in the system. This direct method contributes in its own right to the conceptual foundations of graphical and interactive user interface technology.

New methods that utilize the on-line knowledge (or metadata) for major global query processing tasks are also made possible. They encompass the areas of global query optimization and decomposition, query translation, and result integration. The knowledge needed for these tasks (e.g., implied data items, shortest solution path, and join conditions; local system access paths; query construction across local database schemata; and data equivalency and conversion) is automatically derived from the metadatabase. Without such on-line intelligence and assistance, the required knowledge would have to either be supplied by users at run/compile-time, or be predetermined at design time through schema integration and other standardization approaches.

This work has resolved some interoperability issues of heterogeneous multiple information systems through offering an alternative to the conventional approaches which rely on schema integration. Schema integration is a major source of technical complexity of heterogeneous distributed DBMS at both design-time (efforts and restrictions) and run-time (mappings and architectural overheads). Additional knowledge such as conflicting or alternating data definitions and their resolutions is also supported and stored in the metadatabase for MGQS. Conversion is done in real time through a rule processor firing conversion rules. As a result, the only global modeling effort required of this approach is the development of the enterprise information model itself. It is still challenging, especially concerning knowledge acquisition; but it nevertheless avoids the excessive complexity of integration at the schemata level that would ensue on the enterprise model in the case of conventional approaches.

This approach has also identified and characterized for the first time a definitive model for the notion of "on-line intelligence and assistance" in end user query interface and query processing in term of the enterprise metadata. Therefore, the general concept of an EIM for global query is further made particular and specific in this chapter on the basis of the GIRD model reported in Chapter 7. MGQS is also being employed in a seamless way to facilitate global data management and event-based information flows management in the metadatabase research. This aspect is discussed in Chapter 9 and illustrated in Chapter 6. Finally, information visualization will be a natural extension to MGQS, where an agent can be developed to personalize the metadatabase and a visual/virtual environment can replace the GUI-based user interface used presently. Chapter 11 provides an information visualization model along this line.

9

ADAPTIVE CONCURRENT ARCHITECTURE

This chapter is co-authored with **Gilbert Babin**, Ph.D.
Assistant Professor, Laval University.

The notion of developing a logical layer of an organic architecture using ubiquitous enterprise metadata is brought another step closer to reality in this chapter. A metadatabase supported information architecture using distributed rule-based shells is designed to respond to some of the EIM requirements discussed in chapter 1, especially adaptability and concurrency. With this distributed shell system, the third level of EIM - i.e., data and process management - is also accomplished. The chapter, therefore, concludes the methods of metadatabase model overviewed in Chapter 5, as a solution to the enterprise integration problem.

9.1 CONCURRENT ARCHITECTURES FOR ADAPTIVE INTEGRATION

Dynamic alignment is, by definition, about changes: change of configuration, processes, models, contextual knowledge, and data. The integration that an enterprise seeks and achieves must be adaptive - to stay effective. The previous results for EIM have brought up many good architectures, using elements such as integrated schema, processing knowledge base and shells. These results left unanswered a key question in adaptive integration: how to evolve the architecture when some local systems are changed, deleted, or added? Few of these systems seem to be ready for providing a solution, as judged by their designs. A way to make the judgment is by evaluating the degree of local autonomy that a particular solution has achieved, for autonomy is one of the most distinctive characters of multidatabases and is imperative to adaptability. Autonomy is associated with the level of cooperation needed to control the different operations across the integrated system. The more cooperation there is, the less local autonomy the applications have. From the user's perspective, local autonomy is always needed (so did external schema). From the technical perspective, because of the heterogeneity, it is more difficult to dictate how the different applications will behave. From our perspective, an application is fully autonomous when it does **not** need to comply to any of the following: (1) conforming to an integrated schema (e.g., converting a legacy schema to some global standards), (2) directly cooperating with any global controller (e.g., serialization program or any direct supervision of transactions and their communications), and (3) requiring users to possess specific knowledge about the global environment in which the local systems operate (e.g., cannot use the local system in the same way with the integration as it would be without). Available results on multidatabases still do not support full local autonomy.

Another obvious challenge is performance, which is directly related to the lack of concurrent processing of local systems — or, conversely, to the requirement of a global controller. Regardless of how much pipelining they offer for local systems, virtually all of the previous results which manage data updates call for global serialization at certain point. Factors compounding this bottleneck include network scaling problems and distributed query and transaction processing. The previous results are mostly concerned with small scale networks with a limited number of transactions. Thus, there are questions that remain on the workability of those solutions in larger and widely dispersed environments. At the heart of the distributed processing issue is concurrency and consistency control. In the computing literature, the most accepted criterion for achieving consistency among multiple concurrent jobs is serializability (the Von-Neumann model). It is driven by the objectives of assuring instantaneous correctness for all data in the system. The serializability criterion underlies the basic control method used for the multidatabase manager as well as for the single system database manager. However, to achieve serializability, the multidatabases manager seriously impedes on the performance of the local applications; to achieve serializability, the database manager must lock some data during transaction processing. With new applications and a greater demand for higher data availability, we must define a new criterion for data correctness.

To respond to the basic challenges and implement the conceptual metadatabase solution discussed in Chapter 5, a rule-oriented programming environment (ROPE) is developed for implementing and managing the concurrent architecture of metadatabase. The basic objective of ROPE is to decompose and distribute the pertinent contextual knowledge (for both event-based information flows and data management) contained in the metadatabase into localized shells, and thereby effect concurrent processing and facilitate architecture adaptability under distributed and autonomous control. This knowledge method must be able to (1) control the application logic of local systems without the use of a central controller, (2) enhance the local applications with a distributed knowledge capability for global behavior without changing them, and (3) transfer the needed knowledge both between the metadatabase and the local applications, and among the local applications themselves.

The concurrent architecture is depicted in Figure 9.1. The metadatabase itself provides an integrated enterprise model for the multiple information systems, their databases, and the interactions among the different systems; i.e. the information contents and their contextual knowledge. The metadatabase approach (1) uses the enterprise model to assist end-users performing global queries free of both technical details and a hierarchy of integrated schemata; (2) distributes the contextual knowledge to empower these local systems to update data and communicate with each other without central database control; and (3) incorporates legacy, new or changed local models into its generic structure of metadata to support evolution without system redesign or recompilation. The shells in the concurrent architecture, therefore, implements the distributed (localized) knowledge which, in turn, is managed by the metadatabase.

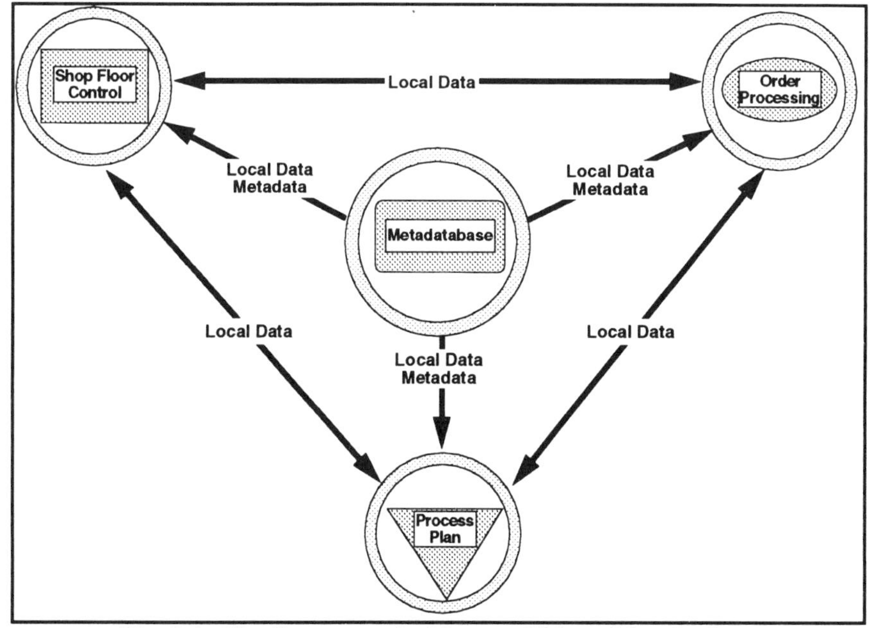

Fig. 9.1. The Concurrent Architecture Using a Metadatabase

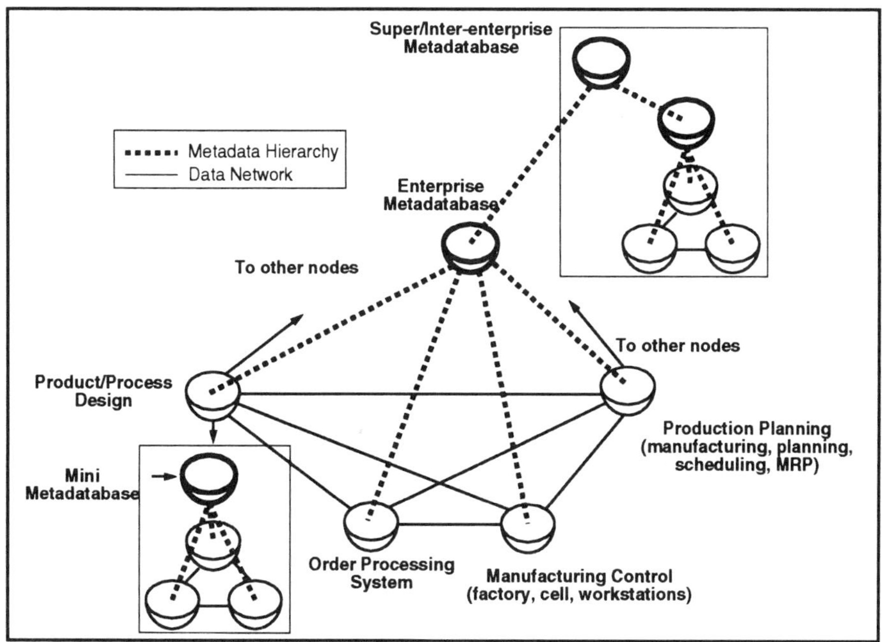

Fig. 9.2. Enterprise Integrated Through Distributed Metadatabase System

In large-scale systems, the metadatabase can be distributed in a recursive manner and constitutes a hierarchy of nodes, illustrated in Figure 9.2, where, for simplicity, only three levels are shown. At the leaf, several of the application systems are represented in a sub- or mini-metadatabase. This mini-metadatabase then can be represented in the main metadatabase system such that the mini-metadatabase becomes the gateway to the application systems it represents. There can, of course, be as many levels of sub-/mini-metadatabases as needed. The real significance of this hierarchy, however, is not its top-down construction, which is the predicament of virtually all other integration models; but rather its ability to effect bottom-up, incremental development and expansion — i.e., scalable integration: the higher level nodes can be constructed from the ones immediately below it. A key element in this bottom-up, scale-up approach is the GIRD meta-model discussed above. This structure allows new application models to be incorporated into a metadatabase without disrupting the current systems. Thus, large scale, overwhelming integration environments can be achieved gradually, by first developing individual nodes in client (application systems) - server (metadatabase) type of clusters and then integrate them in a grand clustering of such clusters. In a similar way, the main metadatabase can be incorporated into a super or inter-enterprise metadatabase and become a mini-metadatabase of the latter. Both the clusters of metadatabases and the clusters of application systems at the leaf nodes are managed by the same active metadatabase method.

The metadatabase model employs a new criterion, event/usage correctness for concurrency control, and thereby removes the need for the global serialization and foster full concurrent processing among local systems. This argument is closely related to some earlier observations, which argue that serialization is impractical if not impossible in multidatabase systems since there is a higher probability of deadlock due to the network.

The event/usage correctness criterion is defined as follows: a data value only needs to be updated when it is needed by an application according to its contextual knowledge. Therefore, the consistency is established on a need-to-know basis, using both operating and integrity rules (also referred to as data management rules) defined in the enterprise model. This criterion eliminates the **requirement** of serialization (making it optional) across multiple systems but entails knowledge methods in its place. One important point to note is that the event/usage correctness criterion defines generally how to synchronize data across different platforms and databases; but does not prohibits serialization from being applied as the operating rules for certain (or all) data items in the enterprise. From ROPE perspective, concurrency control at the local level remains the responsibility of the local DBMS.

The new criterion reduces or even eliminates the need for a central controller depending on the rules used. The rules can be tailored to differentially provide a variable level of consistency for different data items, whereas serialization presumes all data be equally and completely synchronized at any point in time. For data items that require traditional correctness, operating rules can be developed to route them to a serialization controller which can be included in the system on an optional basis.

The concurrent architecture of the metadatabase model (Figure 9.1) is employed as the basic structure to develop the new method and solve the problem. Instead of having the applications changed to fit a control method (e.g., serialization), we use the knowledge about the model (i.e., operating rules and integrity rules) in the metadatabase to build customized control shells around each application. These shells can then operate independently and concurrently with their own control knowledge according to the event/usage criteria; the control knowledge itself is coordinated at the metadatabase. The functionality of each shell depends on the specific knowledge of particular applications, therefore, each shell is in essence different. However, we can create these shells in a manner that allows their basic structure to be identical, with the differences only coming from the specific knowledge they process. The shells must also be able to (1) communicate with each other in a concerted global behavior, (2) react to changes in the local applications that have global repercussions, and (3) process the knowledge they receive from the metadatabase. In addition, the shells should be efficient to implement, change and execute. ROPE is the method developed to satisfy these requirements.

9.2 ROPE: A NEW SOFTWARE METHOD FOR EIM

The ROPE method develops the shells technology needed for the concurrent architecture of the metadatabase-integrated enterprises. It defines: (1) how the rules are stored in the local shells (representation and format used), (2) how the rules are processed, distributed, and managed, (3) how the shell interacts with its corresponding application system, (4) how the different shells interact with each other, and (5) the architecture of the shells. Furthermore, the ROPE approach prescribes three principles: (1) rules representing processing logic are separated from the program code by placing them in a distinct rulebase section for easy modifiability, (2) communications among shells are conducted through a message system, and (3) the rule processing and the message system are implemented into local environments and combined into the shells. As such, the local shells are invisible to the users, but control the "external" behavior of the local systems. These elements are fully described in this section.

9.2.1 The Model of ROPE

Global Query Processing

In ROPE, the EIM capabilities are achieved in three ways. First, ROPE processes global queries at local nodes. Figure 9.3 shows how queries and data flow across the networked shells. The global query system of the MDBMS (metadatabase management system shell; circle in the center) sends requests for local queries to be executed by the different shells. The resulting data are assembled by the global query system. The different local shells can also initiate a request for a global query to be processed at the metadatabase management system shell.

The general process is as follows: a user initiates a global query, either from MDBMS or from a global query interface located in the local application environment, using the Metadatabase Query Language (MQL). This query is sent to MDBMS, where it is processed; its syntax and semantics are validated, and local queries and result integration information are generated. The local queries are then sent to their respective shells, where they will be executed by the local DBMS. The results are then sent back to MDBMS for assembly and post-processing.

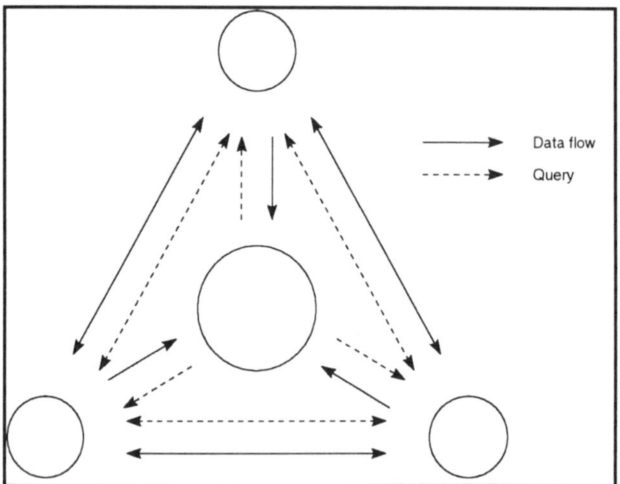

Fig. 9.3. Global Query Processing

Global Updates and Events Processing

The second class of EIM capabilities through ROPE is the global updates and event-based information flows among local databases; which involves direct use of the rulebase sections of ROPE shells but does not require initiation, nor control, from the MDBMS (see Figure 9.4). In this case, the local shells monitor the events happening in an application and the database(s) they're concerned with. Rules are triggered based on the status of the application or the database(s). These rules may generate automatic update commands to be performed by the other shells and query other databases to update their local databases.

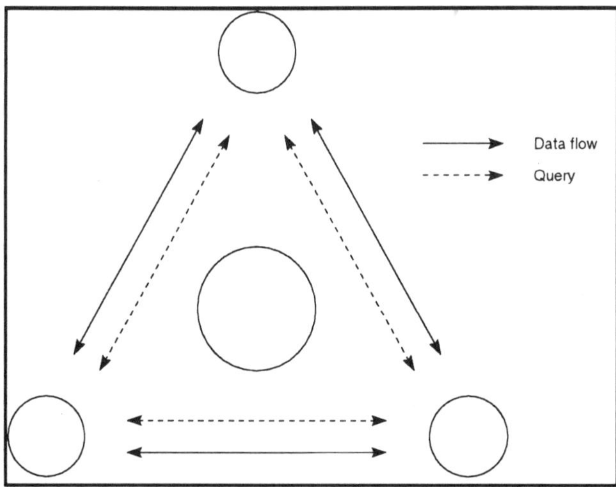

Fig. 9.4. Automatic Enterprise Knowledge Processing

Adaptability and Flexibility.

ROPE assures adaptability (1) by fully modularizing the global behavior of local systems into Metadatabase-supported individual shells, (2) by storing its

knowledge in the form of rules in the shells, (3) by directly processing these rules in local languages, and (4) by automatically updating these rules whenever their logic is modified at the metadatabase. As such, the information processing logic (semantic integrity rules and contextual knowledge) of the multiple systems is managed via rulebase processing. This approach allows the shell to be easily adapted to new situations and provides a flexible interface between the different applications and the metadatabase management system. Any change in the global behavior of local systems as represented in the contents of the metadatabase will trigger the generation of updated rules or new rules by the metadatabase management system in a neutral form, which is then propagated to all pertinent shells and implemented into the rulebase section of the local shells in local forms (see Figure 9.5) by ROPE. Only metadata processing is involved in this management of rules.
When a new system is added to the total environment or, for that matter, deleted therefrom, only three things need to be done to update ROPE in a modularized manner: (1) the metadatabase must be updated (through ordinary metadata transactions), (2) a new shell must be created (or deleted), and (3) pertinent rules in other shells must be updated as ordinary rule updates. ROPE, along with MDBMS, facilitates and automates all three things.

Information Model

The information model of the ROPE method sets the cornerstone for the structure of ROPE's other elements. Consider, based on the above functional description, the creation of shells and the substantiation of their information contents. The pertinent knowledge in the metadatabase is distributed into these shells, when the global rules are decomposed for distribution. The decomposition of a rule itself is straightforward using the decomposition algorithm developed later in this section. This will generate a set of local queries and subrules to be sent to different shells. However, care must be taken when storing that information into the local shells to minimize the processing required at each shell. This can be achieved by storing elements pertaining to one rule separately from elements pertaining to multiple rules. Furthermore, each shell must have sufficient information to perform properly its local tasks and to request processing from other systems.

The information model of ROPE can be subdivided in five functional areas: (1) the shell itself, (2) rule information, (3) trigger information, (4) the queries used to monitor the local application, to fetch data used by the rules, and to store the result from the query, and (5) the information regarding rule chaining, i.e., how the rules are interrelated. The resulting structural model can be used to store all the information needed by ROPE to execute the decomposed global rules. This is illustrated in Figure 9.6, using the TSER representation method.

9.2.2 The Static Structure of ROPE

The static structure of ROPE defines the elements of ROPE that are identical from one shell to another. The local shell structure is shown in Figure 9.7.

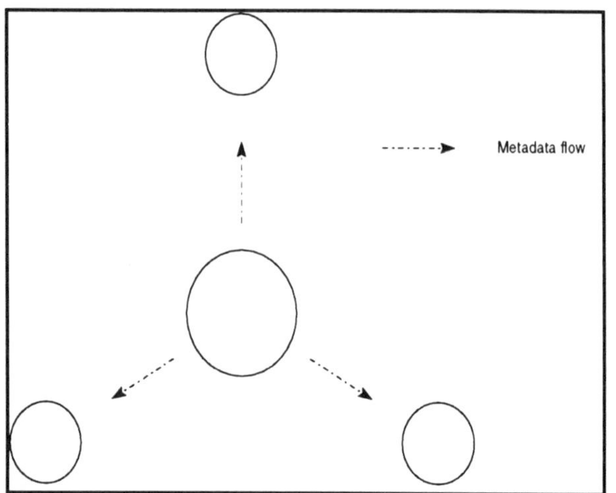

Fig. 9.5 Rule Updating Process

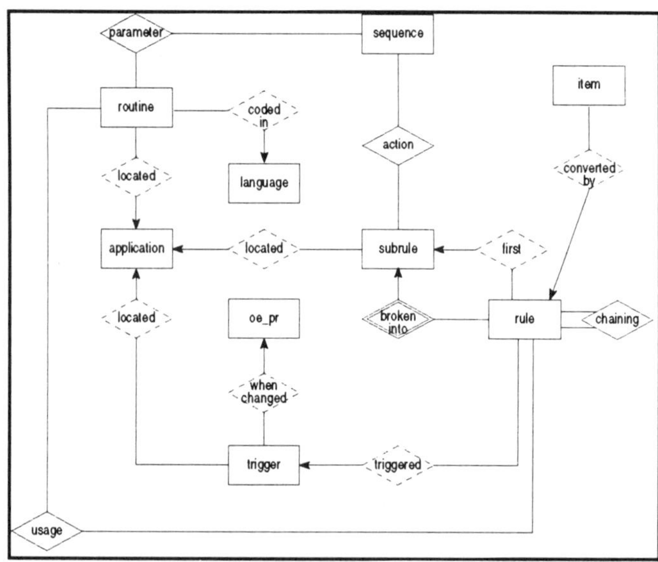

Fig. 9.6. Information Model of a ROPE Shell

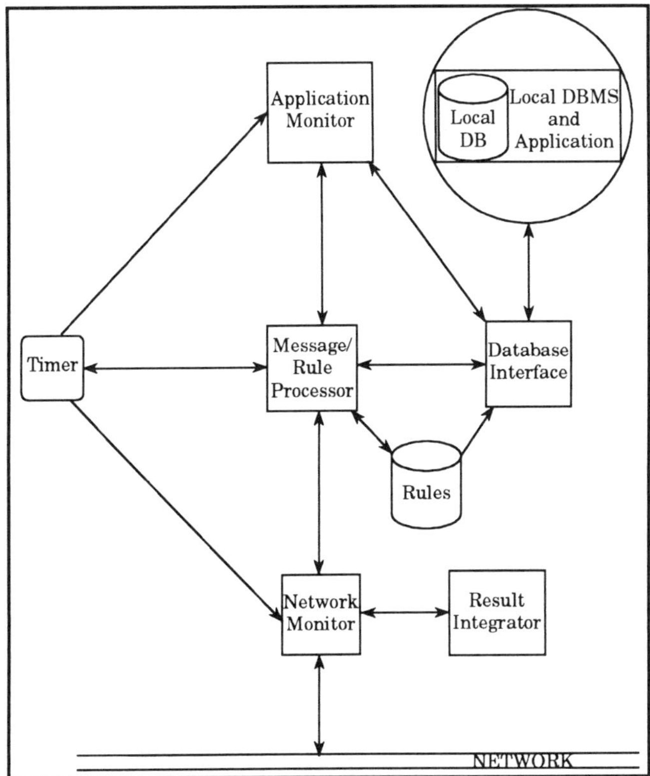

Fig. 9.7. Local Shell Structure

Rulebase Segment

A key element of the shell is the possession of rules. Logically, the Rule Segment implements the intersection of the global rulebase model and the local application logic; physically, it employs a data structure amenable to local software environments. All the rules are originated from and globally managed by the metadatabase. Whenever an operating rule is changed, the change is propagated to all local systems that will be affected by it. Also, when changes occur in the global data model of the enterprise, new data management rules are generated to replace the existing rules in the Rule Segment of different shells. The Rule Segment is presently implemented using flat files, separate from the source code. This allows for easy implementation on different platforms.

Network Monitor

The Network Monitor is the shell's interface with the communications network, thus it provides the window to the outside world for the local application and its shell. It receives incoming messages and passes them to the Message/Rule Processor (see below). It is also responsible for sending messages to other nodes. This module is tailored to the particular network employed for the different applications in implementation, and requires access to the routing information needed to reach the other applications.

Application Monitor

This module interfaces with the local application. It "spies" on the behavior of the application and reports any globally significant event to the Message/Rule Processor, such as changes on the local database that would result in the execution of a global behavior rule. For EIM processing, the Application Monitor functionality can be specified in general terms, allowing implementations on very different platforms. Furthermore, the use of the Global Query System (GQS) facilities discussed in chapter 8 actually removes the need to tailor the Application Monitor to the local database. The biggest challenge with the Application Monitor is how to implement monitoring algorithms while minimizing its dependence on the local database to make it portable. This is achieved by, again, using the GQS facilities, especially the MQL as the global language to automatically generate the logic algorithms and code them in local languages.

Message/Rule Processor

This module is the inference engine of the shell. It is generic and neutral to particular implementations. On the basis of the events it receives from the Network Monitor, the Application Monitor, the Timer (see below), and the local application, it will trigger the appropriate rule(s) stored in the Rule Segment, or execute the appropriate functions of the shell. In addition to rule execution, the Message/Rule Processor performs four other functions: (1) it serves as a dispatcher, transmitting local query requests to the Database Interface (see below); (2) it transmits any structural change notification it receives from MDBMS to the Application Monitor; (3) it updates the Rule Segment and notifies the Application Monitor and Timer, when a rule deletion or insertion notification is received; and (4) it updates the frequency at which events are processed. The Message/Rule Processor consists actually of two processors, the Message Processor and the Rule Processor. The Message Processor deals with dispatching messages and updating the Rule Segment, and the Rule Processor executes the enterprise subrules. Since rules can contain user-defined routines that must be executed by the Message Processor or the Rule Processor, thus the latter must structurally link itself to user-defined routines and dynamically manage the linking to the shell. By separation, the Rule Processor can be linked to any new user-defined routine whenever a rule change occurs, without causing any processing difficulties.

Timer

The Timer manages a list of time events. When a time event is due for processing, the Timer launches the command associated to that time event. This element further mitigates the impact of specificity in local software and hardware environments for the rest of the shell.

The design of the Timer itself is closely related to the local environment. When running in an environment allowing multiple processes (e.g. UNIX), the timer only needs to be an infinite-loop waking up periodically to execute the different events it manages. The single-process environment (e.g. MS-DOS) represents the biggest technical challenge to ROPE implementation. The Timer must be able to run while the regular operations on the hardware can continue. For this to be accomplished, the Timer has to be part of the operating system itself, so it can suspend temporarily regular operations to perform ROPE tasks, or at least, it must behave as if it is part of the operating system.

Result Integrator

The Result Integrator is used to assemble the results of local queries requested by the local system. In addition, it can perform operations on these queries, like producing a sum of the values on the different rows. The functions this module performs are based on MQL and GQS. The processing of the Result Integrator is straightforward. It receives a set of messages as input, one of which contains a script describing (1) the local queries, (2) the integration operations to be performed, and (3) the output file to be used. Then, these scripts are executed.

Database Interface

This module converts the data item values to a neutral format used by the shells. This is to remove the burden of processing conversion rules every time we need to use a data value.

9.2.3 The Dynamic Structure of ROPE

Based on the static structure, specific algorithms are developed for defining the shell's behavior. Just like the structure itself, these algorithms include both a generic nucleus and an implementation-specific interface to enact appropriately for different application systems. These algorithms suggest how the knowledge needs to be structured and what knowledge is needed for the shells to perform their tasks, hence defining the language requirements. The algorithms and languages constitute the dynamic structure of ROPE. There are three major areas where new languages are needed to bring about the application systems' global behavior through ROPE: (1) creating shells for, e.g., new application systems in the integrated environment, (2) defining the global behavior of the local application systems, and (3) communicating across the different shells.

Shell Definitional Language

Shells are created by using this language, which is completely callable by the metadatabase management system or a user of ROPE. The language first defines a shell in generic terms in a global environment, then uses a code constructor to implement the generic structure in the target local environment. Shell definitional constructs include (1) the system functions defining the five elements of the static structure and their attendant algorithms, (2) the system specifications defining the interfaces with the local application, and (3) system parameters defining the requirements of the interfaces and the algorithms. These constructs give rise to a generic shell which is system-independent. This result is then mapped to specific software environments through the code constructor, to allow for maximum portability.

Modeling and Rule Language

The Modeling and Rule Language helps describing the contextual knowledge contained in the metadatabase and the shells. There are two types of actions in the rules: system actions and user actions. The system actions are functions and procedures that are included in every application's shell, as integration tools. They include the routines to process and generate the messages that the shell sends to or receives from other applications' shells. The user actions are all other functions and procedures involved in the rules. The Modeling and Rule Language provides constructs to define: (1) the firing conditions of the rule, (2) the actions to be performed when the rule is fired, (3) the globally significant events (e.g., time event, database event), and (4) how to access the data needed to execute the rule.

Message Protocol and Language

The messages are used to enable communications across the different applications. They are also used to link the metadatabase management system shell with each local system shell. There is some minimal information that the Message Language should express in order to completely specify a message: the message identifier, the function to be performed upon reception of the message and the necessary parameters, and the origin and destination of the message. The functions can be further classified into metadata and data functions. The metadata functions are used to manage the Rule Segment of the shells. The data functions are used to enable cooperation among shells and with the metadatabase. The message types are determined from the functional tasks of a message. The Message Language, an extension of MQL, is ROPE's Manipulation Language.

9.3 THE OPERATION OF ROPE

The following scenarios describe how does ROPE method support the new EIM operations required. We group these scenarios into two classes: (1) rule processing operations (Scenarios 1 through 4) and (2) knowledge management operations (Scenarios 5 through 7). The rule processing operations are mostly concerned with data instances and rule execution; the knowledge management operations deal with the shell's adaptiveness and its ability to change its rulebase. Both will also be illustrate how ROPE works.

9.3.1 Rule Processing Operations

There are five stages of rule execution. The first stage, rule-triggering, varies in the details of execution from one type of rules to another. Once a rule has been triggered and its temporary fact base constructed, the remaining stages of the execution are essentially the same for every type. We will now look more closely at the processing details associated with rule triggering. The following scenarios describe how the shells use the knowledge they store to effect the integration of different application systems illustrated in Figure 9.4.

• *Scenario 1: Time-Triggered Rule (for event-based information flows)*

We define time-triggered rules as rules triggered by the occurrence of a time event, i.e., a specific time has been reached. It is the task of the Timer to manage the list of time events that impact on the shell processing. When the Timer wakes up, it retrieves all the time events due for processing and notifies the appropriate module in the shell.

• *Scenario 2: Data-Triggered Rule (for event-based information flows and data management)*

Data-triggered rules are executed only when a change is detected in the local application database: insertions, deletions, and/or updates. The shell monitors the local database periodically, using the Timer for launching the monitoring based on the time event list. The Application Monitor retrieves: (1) the fields in the table to monitor, (2) the name of the reference table to use, and (3) a monitoring query template. Using this information, it creates a monitoring query and launches the Database Interface, where the query is executed by a call to the local DBMS. The result from the query is preprocessed by the Database Interface to convert local values to their global equivalent values. The result is then transmitted to the Application Monitor to compare the previous result (stored in the reference table) and detect changes, using the monitoring algorithm. If any significant changes are detected, the Application Monitor launches the Message Processor with the changes. Finally, it creates a new event in the time event list to specify when the Application Monitor is to be launched next.

We might mention that there exists two approaches to achieve local application monitoring: (1) the event-driven approach and (2) the timer-driven approach. In the first approach, the triggers become part of the system monitored and the monitoring must be embedded either in the application system itself or in an interface that intercepts all pertinent transactions into the system. The timer-driven approach is more of an external monitoring. At specific time intervals, which are programmable as part of the trigger management by the metadatabase, the application is monitored to see the consequences of change. This approach is less system-dependent and fits the need of event/usage criterion defined in this research just well.

ROPE supports both event-driven and time-driven approaches. For simplicity, the present prototype uses only a timer-driven approach to monitor the databases of the different application systems. To implement the event-driven approach, the prototype would require that some tools exist to define triggers in the local application systems or the DBMSs. The idea is for those triggers to perform the same kind of process as the Application Monitor. The events-synchronization would be undertaken on an optional (selective) basis using the same rule-oriented control that ROPE performs on other contextual knowledge.

• *Scenario 3: Rule-Triggered Rule (for global query and event-based information flows)*

For rule-triggered rules (or chained rules), Stage 1 corresponds to Stage 5 of some other rule: a rule terminates its execution by firing the rules it chains to. Again, in Stage 2, we need to fetch the data needed by the rules to be fired. However, we also need to relate the fact base from the previous rule to the newly retrieved fact base. This is accomplished by (1) using the common fields on which the chaining occurs and (2) expanding the integration script of the chained rule to join the two fact bases on these field values.

• *Scenario 4: User-Triggered Rule (for global query, event-based information flows, and data management)*

The ROPE shell allows for a user to fire any rule, from any shell at any time. There are two ways to fire an arbitrary rule: (1) by triggering a system call to the Message Processor or (2) by sending a message to any application shell requesting the execution of the rule, using the Message Language. The Message Monitor identifies the application shell where the rule execution must start; either where the data or program trigger is located, or where the rule's first subrule is located. The Message Processor dispatches the rule execution message to the appropriate shell and determines according to the message if the rule is triggered by data monitoring; in which case the Message Processor forces the monitoring of the entity/relationship associated to the rule.

9.3.2 Knowledge Management Operations

The following scenarios describe how the local shells will behave when changes are propagated from the metadatabase. They represent the different classes of knowledge modification supported by ROPE.

• *Scenario 5: Structural Model Modification*

Structural model modification includes adding or removing fields or entities/relationships. Once the changes are committed to the local database and the metadatabase, a structural model modification message is sent to the local shell, where it is acquired by the Network Monitor. The message is then transmitted to the Message Processor where it is used to update the global query template of all the rules being triggered by changes in the modified entity/relationship. The next step is to notify the Application Monitor of the changes in the structure and reset the corresponding reference tables by launching the Database Interface to retrieve the current contents of the table after its structure modification.

• *Scenario 6: Rule Insertion and Deletion*

Rule modification is supported in ROPE as an (old) rule deletion followed by a (new) rule insertion. The System Integrator Manager does not need to keep track of where a rule is located. A rule insertion message contains all the details needed to update the different data files of the application shells. The Message Processor performs those changes. The changes could cause any number of the following: (1) updating the list of monitored tables and creating a new reference table for data-triggered rules, (2) inserting a new time event in the time event list for time-triggered and data-triggered rules, (3) updating the list of subrules in the shell, (4) updating the list of user-defined routines located in the shell and rebuilding the Rule Processor and Database Interface (only if adding a new user-defined routine), (5) updating the list of equivalences, and (6) creating query files for the rule. The Message Processor will remove any reference to a rule when receiving a rule deletion message, enforcing the integrity constraints of the ROPE structural model. Any subrule defined for that rule is also deleted. In addition to the constraints implicitly defined in the information model of ROPE, the deletion process includes two more integrity rules: (1) a routine not used by any rule is deleted from the entity "routine" and (2) an item is removed from the entity "item" if there is no conversion rule associated to the item. Finally, any event referencing a deleted rule is removed from the event list. The Rule Processor and Database Interface are updated with a change occurs in the list of user-defined routines.

• *Scenario 7: Monitoring Modification*

ROPE will allow the user to modify the time-string associated to a rule or to modify the frequency at which the Network Monitor will perform its tasks. These changes will only take effect the next time the rule is fired.

9.4 IMPLEMENTATION: A LABORATORY EIM

The metadatabase system is completed when the above operations using ROPE are implemented. A prototype metadatabase is constructed to verify its use as an EIM in an integrated manufacturing laboratory, as demonstrated in Chapter 6. Beyond the core functionality already described, the performance, scalability, and generality of the prototype are also studied in a laboratory environment.

Figure 9.8 illustrates the laboratory environments at Rensselaer in which the prototype was developed. The MDBMS has been implemented on a micro VAX platform using Rdb as the database engine for the metadatabase and has been demonstrated publicly. A new version using RS 6000, AIX, and Oracle has recently been developed to provide a multi-platform and distributed metadatabase environment. The enterprise environment currently consists of (1) a product design database using ROSE (an object-oriented database management system) and EXPRESS (the PDES/STEP data definition language) on an RS 6000, (2) a shop floor control system using Oracle on a PC, (3) an order processing system using Rdb on a microVAX, and (4) a process planning system using dBase on a PC. ROPE shells were then created and incorporated into these local systems as additional application programs against their own database management systems. All major requirements — viz., global query processing, global updates and events processing, and adaptability — are both conceptually and empirically tested against this setting, and proven working properly. A new project management system and in-process inspection system are further candidates to be added to the integration environment; they, again, serve to demonstrate the required adaptability of the metadatabase prototype to function as an EIM.

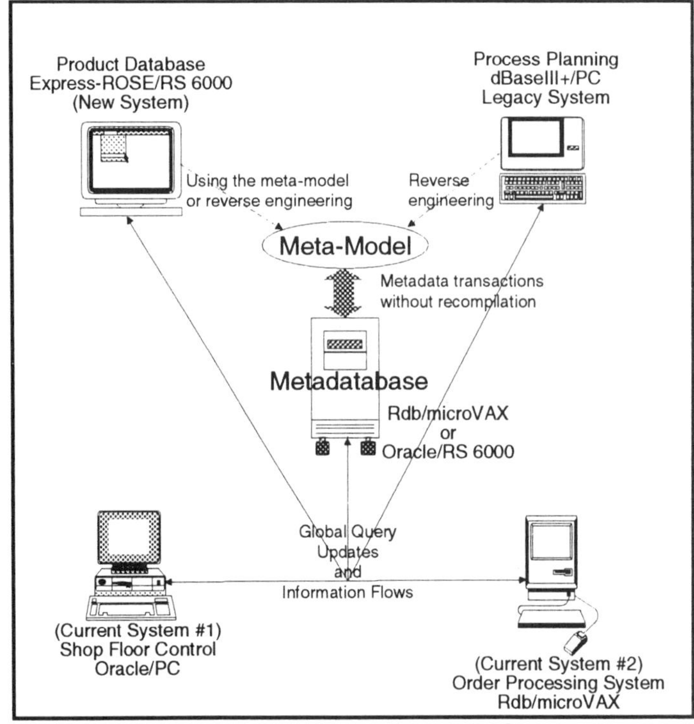

Fig. 9.8. The Adaptability of the EIM Prototype

It is worthwhile to stress that the entire development process incidentally mimics an evolutionary enterprise that the metadatabase model is aimed to facilitate. While the Order Processing system was developed by using TSER, which is the modeling technology in this case, all other systems had been developed independently before the integration commenced. Among them, the design of Shop Floor Control system could be considered as being influenced by the integration technology, while the Process Planning system was completely a legacy system and the Product Database a new technology — which was incorporated into the scope of integration after the MDBMS had been developed. Thus, Figure 9.8 not only depicts a static environment, but more importantly also shows a dynamic process of the integration through the prototype.

Furthermore, the above prototyping gives important practical guidelines to implementing the metadatabase model in a multiple system environment. Researchers in the field of multidatabases have long been confronted with three issues central to creating a multidatabase system: (1) what is the user's view of data, (2) how to translate from the enterprise view of the data to the local view, and (3) how to distribute the translation capabilities. We believe that the metadatabase prototype answers these three issues.

First, the Two-Stage Entity-Relationship modeling methodology captures the essence of each individual application, representing user's views and a neutral structural model of the application. This is valid for both legacy systems, that can be reverse-engineered into a TSER description, and for new applications, that can be modeled using TSER. When the new applications are not modeled in TSER, reverse-engineering (or paradigm translation) of the model for TSER can be performed. Hence, through the isomorphism provided in the TSER model, the user's view on the local application and databases are preserved. Full discussions on these points are provided in.

Second, The metadatabase global query capabilities assures that the consolidated application models can be used to map every query to the local application models. In the GIRD model of metadatabase, there is a clear separation between the enterprise model (including the functional and consolidated structural models) and the implementation of the modeled applications. The relationships between the structural and resource views in the GIRD assure the independence of the model from the implementation. In addition, a translator is to be built for each new DML included in the metadatabase. Note however that there already exists basic tools to incorporate relational, CODASYL, and object-oriented databases; which include translators for dBaseIII+, SQL/Oracle, RDB (Digital Equipment relational system), and ROSE/C++ (for an object-oriented database developed using EXPRESS).

Third, the architecture of ROPE makes use of a global query capability provided by the metadatabase to distribute the translation for interoperability. Specifically, the design prescribes that (1) all ad hoc queries be processed by the metadatabase's Global Query System (GQS) and (2) all planned queries (i.e., the queries needed to retrieve rule information) are preprocessed using GQS capabilities and encapsulated into local shells. This way the architecture of the local application shells is simplified and the performance enhanced. In addition, because all the translators are managed in the metadatabase environment, their design can be optimized to use all the information available from the GIRD model. ROPE languages and other constructs facilitate the construction of shells for member application systems and achieve the adaptive integration goals for the concurrent architecture of the EIM.

In order to assess the performance of executing (original) global rules in the distributed shells, the following assumptions are made: (1) it takes s steps to execute a ROPE job for a global rule, (2) each step occurs on a different shell, (3) it takes on average t units of time to execute an operation for a step (i.e., execute a subrule, a local query), (4) it takes n units of time to transmit a message, and (5) messages are processed every d unit of time. In the best case, there are no delays, hence it takes $s.t$ units of time to perform the operation. In the worst case, we have to wait $d+n$ units of time between each step, thus, the execution time is $s.t+(s-1).(n+d)$.

The worst case equation provides some insight on how to optimize the performances of the system. The only theoretical variable in the formula is the number of steps; the more steps we have per rule, the longer it will take to execute the rule. This is why the decomposition algorithm minimizes the number of subrules to reduce the number of times a message is passed to another system. The rest are technological parameters: the performance can only be improved by (1) reducing the processing time t with a faster rule processing, (2) increasing the speed of the network, hence reducing n, and (3) increasing the frequency at which messages are processed ($1/d$).

9.5 SATISFACTION OF EIM REQUIREMENTS

The conceptual promises of the adaptive concurrent architecture using ROPE for EIM are reviewed, with respect to wide-area, scalability, adaptability, parallelism, and autonomy. There are two levels of analysis to this review: the conceptual model and the execution model. The former is provided in Section 9.1, where parallelism and scalability were explicitly illuminated in Figures 9.1 and 9.2, respectively; and all four were discussed as to how the proposed model accomplishes these goals. The execution model consists of (1) MDBMS which was established earlier in the book, and (2) ROPE, which was presented in Sections 9.2 and 9.3 above. To further solidify our review, the issue of ROPE's satisfaction of open system requirements is discussed here. This issue encompasses interoperability and portability, and underlines a technical basis to all four issues above.

The open system architecture defined by ROPE is composed of three layers: (1) the local environment layer, (2) the shell layer, and (3) the network layer. The link between the local environment and the shell layer is achieved by (1) the Database Interface in charge of translating any local value into its global equivalent, (2) the Definitional Language that unifies the system calls performed by the shell, and (3) the Message Language. Because there are but a few connection points, the shells can be easily implemented in very diverse environments. The ROPE shell design assumes some basic and generic database and network capabilities of the local application systems, but are otherwise independent of the implementation environment.

ROPE deploys the model integration knowledge in the metadatabase to effect interoperability among the heterogeneous application systems it integrates. Model integration knowledge is acquired from this modeling process: First, each application has its own data model, which is translated into TSER using two modeling primitives (functional dependencies and rules) and a mean to associate, or "package", them. Model discrepancies are solved by defining equivalent data items as contextual knowledge within an application or across applications. This knowledge also includes conversion rules to resolve data format discrepancies between equivalent data items are solved by the definition of conversion rules. Implementation discrepancies in database organization are addressed by mapping the model into the actual implementation. This way, the implementation can differ from the model, but the metadatabase can always be used to trace back and resolve these discrepancies.

The concurrent processing method and the event/usage concurrency control approach make it possible to fulfill the need for local system independence. The ROPE shell provides an interface between the enterprise knowledge and the application systems. It is used to translate any result from the global knowledge processing into a format suitable for the local application systems, and vice versa. The distributed knowledge processing and management method enables the shells to communicate partial rule processing results as well as the MDBMS to transmit new or updated knowledge to the shells. The decomposition algorithm is designed in a holistic view of knowledge processing in a distributed environment, meeting the requirements of such a task. Furthermore, the shell's linkage to the local application and the network is minimized by ROPE. However, after that linkage is accomplished, the application has the option of tapping into the ROPE capabilities as an extension to its own environment. In instances where the local application system would execute a ROPE command, it would do so by sending a message using the Message Language, or by directly calling the Message/Rule Processor.

A level of open system architecture is evident in the above review. In the prototype, as discussed in Section 9.4, this property is proven in a laboratory setting. With the open system architecture and the new event/usage correctness criteria, the satisfaction of the above four requirements also leads itself to the fifth, wide (global) area operation (see Figure 9.2). On this basis, the five requirements are considered sufficed by the metadatabase model through the ROPE-supported implementation.

Finally we review the big picture of IT, beyond the EIM technology, for enterprise integration. To compare the metadatabase approach against the efforts in the field of enterprise IT, we might mention first the emerging standards and technologies in the information industry, especially the national-scale information superhighway. A key premise for National Information Infrastructure is the ability to link, interoperate, integrate, and manage the distributed information resources for enterprise users, satisfying the requirements discussed above. This has thus become a central goal of research in both industry and university communities. Prime efforts range from multiple databases, the International Standards Organization's Distributed Applications Environment (DAE) and the Object Management Organization's Common Object Request Broker Architecture (CORBA) all the way to the recent National Industrial Information Infrastructure Protocols (NIIIP) initiatives co-ordinated by IBM and sponsored by ARPA.

From the perspective of dynamic alignment, there are three basic classes of criteria that can be recognized for assessing the nature of these technologies: (1) meta-data assisted networking for interoperability, (2) global modeling for enterprise views, and (3) managing the networking architecture using the global models for feedback. The metadatabase model claims its unique strengths in the third area, feedback, which is critical to true scalability and adaptability. It also claims some unique promises in the modeling area (with its attendant meta-modeling methods) and the interoperability area (with its rule-oriented concurrent architecture), as well. In contrast, much of the ongoing efforts elsewhere have been focused on turning out standards and technologies for the first two areas. The metadatabase model is established on this basis as a solution to some of the problems facing enterprise integration and modeling that Chapter 1 discusses. In particular, an EIM is provided.

10

MANUFACTURING INTEGRATION

The concept of enterprise integration and modeling is particularized for manufacturing in this chapter. The metadatabase approach is applied to integrate basic manufacturing information systems. A core information model and a specific procedure of using this model to develop a metadatabase system is provided. In this sense, this chapter offers an elaboration of the metadatabase solution to manufacturing integration that chapter 1 indicates.

10.1 INFORMATION MANAGEMENT FOR MANUFACTURING ENTERPRISE INTEGRATION

Information technology plays a key role in modern manufacturing at two levels: facility and enterprise. Facility-level manufacturing information systems are responsible for mundane tasks such as production planning and shop floor control. Figure 10.1 depicts the major functions of a generic computer-integrated manufacturing (CIM) facility, which includes process planning (PP), material requirements planning (MRP), shop floor control (SFC). work stations operation, and material handling. Typically, touch labor takes place only in the last two functions and accounts for no more than 40% of the total effort-the rest is entirely information processing. Even the share of touch labor involves a significant use of information technology for, e.g., data entry and display in in-process verification, statistical process control (SPC), and electronic data interchange (EDI). Therefore, it is appropriate to say that today's manufacturing systems rely on information technology, and the job of information management is both to support these systems and to enable them achieving their objectives. At the enterprise level, however, the goal for the information management is nothing short of effecting the synergies among all stages of the life cycle of manufacturing, including its customer, supplier, and dealer as well as design, production, and business. In fact, information has become the agent of integration for manufacturing enterprises competing in today's global market place. When manufacturing technology and institutional factors are largely exogenous to the management, information is virtually the single most fundamental factor that determines an enterprise's maximal productivity, quality, and customer service. Thus, in this sense, information has become the fourth basic factor of production, along with labor, land, and capital.

The discussion of manufacturing information systems begins with an enterprise-level vision and from there moves down to a facility-level review. The functionality and information requirements, systems development, using a core information model, and the application of the metadatabase model for information management are then discussed in this context. A basic CIM case is used throughout to illustrate the various concepts and techniques discussed. The discussion will be concluded with emerging concepts. architectures. and systems pursuing the enterprise level Vision of the future. Introduced below is a vision to provide a big picture as the anchoring point for the discussion.

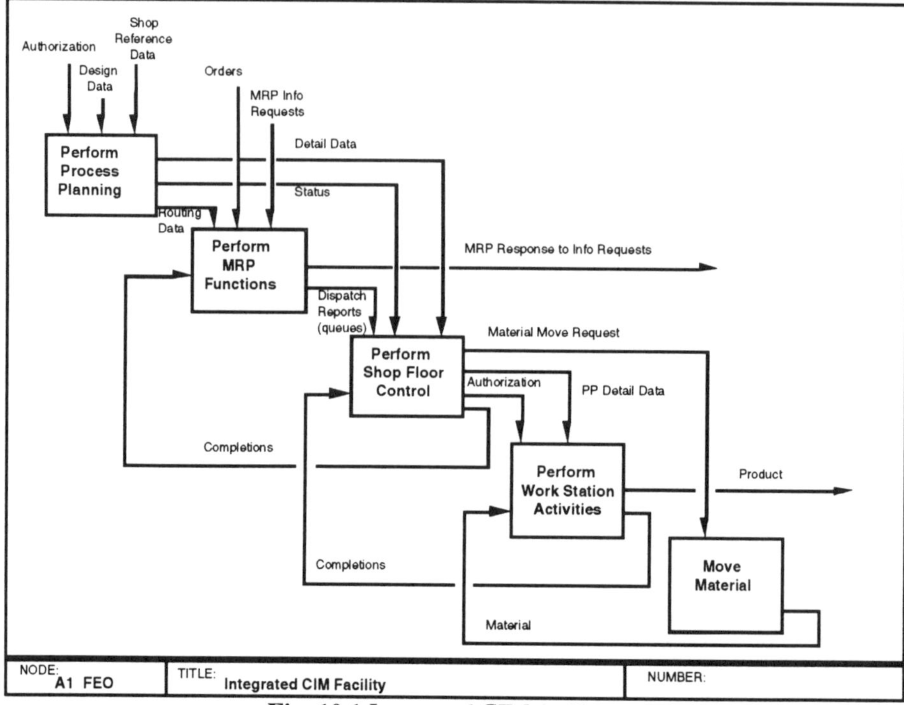

Fig. 10.1 Integrated CIM facility

10.1.1 Adaptive Manufacturing through Information Technology: A Vision

From "islands of automation" (e.g., CAD-CAM) to enterprise-level CIM, the notion of computerized manufacturing has undergone a far-reaching evolution. The new information technologies this effort has brought out also prompted whole new industries in systems integration and processes reengineering and continue to result in new standards and applications for both manufacturing and service enterprises. Now that integration is effectively a given and CIM an objective in sight. is there life after CIM? Or. asking the question from a users perspective. is there a fundamental need for a new vision beyond CIM to address further the entrenched competitiveness problem facing manufacturing enterprises in today's global marketplace? The answer is a resounding yes, as evidenced by the emerging calls for agile manufacturing, flexible CIM, and virtual corporation. The key reason is simple: previous visions, efforts, and results of integration worldwide have yet to consider sufficiently the customer's evolving needs. Solutions emphasize the achievement of synergism across enterprise functions given requirements fixed at a particular point in time. These requirements, however, rarely stay unchanged for long. In fact, due to global competition and ever heightening customer demands, the basic competitive strategy of a corporation increasingly requires that the enterprise be able to respond rapidly to market conditions with a high degree of product differentiation and value-based customer services. These requirements cause rapid changes in the enterprise that can no longer be dealt with by using managerial savvy alone. This trend is clearly established and in all likelihood will become more pronounced as we enter the next century.

Therefore, for improved productivity and quality, manufacturing requirements for the next century must focus on achieving adaptiveness to consolidate and extend the substantial gains made to date in integration. The result will be an enterprise with the ability to effect shorter cycle times, with lower volumes of identical items and higher mixtures of different items on the same assembly lines. It will also lead to greater flexibility in the organization of physical facilities that potentially are distributed globally, with increased customization, greater parallel activity across business functions and processes, and closer coupling with vendors and customers. This adaptiveness must be fully characterized with established scientific principles to clearly illuminate the technological gaps between the objective and the previous results, and hence it will be more robust than a casual notion of agility or flexibility that may not lead to the understanding of the problem necessary for guiding the search for new fundamental solutions.

A scenario might best illustrate this vision. A customer calls the manufacturer to order a product that has a personalized logo or other custom features. Some of these custom requirements might be handled easily from a standard Options package, some might require changes in standard processes for the product, and others might entail a revised design or even new materials. Thus the cost and production time varies widely, depending on the specific customization. The objective is not only to be able to offer this kind of customized product at market-able prices but also to provide a firm price and delivery date to the customer on the spot while the customer is still on the telephone Line completing the order(Figure 10.2).

Accommodating these requirements challenges the ingenuity of all members of the enterprise and demands innovative techniques for designing the product and the processes needed to build it, including verification of the product and global planning and control of the enterprise. Throughout this process, the entire product life cycle must be considered, including adaptability to change after initial manufacture and the ability for obsolete products to be recycled or safely and economically destroyed. But above all, a key ingredient of this new capability is information technology. The modeling, management, utilization, storage, and processing of information must be adaptive as well as integrated to support parallel functions and processes through out the enterprise. The manufacturer must set out to acquire the necessary new technology to enable these new fundamental regimes, where managers are simply process owners working with other types of employees across the organization. In a nutshell, a corporation must be able to separate its functional groupings of personnel, facilities, and other resources from its physical organizations-or, in other words, to form multiple "virtual organizations" simultaneously out of the same physical resources and adapt them without having to change the actual organizations. The justification is simple: there exists only one physical organization at any point of time regardless how adaptive it is, and it is always subject to organizational inertia. Thus, for example, a design engineer of an auto manufacturer in Detroit, can be an effective team member with industrial designers in Milan, Italy, and manufacturing engineers throughout the Midwest, while at the same time be involved with other teams that deal with customers, dealers, suppliers. and other vendors vertically or horizontally associated with the enterprise. Only through information can this virtual organization become meaningful and only effecting a new generation of information technology can this vision be realized.

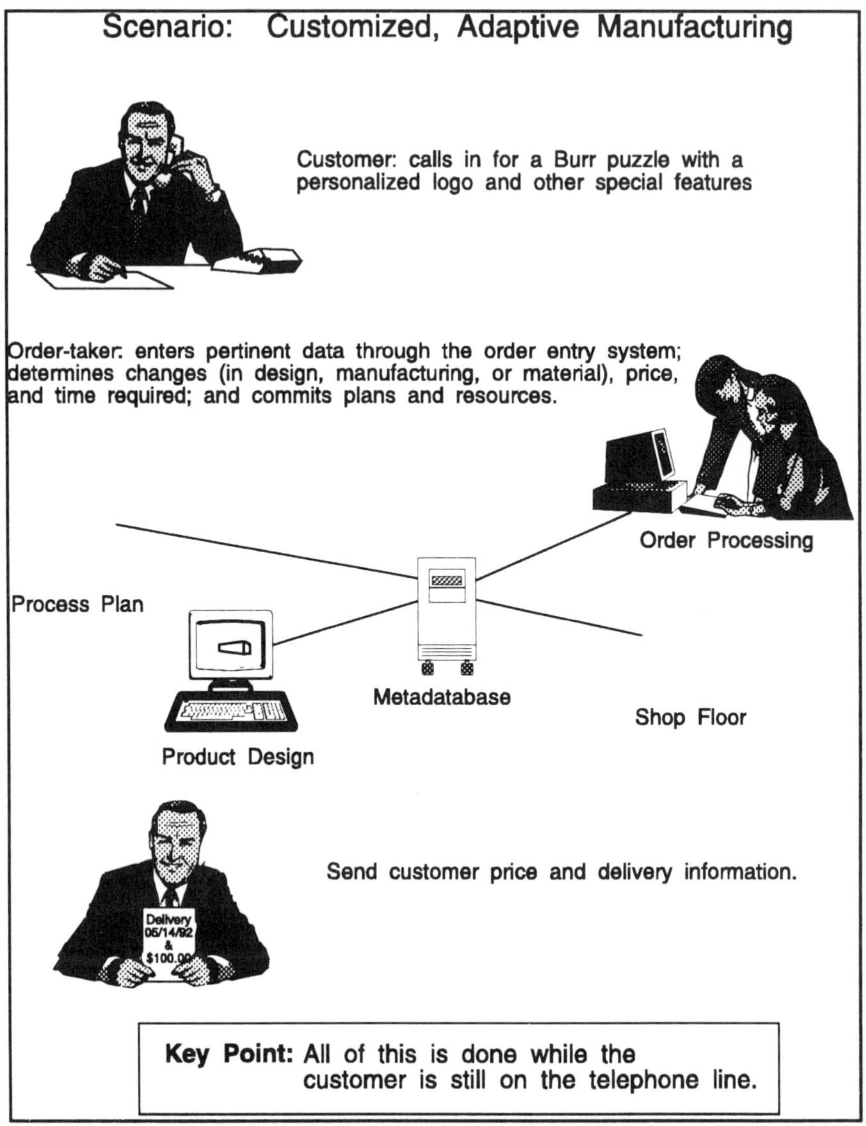

Fig. 10.2. Scenario: customized, adaptive manufacturing

10.1.2 Basic Concepts of Manufacturing Information Systems

To understand, use, and manage a manufacturing information system, there are three key questions to ask and answer: (1) what manufacturing functions and processes does this system support? (2) what information resources-i.e., data resources, knowledge bases, and decision models-does it require? and (3) what information technology does it employ? These questions apply equally well to both facility- and enterprise-level systems, although the answer would have significantly different implications for the manufacturer from one level to another.

Facility-level Systems

Information systems support many mundane jobs in a facility. An example is shown in Figure 10.3, which indicates some basic functions on a shop floor and the support these functions need from a shopfloor information system. Similar situations exist with virtually all other engineering and production activities. Below is a list of common functions and processes for which information systems have been developed.

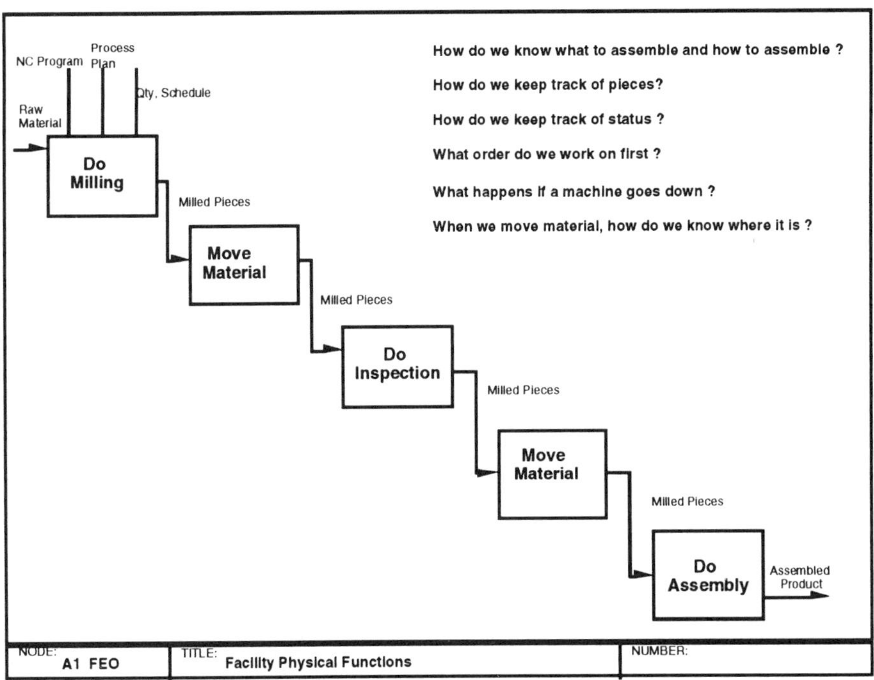

Fig. 10.3. The need for a shop floor information system

- CAD.
- Computer-aided engineering (CAE).
- Computer-aided manufacturing (CAM).
- Computer-aided process planning (CAPP).
- Production planning and scheduling.
- Inventory control and forecasting.
- SPC.

- Material handling.
- Inspection and in-process verification.
- Warehousing.
- Flexible manufacturing (FMS) and cell control.
- SFC.
- MRP.
- Manufacturing resources planning (MRP II).
- Integrated computer-aided production planning (ICAPP).

Enterprise-level Systems

Five basic elements comprise a manufacturing enterprise:

- Engineering (product and process design).
- Business (marketing, distribution, finance, and other administration).
- Production (manufacturing facilities and processes).
- Vendor (supplier, dealer, and collaborator).
- Customer (individual or organization).

Enterprise-level systems, therefore, typically cut across the boundaries of these elements and strive to achieve synergism through the integration of information. As discussed earlier, this integration often is driven by the following goals, which have in effect become the underlying principles of enterprise information integration:

- Shortening and managing the product life cycle ranging from market study, product development, and production to customer service.
- Maximizing parallelism among decision processes and activities throughout the life cycle.
- Effecting virtual and horizontal organization of all resources involved in the life cycle.

These three principles all entail adaptiveness in the integration across all elements of the enterprise. They, in part or in whole, drive the theme of the common information systems at the enterprise level as manifested in these integration efforts:

- Concurrent or simultaneous engineering (CE), for engineering, production, and business.
- CIM enterprise, for production, engineering and business.
- Just-in-time (JIT), for production and vendor.
- Design for manufacturing (DFM), for engineering and production.
- Total quality management (TQM), for customer, business, engineering, and production.
- Adaptive integrated manufacturing enterprise (AIME), for production, engineering, business, vendor, and customer.

Methodology and Technology

Information systems at both levels together constitute a total supersystem for the manufacturer. Thus, regardless of how many and what kinds of system exist in an enterprise, there must be a cohesive information architecture to consolidate the physical facilities, communications infra-structure, and information resources that these systems require, and to reconcile them with the enterprise's managerial control systems and organizational structures. Such an architecture is sometimes referred to as an enterprise model. Obviously, an enterprise model will not and should not be static; rather its detailing is a function of the strategic planning or integration that the enterprise undertakes at the time and depends on the scope of the systems. Nevertheless, an enterprise model must he maintained for the enterprise at all times to ensure that there will be no fundamental conflicts and barriers among present and future systems. Enterprise modeling can be greatly facilitated by using a reference model that provides requirements and economical assessments for the particular industry to which the enterprise belongs.

Given an enterprise model. the development of an information system typically includes five activities:

1. Project planning and feasibility study.
2. Structured systems analysis for determining information resources requirements.
3. Structured systems design, focusing on (1) data modeling for databases and files, (2)process modeling for application programs, (3) knowledge modeling for production rules and other operation logic, (4) decision modeling for decision processes and user interface requirements, and (5)software engineering of the above models for implementation design.
4. Implementation of the system into the organization and users training.
5. Control, change, and growth of the system.

10.2 PROTOTYPICAL MANUFACTURING INFORMATION SYSTEMS

Information technology has been applied since the early loss to the production planning and inventory control functions in manufacturing facilities. In the 1970s, its application was expanded in parallel to shop floors for actual (or work order-level) production control and to engineering laboratories for product design functions. In the 1980s, prompted by both the opportunity for integration and the problems of disjoint systems (the so called islands of automation), the focus started to shift from individual systems to facility wide and, most recently, enterprise-level integration of systems. The shift is an evolution marked by several conceptual milestones: initially, the integration problem was equated with connecting the islands of automation through local area networking and linking disjointed application systems through software interfacing (i.e., file conversions and transfer). The need to manage the complexities of file structures and to reconcile the inconsistencies of the file contents led to emphasis on data standards, communications protocols, and open systems architectures. The need to promote parallelism in processes and to facilitate the synergy among all functional applications across the enterprise, whose individual users' particular views and requirements created the complexities and inconsistencies in the first place, revealed a higher dimensionality of integration and placed major emphasis on enterprise information models, reengineering, and information integration technology. This has naturally been followed by the current calls for adaptive manufacturing, total quality management, and international standards on data and knowledge interchange using a conceptual model.

10.2.1 Production Planning and Business Functions: MRP and MRP II

MRP. MRP is a classic of manufacturing information systems and continues to be a backbone of information management functions for many manufacturing facilities of all sizes. Its core is a master production scheduler that coordinates detailed production plans at all stages of production from (raw materials) input to semi-finished product to finished product--for a fixed planning horizon (usually weeks or months). The scheduling starts with the bill of materials (BOM) for the finished product and the quantity required at the end of the planning horizon. The BOM is exploded level by level to reach the end items, while the scheduler also works backward to determine when and how many of each item will be needed. The process is completed when every part and component in the BOM has a determined production schedule. The major advantage (and acid test) of an MRP system over traditional production planning and inventory control systems is its ability to coordinate the entire BOM of a product or even many products. An ideal MRP system will achieve a seamless pattern of work flows throughout the multistage production process with (1) no work-in-process (WIP) inventory and minimal overall inventory, (2) no stockouts for WIPs, and (3) minimal make span or time required to go through the entire process. The major limitation of MRP is that, like other production planning systems, it relies entirely on estimated parameters of the production system and performs only static scheduling for a long time period (as opposed to real-time, adaptive control). Its output, the detailed plans, are invariably point estimates that can only be used as possible reference points for actual shop floor scheduling. In practice, MRP is meant to be employed not for shop floor control, but for master production scheduling; for this purpose it is clearly an extension of the traditional schedulers and serves as a super-scheduler integrating many parts of production scheduling by using the computer power of modern information technology.

MRP's major information requirements include forecasting, supply delivery, and production capacity on the data side and decision rules, heuristics, and analytical models on the knowledge side. The quality of these information resources-their timeliness, accuracy, and comprehensiveness-determines that of the MRP output. With the latest information technology, especially knowledge bases and distributed data processing, even a static MRP can be enhanced to (1) support near real-time planning within a shorter time frame by rerunning the MRP every day, (2) offer better information from other sources (marketing, purchasing, and shop floor), and (3) supply more scheduling power by incorporating databases and knowledge-based techniques.

MRP II. MRP II employs information technology concepts that were developed after the original MRP systems. Specifically, it extends the scope of information from focusing on production planning per se to also including some business sources such as customer orders, accounting ledgers, and deliveries. Furthermore, it broadens the link to shop floor control by incorporating updated estimates of capacity and other production parameters into the scheduling to generate workorders for shop floor systems. Therefore, MRP II can be considered an attempt at integrating several functions in production planning, shop floor control, and business through a common database to manage the capacity of a manufacturing facility. Its proven functionality, however, is still the static and time-phased scheduling for production, albeit more elaborate than MRP. Its connection to shop floor activities and business databases is inherently off-line, or batch-processing based, due to its underpinning decision logic. Like MRP, MRP II uses a life cycle of scheduling processes that has clear stage boundaries and domain perspectives leading to separate, self-contained units of functionality. For example, lead time and priority are two parameters central to scheduling work. They are determined *a priori* in each unit, rather than being estimated directly and dynamically from actual conditions on the shop floor and the source data in other units when they are needed in computation.

The information requirements of MRP II are essentially those of MRP plus process planning, capacity planning, work order, customer order entry, warehousing, general ledger, and various other financial and shop floor activities, depending on the particular implementation in the marketplace. With the added capability of processing orders and incorporating this information into planning, MRP II allows a degree of flexibility in production planning for make-to-stock and, to a lesser extent, make-to-order environments. The information model used by MRP II thus differs from the one for MRP in that it contains many information resources that other systems are responsible to generate and maintain. These overlaps indicate the need for managing cross-system data resources as well as information integration. New knowledge capabilities will be needed to improve MRPII's underlying decision logic from one that is segmented to one that fuses the pertinent units into global parallel processes.

10.2.2 Production Control and Extended Planning for Vendors: SFC, FMS, and JIT

SFC and FMC. Shop floor control is a generic function in manufacturing that executes the production plans and coordinates the operations as depicted in Figures 10.1 and 10.3. Its time frame is typically much shorter than that of MRP and MRP II and is determined by the operational jobs that it controls. Therefore, the complexity of an SFC depends largely on the flexibility of the configuration of workstations in the shop, ranging from a near-continuous flow shop (which tends to be the simplest case) to a batch-based job shop all the way to a mixed-part-virtual-cell shop (the most complex). The scope of control also varies, depending not only on the type of shop but also on the level of automation. In highly automated facilities, SFC may include material handling (e.g., automated guided vehicles) and workstation control as well as cell-hierarchical administration. while less automated production systems may only need SFC to keep track of work orders, work-in-process, and other traditional management jobs. In a similar way, such systems as inspection, in-process verification and statistical process control may or may not be incorporated into SFC. Clearly, unlike MRP and MRP II, SFC is not a sufficiently standardized function. It tends to be developed on an ad hoc basis and requires comprehensive modeling effort to meet specifications for the host enterprise. FMS, on the other hand, constitutes particular types of shop floor capabilities and configurations and hence is more likely to identify a generic basis for developing off-the-shelf information and control systems. Nonetheless, FMS information and control systems tend to be bundled with a particular hardware environment--workstations and other infrastructures--so that they require customization and significant modeling effort to fit into individual situations. Despite the variance in the complexity of their control mechanisms, SFC and FMS information systems all required similar basic functionality as covered in the generic description in Figures 10.1 and 10.3.

The information requirements of SFC and FMS are more or less straightforward for data resources but quite involved and time frame dependent for knowledge resources (including decision models). The data resources required are basically process plans and operations, workorders, work-in-process, data on mechanisms (machines, cells and facilities), routing, machine loading, and part data. Many of these data resources are also needed or used for MRP and MRP II; the difference is usually the degree of detail (associated with the time frame found in work orders routing and other operation-based data). Knowledge resources, on the other hand, involve flows, controls, and other operating rules and models using the data resources. They are particular to the specifics of the system. A flowshop may be operated by using some fixed schedules, a batch-based SFC may call for significant knowledge resources on feedback to respond to real events taking place on the shop floor, and a cellular cell-based FMS may require advanced information sharing across cells to regroup parts and jobs on an on-line and real-time basis, thereby entailing complex knowledge bases. Similarly, when additional functions such as inspection, statistical process control, and quality assurance are included on top of the basic SFC-FMS functionality, the additional information requirements tend to stem more from the use of data (or contextual knowledge) than from data resources per se. Evidently, information systems for SFC and FMS cannot be built from standard package without involving extensive modeling effort to customize them for the host enterprise. Acquiring particular contextual knowledge for common data resources would be at the heart of such custom modeling. Building blocks that can be employed to implement an SFC information system include control packages for workstations and cells, on-line scheduling and WIP monitoring systems, and modules for various process controls. Factory data entry and display techniques (e.g., bar-code systems and personal-computer-based interactive operator support systems) would be of great value in successfully involving factor operators in SFC-FMS.

JIT. The nature and promises of JIT are best understood from an extended enterprise view. Essentially, JIT is an (extended) enterprise SFC system that regards suppliers' production functions as an integral part of the enterprise's overall life cycle of production and sets out to minimize or even eliminate the manufacturer's own inventory, which is nothing more than a work-in-process in between the supplier and the manufacturer when organizational boundaries are discounted. After all, the elimination of WIPs is precisely what any SFC-FMS or MRP-MRP II systems strives to accomplish to achieve smooth shop floor production. It follows from this enterprise view that. minimally, a JIT system would require the coordination between the SFC's time frame and the suppliers' time frames of delivery and would link them through certain formal mechanism. More adequately, such coordination would be extended to involve the production planning and control functions of both the manufacturer and its suppliers. The formal connections obviously require organizational changes and have proven to be a major obstacle to US. manufacturer's full use of the possibilities offered by JIT. In Japan. major manufacturers that pioneered the practice of JIT often own their suppliers as "satellite" companies or influence their supplier in substantive ways, hence the required organization is usually already in place for the manufacturer to implement JIT. Given this hierarchical structure between manufacturers and supplier, it is a small wonder that the enterprise-oriented perspective of JIT naturally evolved and flourished in Japan. However, organizational connections are not a premise of JIT: many of the connections needed for effective coordination can be accomplished through information technology. In other words, to effect JIT, a proper cross-organizational information system linking the pertinent information resources of both sides' production planning and control functions (so that, under the guidance of an enterprise model, each could share in the other's processing) would suffice. The enterprise model would address control issues such as ownership, usage, and processing of this information and would in practice amount to a virtual organization as discussed in Chapter 1. The required information resources are no different from those discussed for MRP-MRP II and SFC-FMS, except that the organizational boundaries would be removed under the concept of (extended) enterprise.

10.2.3 Engineering Functions: CAD-CAM, CAE, and CAPP

CAD-CAM, CAE, and CAPP provide product designs and process plans using engineering methods and feed the designs and plans into production. The basic functions of CAD include automatic engineering drawing, solid modeling, and product data management; CAE analysis and simulation; and CAPP instructions needed by CAM for actual machining. Therefore, just like production planning, these functions are performed sequentially in self-contained stages prior to the actual production stage in the product life cycle. The computerization of these functions is focused on automating the engineering methods and principles used in the design process. For example, CAPP takes results from CAD in batch and derives manufacturing processes for CAM from the product designs according to predetermined fixed algorithms or planning rules. The process plans are then transferred in batch to SFC for execution on work-stations, computer-based numerical controlled machines, and other CAM system and are expected to remain unchanged throughout the useful life of the product design and the machines used.

CAD-CAM and CAE. The information requirements for CAD-CAM and CAE are well known: they are determined by and rooted in the long-established engineering sciences and their practice. Their computer implementation is, therefore, dominated by generic but proprietary software systems, combining computer graphics (for electronic drawing and imaging) with high powered computation for processing and managing product definitional data and engineering algorithms (e.g., tolerancing and analysis); both of which are the core information requirements for CAD, CAM and CAE functions. Vendors of CAD-CAM and CAE systems traditionally developed their own proprietary design of databases to optimize the computing performance of their engineering environments. Consequently, a formidable barrier was created preventing users of different vendors from interchanging their product data either horizontally among engineers or vertically across stages of the enterprise. As a response to this problem, the industry has collaborated with national and international standards-setting organizations such as the National Institute of Standards and Technology (NIST) of the United States and the International Standards Organization (ISO) to bring compatibility to the field. The most significant and growing effort is the product data exchange using the STEP model, which combines a leading standard under NIST-the previous PDES specification-with ISO's standard for the exchange of product model data (STEP). The model has gained acceptance in the United States, E.C., and Japan. Incidentally, the old PDES under NIST itself symbolized a decade-long quest for standards to support CAD systems' interoperability; tremendous efforts were undertaken by both NIST and the U.S. Air Force through such projects as IGES (the effort to develop a neutral file format for geometric data to be used by different CAD systems to transfer between proprietary formats when interfacing with each other) and PDDI (the specification of product definitional data to facilitate seamless interchange of part design files among air force contractors and vendors involved in aircraft design). The evolution from IGES, PDDI, and other early standards to PDES also underlines a simultaneous evolution of the scope of information resources used. The scope increased from IGES to PDDI mainly due to the complexity of products considered, but the change from PDDI to the old PDES and then to the new international PDES represents an enterprise view beyond CAD and CAE functions. The new PDES (i.e., STEP) model emphasizes concurrent engineering not only among engineers within and without an organization but also between engineering design and production. This model includes process planning requirements and is presently embarking on major new initiatives to develop enterprise information models containing both data and knowledge resources for product and process design and ultimately for production itself. The effort could take minimally several years before any concrete results are achieved. Again, the key to this integration effort (from product and process design to production) is information, characterized by information requirements and consolidated through information modeling. A word of caution regarding standards is warranted: standards tend to be too comprehensive to be employed economically by the average-size manufacturer and could be too overwhelming to adapt to future technology.

CAPP. The counterpart of CAD in process design is CAPP. Its required information resources are characterized by process definitional data and process plan generation knowledge. A CAPP system often works together with particular CAD systems so that the latter feed product deign files into the former and drive its processing. The complexity of CAPP systems depends essentially on whether the process plans are generated on the fly for the inputting product design or chosen from a library of existing plans. Obviously, generating process plans at runtime demands more refined data resources and significant knowledge-based capabilities. The most dynamic systems would, in addition, possess data resources on the real conditions of the particular manufacturing facilities that the processes are designed for and take them into account when generating process plans. The shorter the time frame between the generation and execution of process plans, the more dynamic the CAPP systems need to be. A clear direction for the extension of CAPP is its connection with SFC and/or MRP-MRP II so as to effect better adaptiveness to process planing. Incidentally, this connection would also benefit the adaptiveness of the production planning and control systems in a similar way. CAPP systems with these extensions are emerging in the industry. Ironically, as CAPP systems are extended to integrate into actual production, they become less generic and require more particular modeling for the host enterprises. The savings are, hence, found in hieghtened effectiveness, particularly, good quality (due to the dynamic alignment capabilities), rather than in processing CAPP systems per se. This argument holds true for virtually all enterprise integration endeavors.

10.2.4 Integration of Engineering, Production, and Business: CE and CIM

CE. Concurrent engineering started out as an initiative on engineering integration by the Defense Advanced Research Projects Agency (DARPA). The effort was soon extended to include manufacturing processes and emphasized parallel processing between design and production functions. Recently, the notion of concurrence was further extended to business activities that feed into design, such as marketing. Nonetheless, the basic orientation is still engineering design, and the focus is the shortening of the new product development cycle. The DARPA initiative resulted in many good solutions addressing various aspects of the problem. A commonly used solution is the team approach to the process of engineering itself, which calls for grouping design engineers with manufacturing engineers and marketing professionals to facilitate interactions and synergy among these traditionally sequential tasks. Another solution is the design for manufacturability (or for other things) approach, which provides new methodology to reorient design from optimizing for engineering to optimizing for production. Other results of the DARPA initiative include total quality management and quality function development, which are considered functional tools for CE.

The most concrete accomplishments of CE seem to belong to the areas of computing technology and software engineering for integrating CAD-CAM-CAE models, systems, and environments: a prime case is the PDES-STEP effort discussed above, which has become a rallying point of enabling technology for many aspects of CE. As a whole vision, CE remains a goal for individual manufacturers to strive toward; it does not have off-the-shelf solutions that a company can easily put together. Its very basis is still the notion of enterprise information integration. The modeling effort and the scope of information requirements depend, as always, on the vision of CE of the particular enterprise. For instance, to truly and fully implement the team approach and the design-for-manufacturing methodology, the CE information systems should be able to support the formation of virtual teams (multiple teams formed from the same actual organization or from multiple organizations) and the real-time feedback from production to design.

CIM. While CE comes from the perspective of engineering, computer-integrated manufacturing was prompted by the need to integrate production planning with control. It was later extended to include both business functions and engineering. Earlier conceptions of CIM placed efforts mainly on manufacturing facilities, local area networks, and automatic control technology to effect the integration of MRP-MRP II, SFC-FMS, and CAPP-CAD. Software interfacing techniques and control and communication protocols were commonly sought for as the solutions. Soon after, however, it became clear that protocols (e.g., NIST's TOP and GM's MAP) and software connectors (e.g., application program interchange (API)) are only pieces of the solution to CIM, rather than being the solution itself, because integration requires fusion of the logic of all systems that cannot be achieved by straightforward patch-up using APIs and the like. The focus then shifted to information integration, and fundamental results started to emerge. These new results not only advanced the methodology for integrated enterprise modeling and the technology for managing multiple systems (e.g., heterogeneous, distributed, and autonomous databases) but also converged on the same enterprise vision as CE was revealing to itself. It is now commonly accepted that both CIM and CE are an information integration vision for the whole enterprise, which entails the same set of information technology solutions.

A large number of organizations and research groups have contributed to making the vision of CIM a reality. Some representative efforts include Europe's ESPRIT (an E.C. consortium that oversees numerous individual projects in industry and academe), the U.S. Air Force's ICAM project, and the multiyear, multidisciplinary CIM research projects at industrial companies and universities. Open systems architecture and metadata (enterprise models) technology are among the most noticeable new results that have come from the quest for CIM. On this basis, a CIM information system would feature an enterprise model and use this model to guide and facilitate the management of functional information (sub)systems in a concurrent manner.

10.3 INTEGRATION USING THE METADATABASE MODEL

Throughout this chapter, the significance of an enterprise view in manufacturing information management and the need of enterprise modeling for the development of integrated systems were emphasized. The enterprise model itself is increasingly recognized by both academia and industry as a central part of the information architecture for integrated manufacturing. Actually, as discussed in chapter 1, one can say that enterprise metadata (including information models and other data about data resources) play an ever more critical role in information management as the scope of systems becomes ever larger and moves toward enterprise-level integration. To point out this trend, which is bound to become more pronounced in the future, some of the basic problems facing manufacturing information integration are briefly reviewed.

10.3.1 Complexity of Manufacturing Enterprises

As discussed above, manufacturing enterprises all feature multiple information systems that have the following characteristics:

1. They are developed and maintained at local sites for particular applications and user groups according to local conditions.
2. They interact with each other in high volume, wide-area or even global networks.
3. They involve numerous different data resources (e.g., product design and manufacturing processes) and contextual knowledge (including operating rules and information flows).
4. They or their contents are frequently revised as technology and needs evolve.

These characteristics together extend beyond the capabilities of available information technology. A great deal of research in CIM and CE has been devoted to developing new integration technologies and a great deal of success has been accomplished. However, major problems remain to be solved. They range from specific technical issues such as managing updates and views in multidatabases and accommodating legacy systems and new systems in integrated environments all the way to conceptual modeling of the requirements for real-time information flow between manufacturing and design (as opposed to only from design to manufacturing). At one level or another, these problems arise from the common limitation of past efforts that achieved integration against a fixed set of requirements without considering fully the adaptive nature of multiple manufacturing systems.

Management of Multiple Systems. Commercially available results do not manage multiple information systems with satisfactory performance. Most of these results employ as a cornerstone of their approaches, the traditional Von Neumann model of synchronization, which integrates schemata and serializes transactions across local systems under a central administrator. Consequently, there are fundamental limitations imposed by the architectures of these systems. These limitations place restrictions on local autonomy because of the requirements for schema integration and standardization of system structures, on global computing because of the complexity of serialization, and on system evolution because of the need to recompile or even redesign major elements of the global system when changes are made. Alternative approaches must be found to resolve these limitations, placing the solution to this problem at the heart of the adaptiveness issue.

Achievement of an Open Systems Architecture. Another key challenge for adaptiveness is an open system architecture, which is a prevailing concern in efforts such as CIMOSA and the industry-led Open Software Foundation. This capability is critical to a manufacturing enterprise's ability to respond rapidly to change as well as to incorporate heterogeneous systems. Despite the vast progress made in the past decade on standards, current technology still cannot support adaptiveness. These standards tend to emphasize standardization on designs and structures, rather than separating the underlying logic from systems. Thus in a manner related to the issues discussed above current results do not accommodate legacy systems, revising or deleting existing systems, and adding new systems without necessitating major redesign or recompilation of existing systems. For example. all the conventional systems require large scale schema restructuring at least at the global level to accommodate nontrivial changes. This often leads to unrealistic costs in practice. Standard or neutral structures alone cannot solve this problem. Techniques must be found to allow systems that do not use standards to work with systems that do and to make the global architecture and its administration independent of the local systems.

10.3.2 Solution Through Enterprise Metadata

A solution approach to the above problems that is currently emerging is not only to develop rigorous enterprise models but also to employ them using new metadata technology to provide on-line knowledge for the enterprise's information management and integration. Because the on-line enterprise models (i.e., metadatabases) are easier to be made adaptive, an information architecture that is based on a metadatabase would also be adaptive. Chapter 5 has provided an overview to this architecture and chapters 6 to 9 have detailed it in technical discussions. Virtually all ongoing major efforts on enterprise information integration in the industry have explicitly or implicitly embraced the use of a metadatabase of some kind(or repository) in their architectures. With appropriate attendant software technology such as metamodels and rule-based shells, both new and legacy systems can be added to an integrated environment without causing any part of the total environment, including the systems being added, to experience disruption. All that would be required is reverse modeling and automatic update to the global coordination system through the metadatabase. Modification to any part of other systems would involve only ordinary metadata transactions, too. Although particular future products will certainly use their own versions of implementation technology for enterprise metadata, we believe, nonetheless, the general principles shown in the metadatabase model will stand.

A problem facing this approach, however, is the development of a global model of data and knowledge that is both sound and practical. This task in actuality can easily overwhelm even a major organization. Thus, the enterprise integration industry is dominated by consulting companies and their multi-million dollar projects. Small and medium-sized manufacturers are especially hard-pressed for finding affordable solutions to their integration needs. One approach to improving the feasibility of modeling is to develop core reference models that particular enterprises can adopt and customize for their respective environments. This way, some common modules can be developed in a standard way to hold down the total cost of custom design and reduce the effort required for integration. The CIM-OSA (Computer Integrated Manufacturing Open System Architecture) project at Europe is among the first to advocate such an approach. It has developed generic constructs for the structured description of the enterprise system model and a general framework in designing and implementing systems. While calling for a comprehensive "particular model" to further specify the information contents for each particular industry concerned, the CIM-OSA model presently stops short of delivering just that.

A more focused information requirements model is developed at Rensselaer which provides an integration theory constructed from the literature and determines the basic classes of data and knowledge required for integrating manufacturing planning and control functions according to the theory. Its data classes lead directly to structural models of data resources for database analysis and design. Similarly, the knowledge classes and decision logic associate the data classes with the myriad of integrated functions and sub-functions that need to take place, leading to particular production rules and assertions for an enterprise. This particularization of the model is called instantiation.

The resulting reference mode can be used as a road map to facilitate information planning for three cycles of manufacturing enterprises: Product (life) cycle, production cycle (based on customer orders), and part cycle (based on work orders). Corresponding to the information planning framework shown in Figure 2.1 of chapter 2, (1) the reference model provides specific directions for such strategic planning goals as process re-engineering, (2) the data classes and knowledge classes of the model indicate the needs and opportunities for information systems integration for top-down IS planning, and (3) the instantiation of the reference model supplies a core checklist for bottom-up evaluation of existing functional area systems. The product cycle planning corresponds to the top-down process in the framework, while the part cycle is bottom-up and the production cycle links both. The reference model can also be instantiated into a core information model serving as a starting point of information system development in particular manufacturing enterprises (in conjunction with organization-specific details). Such a instantiation is provided next.

10.3.3 A Core Information Model

The objective for this instantiated core model is soundness and compactness: to include fundamental data structures and, expressly, operating rules for integration and yet remain unimposing for small to medium-sized enterprises. The model is completed with empirical investigations based on industrial scenarios tested at Rensselaer's Computer Integrated Manufacturing (CIM) research facility (by representatives from Alcoa, Digital Equipment Corporation, GE, GM, and IBM).

The data part of the core model is represented as structural models shown in Figures 10.4(a,b,c,d) (individual systems) and 10.5 (the CIM system); while the knowledge part is documented below. The modeling process used and the semantics of the modeling constructs presented are discussed in section 3.1 of chapter 3, and defined in chapter 4. The functional modeling for CIM is presented in Section 3.5 of Chapter 3.

Operating Rules

```
IF      (changes_in_oepr
("PROCESS_PLAN","PLAN",TRUE,FALSE,TRUE,FALSE,-1,-1,-1,2,-1) AND
        (ROUTING >0) AND
        (ORDER_PROCESSING.COST =0) AND
        (PLANSTATUS <> "RELEASED"))
THEN    PLANSTATUS := "RELEASED" ;
        ORDER_PROCESSING.COST := TTLDIRECT ;
        OI_STATUS := "ENGNRD" ;
        enter_new_plan (PROCESS_PLAN.PLANREV<-(PLANREV)) ;

        IF      ROUTING code is assigned and routing is available (greater than 0)
and     /* OPS_PPS */
                ORDER_PROCESSING.COST is not assigned and
                process PLANSTATUS is not “RELEASED”
        THEN    set PLANSTATUS := "RELEASED";
                set ORDER_PROCESSING.COST := TTLDIRECT ;
                set OI_STATUS := "ENGNRD" ;
                do plan for next part.

IF      (changes_in_oepr
("PROCESS_PLAN","PLAN",TRUE,FALSE,TRUE,FALSE,-1,-1,-1,2,-1) AND
        (ROUTING >0) AND
        (COST <>0) AND
        (PLANSTATUS <> "RELEASED"))
THEN    PLANSTATUS := "RELEASED" ;
        OI_STATUS := "ENGNRD" ;
        enter_new_plan (PROCESS_PLAN.PLANREV<-(PLANREV)) ;

        IF      ROUTING code is assigned and routing is available (greater than 0)
and     /* OPS_PPS */
                ORDER_PROCESSING.COST is already assigned and
                process PLANSTATUS is not “RELEASED”
        THEN    set PLANSTATUS := "RELEASED";
                set OI_STATUS := "ENGNRD" ;
                do plan for next part.

IF      (changes_in_oepr
("PROCESS_PLAN","PLAN",TRUE,FALSE,TRUE,FALSE,-1,-1,-1,2,-1) AND
        (ROUTING = -1))
THEN    PLANSTATUS := "HOLD" ;
        request_design_revision (PROCESS_PLAN.PARTREV<-(PARTREV)) ;

        IF      ROUTING code is assigned and routing is not available (= -1)
        /* PPS_PDB */
        THEN    set PLANSTATUS := "HOLD" ;
                Request design revision.
```

```
IF      (changes_in_oepr
("ORDER_PROCESSING","ORDER_ITEM",TRUE,FALSE,TRUE,FALSE,-1,-1,-
1,-1,30) AND
        (OI_STATUS = "ENGNRD"))
THEN    enter_remote (CUST_ORDER_ID<-
(ORDER_LINE_ID),ORDER_PROCESSING.PART_ID<-
(ORDER_LINE_ID),QUANTITY) ;
        OI_STATUS := "IN SFC" ;

        IF      the new routing is ready     /* SFC_OPS */
        THEN    copy work order information from OPS D/B to SFC  D/B.
                set OI_STATUS := "IN SFC" ;

IF      (changes_in_oepr
("ORDER_PROCESSING","ORDER_ITEM",TRUE,FALSE,TRUE,FALSE,-1,-1,-
1,-1,30) AND
        (B.OI_STATUS = "NOT ASSGND") AND
        (exists(B.ORDER_PROCESSING.PART_ID<-(ORDER_LINE_ID) =
A.PROCESS_PLAN.PARTID<-(PARTREV),B.ORDER_LINE_ID)))
THEN    B.OI_STATUS := "IN SFC" ;
        enter_remote (B.CUST_ORDER_ID<-
(ORDER_LINE_ID),B.ORDER_PROCESSING.PART_ID<-
(ORDER_LINE_ID),B.ORDER_PROCESSING.QUANTITY) ;

        IF      OI_STATUS = "NOT ASSGND"   and        /* SFC_OPS_PPS */
                process plan for the part already exists
        THEN    set OI_STATUS := "IN SFC"   and
                copy order information from OPS D/B to SFC D/B  and

IF      (changes_in_oepr
("ORDER_PROCESSING","ORDER_ITEM",TRUE,FALSE,FALSE,FALSE,-1,-
1,-1,-1,1) AND
        (WO_QUAN <> ORDER_PROCESSING.QUANTITY))
THEN    WO_QUAN := ORDER_PROCESSING.QUANTITY ;

        IF      there is any update in ORDER_ITEM table and          /*
SFC_OPS */
                work order quantity changes.
        THEN    copy new work order quantity  to  WO_QUAN in SFC ;

IF      (every_time (-1,-1,-1,1,0) AND
        (is_assembly (ORDER_PROCESSING.PART_ID<-(ORDER_LINE_ID))
AND
        (SHOP_FLOOR.STATUS = "ENDED")))
THEN    ORDER_PROCESSING.OI_STATUS := "ASSEMBLED" ;

        IF      the part is in assembly process and  /*  SFC_OPS */
                SHOP_FLOOR.STATUS is "ENDED"
        THEN    set ORDER_PROCESSING.OI_STATUS := "ASSEMBLED" ;

IF      (every_time (-1,-1,-1,1,0) AND
```

```
        (is_assembly (ORDER_PROCESSING.PART_ID<-(ORDER_LINE_ID))
AND
        (SHOP_FLOOR.STATUS = "START")))
THEN    ORDER_PROCESSING.OI_STATUS := "ASSEMBLY" ;

        IF      the part is in assembly process and  /* SFC_OPS */
                SHOP_FLOOR.STATUS = "START"
        THEN    set ORDER_PROCESSING.OI_STATUS := "ASSEMBLY" ;

IF      (every_time (-1,-1,-1,1,0) AND
        (NOT   is_assembly   (ORDER_PROCESSING.PART_ID<-
(ORDER_LINE_ID)) AND
        (SHOP_FLOOR.STATUS = "ENDED")))
THEN    ORDER_PROCESSING.OI_STATUS := "MILLED" ;

        IF      the part is not in assembly process and       /* SFC_OPS */
                SHOP_FLOOR.STATUS = "ENDED"
        THEN    set ORDER_PROCESSING.OI_STATUS := "MILLED" ;

IF      (every_time (-1,-1,-1,1,0) AND
        (NOT   is_assembly   (ORDER_PROCESSING.PART_ID<-
(ORDER_LINE_ID)) AND
        (SHOP_FLOOR.STATUS = "START")))
THEN    ORDER_PROCESSING.OI_STATUS := "MILLING" ;

        IF      the part is not in assembly process and       /* SFC_OPS */
                SHOP_FLOOR.STATUS = "START"
        THEN    set ORDER_PROCESSING.OI_STATUS := "MILLING" ;

IF      (every_time (-1,-1,-1,0,10) AND
        (NUM_SCRAPPED > (0.01 * WO_QUAN)))
THEN    SHOP_FLOOR.STATUS := "HOLD" ;
        move_to_end_of_queue (WO_ID<-(WO_ID SEQ_ID)) ;
        notify_operator (WO_ID<-(WO_ID SEQ_ID)) ;

        IF      number of scrapped item is greater than 1% of work order       /*
SFC_INSPECT ION*/
        THEN    set SHOP_FLOOR.STATUS := "HOLD" ;
                move it to end of queue;
                notify  operator

IF      (changes_in_oepr
("ORDER_PROCESSING","ORDER",TRUE,FALSE,TRUE,FALSE,-1,-1,-1,12,-
1) AND
        ((OD_STATUS = "DONE") AND
        (max (END_DATE) > DATE_DESIRED)))
THEN    request_process_revision (PART_ID<-(WO_ID)) ;

        IF      OD_STATUS = "DONE" and        /* OPS_SFC_PPS */
                any of order is past_due
        THEN    request process planner for future revision.
```

```
IF      (changes_in_oepr
("ORDER_PROCESSING","ORDER_ITEM",TRUE,FALSE,TRUE,FALSE,-1,-1,-
1,6,-1) AND
        (A.OI_STATUS = "NOT ASSGND") AND
        (NOT exists (A.ORDER_PROCESSING.PART_ID<-(ORDER_LINE_ID)
= B.product_ID<-(product_ID),A.ORDER_LINE_ID))))
THEN    A.OI_STATUS := "IN DESIGN" ;
        prepare_new_design_request (A.ORDER_PROCESSING.PART_ID<-
(ORDER_LINE_ID)) ;
        A.$Product_Version<-($Product_Version) := new_revision
(A.ORDER_PROCESSING.PART_ID<-(ORDER_LINE_ID)) ;

        IF      OI_STATUS is not assigned and    /* OPS_PDB */
                there is no existing design for the PARTID
        THEN    set OI_STATUS "IN DESIGN" and
                prepare new design request (Copy order information in OPS to
PDB) and
                assign new Product_Version number

IF      (changes_in_oepr
("ORDER_PROCESSING","ORDER_ITEM",TRUE,FALSE,TRUE,FALSE,-1,-1,-
1,6,-1) AND
        (A.OI_STATUS = "NOT ASSGND") AND
        (exists (A.ORDER_PROCESSING.PART_ID<-(ORDER_LINE_ID) =
B.product_ID<-(product_ID),A.ORDER_LINE_ID))))
THEN    A.OI_STATUS := "DESIGNED" ;
        prepare_new_Pro_plan_request (A.ORDER_PROCESSING.PART_ID<-
(ORDER_LINE_ID)) ;

        IF      OI_STATUS is not assigned and    /* OPS_PDB_PPS */
                there exists a design for the PARTID
        THEN    set OI_STATUS "DESIGNED" and
                request new process planning.

IF      (changes_in_oepr
("PRODUCT_DESIGN","Product_Version",TRUE,FALSE,FALSE,FALSE ,-1,-1,-
1,-1,1) AND
        (exists (A.ORDER_PROCESSING.PART_ID<-(ORDER_LINE_ID) =
B.INSPECTION.PART_ID,A.ORDER_LINE_ID))))
THEN    A.OI_STATUS = "DESIGNED" AND
        A.INSPECTION.STATUS<-(PART) := "ASSGND" ;

        IF      the design is updated or added and    /* INSPECTION_OPS_PDB
*/
                inspection plan for the part exists
        THEN    set OI_STATUS "DESIGNED" and
                set INSPECTION.STATUS = "READY"

IF      (changes_in_oepr
("PRODUCT_DESIGN","Product_Version",TRUE,FALSE,FALSE,FALSE ,-1,-1,-
1,-1,1) AND
```

```
        (NOT exists (A.ORDER_PROCESSING.PART_ID<-(ORDER_LINE_ID)
= B.INSPECTION.PART_ID,ORDER_LINE_ID))))
THEN    A.OI_STATUS = "DESIGNED" AND
        convert_design_model_to_inspection_model (A.Product_Version<-
(Product_Version),A.product_ID<-(Product)) ;
        Inspection_plan_request (A.Product_Version<-
(Product_Version),A.product_ID<-(Product)) ;

        IF      the design is updated or added and    /* INSPECTION_OPS_PDB
*/
                inspection plan for the part not exists
        THEN    set OI_STATUS "DESIGNED" and
                convert design data to inspection data and
                request new Inspection plan

IF      (changes_in_oepr
("PRODUCT_DESIGN","INSP_PART",TRUE,FALSE,FALSE,FALSE ,-1,-1,-1,-
1,5) AND
        inspection.status = "COMPLETE")
THEN    record_ins_result (Pard_ID,Serial#,Actual_tol).
        IF      inspection is done          /* INSPECTION_SFC */
        THEN    record inspection results into PDB
```

The core information model in Figure 10.5 implies some global integrity rules that need to be implemented to manage the inter-relationships among the data semantics in the individual databases (SFC, PP, OPS, and PDB)> Integrity control rules are derived directly from interpreting the integrated OER model (see Chapter 4). These rules can be implemented at the CIM system manager's discretion using any method deemed sufficient. A full fledge metadatabase, however, will automatically recognize the local databases involved in these global integrity rules and enforce the rules on them just like it implements operating rules (i.e., through the distributed shells - see Chapter 9). The specific data items (types) requiring these rules are listed next. Note that the forms of the two types of rules (functional and mandatory relationships) are given in Section 4.2.1 of Chapter 4.

Functional Relationship

Appl	**Functional Relationship**	**Determinant**	**Determined**	**Determinant Data Item(s)**	**Determined Data Item(s)**
OPS	IS_ORDER_OF	ORDER_ITEM	ITEM	ORDER_LINE_ID	PART_ID
	PLACED_BY	ORDER	CUSTOMER	CUST_ORDER_ID	CUST_ID
SFC	WO_SEQ_WS	WO_SEQ	WK_STATION	WO_ID, SEQ_ID	WS_ID
PPS	PART_MATERIAL	PARTREV	MATERIAL	PARTREV	MATCODE
	OP_RESOURCE	OPERATION	RESOURCE	OPID	RESID
PDB	SmFeature_Feature	Sheetmetal_Feature	Feature	$Sheetmetal_Feature	feature_ID

GD2D_P_2D	Global_Datum_2D	Point_2D	$Global_Datum_2D	$Point_2D
SmFeature_P_2D	Sheetmetal_Feature	Point_2D	$Sheetmetal_Feature	$Point_2D
Arc_P_2D	Arc	Point_2D	$Arc	$Point_2D
SmFeature_LT_2D	Sheetmetal_Feature	Loc_Tol_2D	$Sheetmetal_Feature	$Loc_Tol_2D
Rect_Size_Tol	Rectangle	Size_Tol	$Rectangle	$Size_Tol
Line_P_2D	Line	Point_2D	$Line	$Point_2D
U_Tab_Size_Tol	U_Tab	Size_Tol	$U_Tab	$Size_Tol
RectPattern_Size_Tol	RectangularPattern	Size_Tol	$RectangularPattern	$Size_Tol
Keyhole_Size_Tol	Keyhole	Size_Tol	$Keyhole	$Size_Tol
Hole_Size_Tol	Hole	Size_Tol	$Hole	$Size_Tol
Slot_Size_Tol	Slot	Size_Tol	$Slot	$Size_Tol
P_Version_Part	Product_Version	OE_product_ID	$Product_Version	product_ID

Mandatory Relationship

Appl.	Mandatory Relationship	Owner	Owned	Owner Data Item(s)	Owned Data Item(s)
OPS	ON_ORDER_ITEM	ORDER	ORDER_ITEM	CUST_ORDER_ID	ORDER_LINE_ID
SFC	HAS_WO	PART	WORK_ORDER	PART_ID	WO_ID
PPS	HAS_REV	PART	PARTREV	PART_ID	PARTREV
	HAS_PLAN	PARTREV	PLAN	PARTREV	PLANREV
	HAS_OP	PLAN	OPERATION	PLANREV	OPID
	HAS_DETAIL	OPERATION	DETAIL	OPID	DETAILID
PDB	Feature_OE$Cloop	Feature	OE_$Closed_Loop	feature_ID	$Closed_Loop
	Feature_GD2D	Feature	Global_Datum_2D	feature_ID	$Global_Datum_2D
	OE$Cloop_SmFeature	OE_$Closed_Loop	Sheetmetal_Feature	$Closed_Loop	$Sheetmetal_Feature
	OE$Cloop_Other	OE_$Closed_Loop	Other	$Closed_Loop	other_ID
	SmFeature_U_Tab	Sheetmetal_Feature	U_Tab	$Sheetmetal_Feature	$U_Tab
	SmFeature_Rect	Sheetmetal_Feature	Rectangle	$Sheetmetal_Feature	$Rectangle
	SmFeature_RectPattern	Sheetmetal_Feature	RectangularPattern	$Sheetmetal_Feature	$RectangularPattern

SmFeature_Keyhole	Sheetmetal_Feature	Keyhole	$Sheetmetal_Feature	$Keyhole
SmFeature_Hole	Sheetmetal_Feature	Hole	$Sheetmetal_Feature	$Hole
SmFeature_Slot	Sheetmetal_Feature	Slot	$Sheetmetal_Feature	$Slot
Line_geoEntity	Line	geometric_Entity	$Line	$geometric_Entity
Arc_geoEntity	Arc	geometric_Entity	$Arc	$geometric_Entity

10.4 THE PROCEDURE OF SYSTEMS DEVELOPMENT USING THE CORE INFORMATION MODEL

The structural models presented above can be immediately implemented using commonly available database management systems (DBMS), either relational or object-oriented. The object-oriented DBMS technology is less mature commercially than the relational, and its implementation tends to require more custom refinements. Thus, regarding implementation into object-oriented systems, we content ourselves with a general rule stating that the (hierarchy of) SUBJECTs from the functional models will be linked with Entities and Relationships from the structural models and thereby form a class hierarchy, where Entity-Relationship constructs constitute the leaf level objects. One specific example of such an approach is provided in chapter 4.

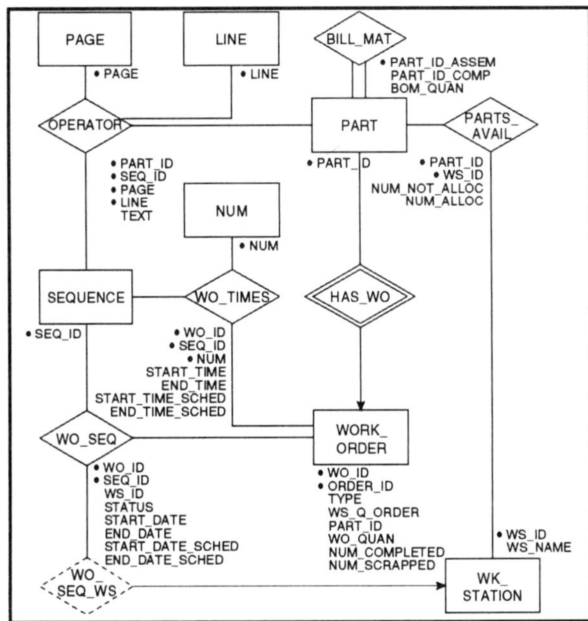

Fig. 10.4.(a) Shop Floor Control System

ITEM
DETITEM
DETAIL
HAS_DETAIL

• ITEMID
ITEMTYPE
ITEMDESC
LOCATION

• DETAILID
• ITEMID
QUANTITY

• DETAILID
OPID
DETAILDESC
MFGTEXT
QCTEXT

HAS_PLAN
PLAN
HAS_OP
OPERATION

• PLANREV
PARTREV
PLANNER
PLANDATE
GTCODE
EFFSTART
EFFSTOP
PLANSTATUS
ROUTING
ISSTKTRSHR
INSTKTRSHR
TTLDIRECT
PLANNRCODE

• OPID
PLANREV
OPDESC
RESID
SUTIME
CYCLETIME
RESPEROP
TRANSITHRS

OP_RESOURCE

PARTREV
PART_MATERIAL
MATERIAL

• PARTREV
PARTID
MATCODE
LENGTH
WIDTH
HEIGHT
UNITS
ABCCLASS
CYCLCNTCLS
RECORDTYPE
SOURCECODE
UNITMEASURE

• MATCODE
MATDESC
MATWEIGHT
STUNITS
YSTRENGTH
TSTRENGTH
BHN
RHN
MCHNABLITY

RESOURCE

• RESID
RESTYPE
DEPARTMENT
HOURLYRATE
TONNAGE
MAXX
MAXY
MAXZ
MAXWEIGHT
HP
RESDESC

HAS_REV
PART

• PARTID
PARTDESC

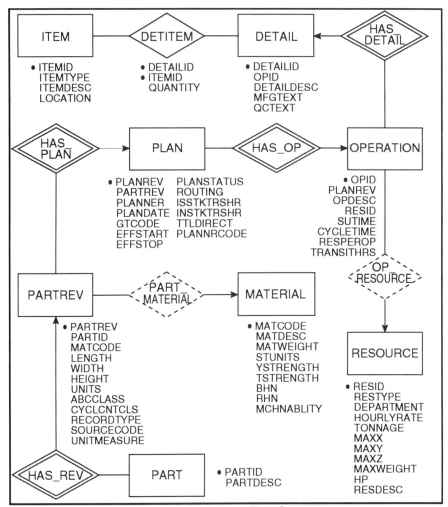

Fig. 10.4.(b) Process Plan System

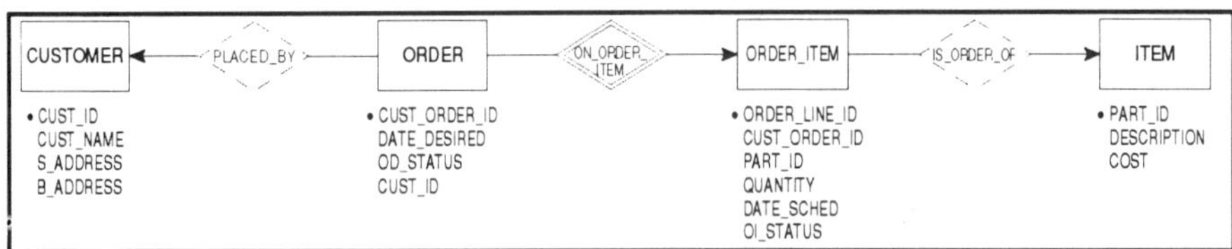

Fig. 10.4.(c) Order Processing System

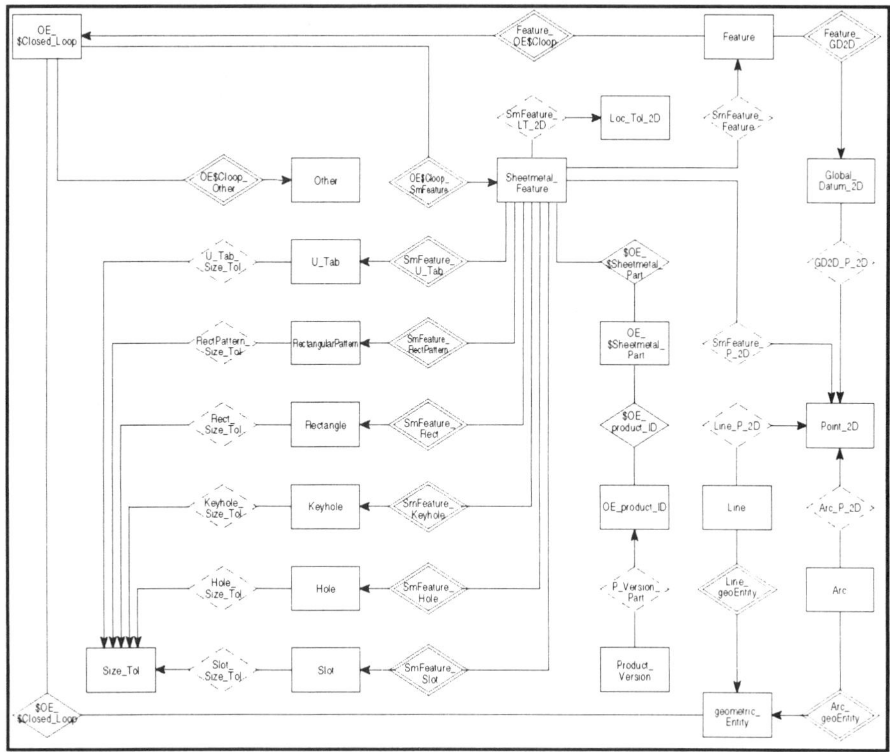

Fig. 10.4.(d) Product Design Database System

10.4.1 The Procedure

The procedure of developing a CIM information system using the core model is summarized below (assuming that the manufacturer will use off-the-shelf relational DBMS's for the development):

(**a**) Each of the structural models in Figure 10.4 maps directly into a relational schema for the particular application system, where ENTITY and PLURAL RELATIONSHIP become base relations with exactly the same primary keys and attributes as in the model. An example for Shop Floor Control is provided in Table 10.1. At the user's discretion, this starting design can be fine tuned in the usual manner. At this point, a sound information environment encompassing certain basic CIM systems amenable for integration, but not yet integrated, is in place. Each system will operate in a standalone manner and the integrating information flows must be effected through managerial measures.

Table 10.1. Base relation of the Shop Floor Control System

Relation Name	Definition : (Key item(s), attribute[1],...attribute[n])
WK_STATION	(WS_ID, WS_NAME)
WORK_ORDER	(WO_ID, NUM_COMPLETED, NUM_SCRAPPEDORDER_ID, TYPE, WS_Q_ORDER, PART_ID, WO_QUAN)
WO_SEQ	(WO_ID, SEQ_ID, WS_ID, STATUS, START_DATE, END_DATE)
BILL_MAT	(PART_ID_ASSEM, PART_ID_COMP, BOM_QUAN)
PARTS_AVAIL	(PART_ID, WS_ID, NUM_NOT_ALLOC, NUM_ALLOC)
WO_TIMES	(WO_ID, SEQ_ID, NUM, START_TIME, END_TIME)
OPERATOR	(PART_ID, SEQ_ID, PAGE, LINE, TEXT)

(b) The integration knowledge - including both operating rules and data management rules - is implemented at each local system using its own programming environments. For instance, the tracking of orders will be coded as application programs or database shells at the process planning system, the shop floor control system and the order processing system, as well as any other systems involved in the operating rules. This, of course, promises to be no small undertaking; but should not be overwhelming, either, especially when compared to the integration efforts where no such core model is provided. The knowledge can be selected and implemented in an incremental manner to further alleviate the effort required. A basic system of integration is obtained, where the integrating knowledge is not globally managed and the individual systems are not supposed to be changed, added, or deleted. Nonetheless, such a basic integration is precisely most manufacturers (large and small) would be more than happy to acquire for the present.

(c) A metadatabase is created to provide further integration modeling capabilities when needed, such as that the core model will be expanded to incorporate new systems. In addition to models in Figure 10.4, the integrated model in Figure 10.5 will also be created and stored in the metadatabase, along with the functional models in sec. 3.5 of chapter 3. Thus, a global data and knowledge integration is achieved at the model level by virtue of the metadatabase. The same modeling process discussed in chapter 4 will be able to perform the task of developing models for new systems and integrating them with existing environments. The implementation of the new model will follow the same procedure here, plus necessary modifications to the code implementing rules, according to the newly consolidated contextual knowledge. An inroad into the hard task of integration management is achieved with the inclusion of the metadatabase, although the contextual knowledge and the integration architecture/configuration are not managed automatically, yet.

(d) The metadatabase is optionally augmented with an integration technology called Rule-Oriented Programming Environment (ROPE) technology (see chapter 9) to automatically distribute the contextual knowledge from the metadatabase (containing the global CIM model) to local application systems and implement them into rule-based shells at individual systems. Albeit not completely automated, most of the

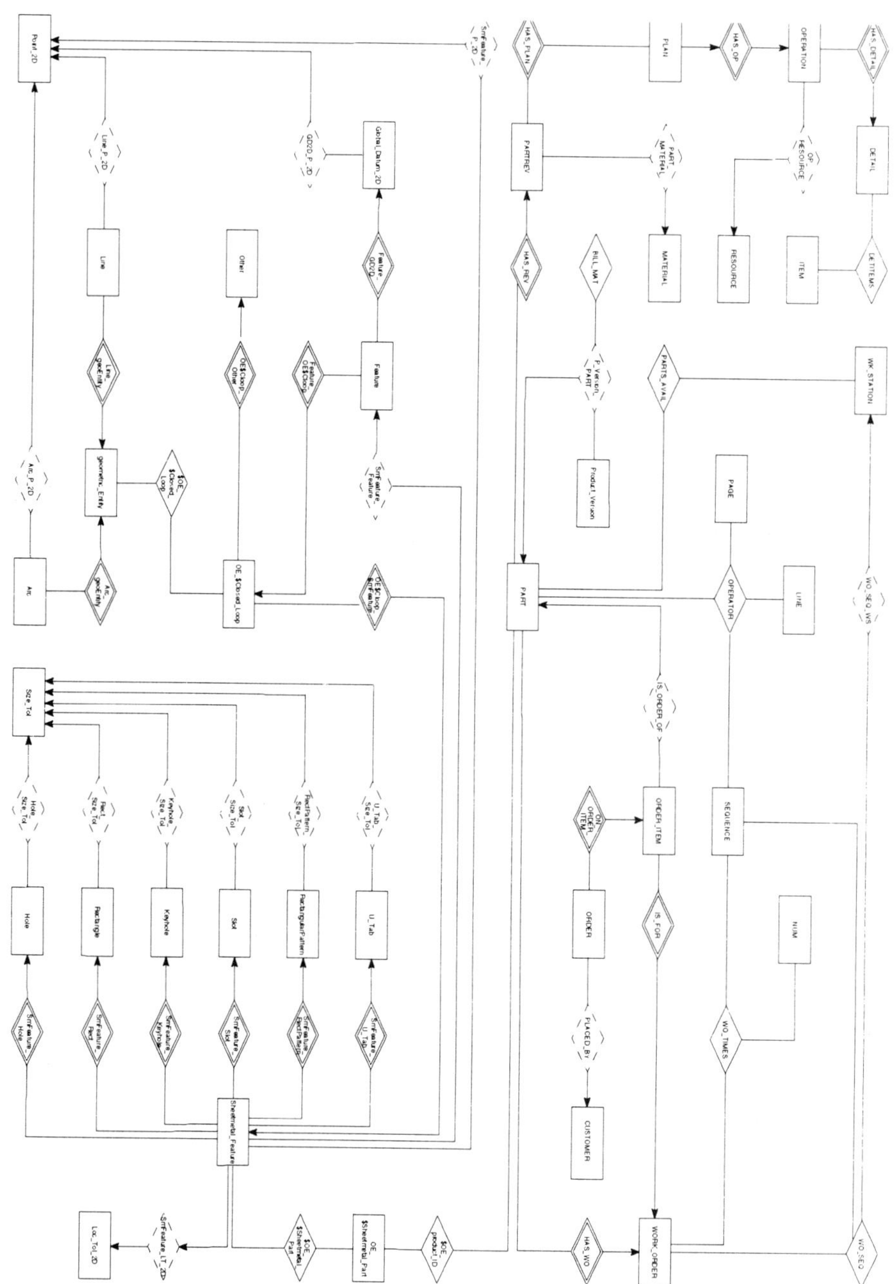

Fig.10.5. Integrated structural diagram of CIM Enterprise

implementation tasks described in (b) and (c) above for rules are carried out by ROPE. At this final stage, the complete integration is accomplished in an on-line and automated manner.

The above procedure itself is incremental; the user can opt to implement only the first one, as well as proceeding to any of the next three levels. Next, we discuss some implementation techniques in detail; the first three steps are combined in the discussion.

10.4.2 Implementation of a Basic System with a Metadatabase

Corresponding to step (c) in the above procedure, the metadatabase serves mainly as a standalone global information resources dictionary system. It contains the global catalog of information resources across the enterprise, their functional interrelationships, the transformation between information models, and the production knowledge and the interactions among the subsystems. Thus, the metadatabase may be queried of information models and control knowledge for use in further modeling or information resources management.

Both the metadatabase and the local application models can be implemented into some target (commercial) DBMS using the same techniques. For illustration, consider the structural model in Figure 10.4(a), using a relational DBMS. The detailed implementation of the database scheme can be described as a two-step process: 1) implementing the base relations, and 2) implementing the integrity constraints and operating rules. When the chosen DBMS explicitly supports the notion of Integrity Constraints (primary key and foreign key definition) and Database Triggers (e.g., ORACLE Version 7), the base relations and integrity rules can be implemented in a straightforward way using built-in data definition languages (DDL) as shown in Figure 10.6. The *pk_partrev* constraint in the figure identifies the *partrev* column as the primary key of the *partrev* table, and ensures that no two part-revision codes in the table have the same part-revision id and no partrev is NULL. The operating rules can also be implemented with a non-declarative approach using Database Triggers, which are automatically fired when triggering INSERT, UPDATE, or DELETE statements.

```
CREATE TABLE partrev
        ( partrev           CHAR (5)          CONSTRAINT   pk_partrev
        PRIMARY KEY,
         partid  CHAR (10),
         matcode            CHAR (15),
         length  NUMBER,
         width   NUMBER,
         height  NUMBER,
        ..........
         units   CHAR (10),
         sourcecode         CHAR (2),
         unitmeasure        CHAR (2) );
```

Fig. 10.6 A DDL sample for creating a base relation

For systems that do not fully support integrity rules, a document file can be produced which details data management rules and operating rules. Next, a software tool (software development library) can be either adopted (from the field) or developed to *automatically* generated a set of procedures for the documented rules and operationalize the contextual knowledge. Such a callable library of procedures can easily be generated in a manner similar to the (much more complicated) standard embedded SQL for the C language. It is to be triggered by the database application or the user whenever transactions of *insert*, *delete*, and *update* which affect the data-items are involved.

It is worth noting that referential integrities across different systems cannot be enforced by a single DBMS, but rather must have the global rules distributed and localized into these systems. Same global monitoring capabilities are also needed to maintain the consistency of rules. This is addressed by ROPE, as discussed next.

10.4.3 Advanced System: Growth And Change

The metadatabase can be utilized as a knowledge-based systems integrator through ROPE. This software technology calls for a new "rule" section to overlay on top of the usual data typing for efficient execution, management and maintenance of distributed knowledge models; which are implemented as rule-based shells for the component applications. Empowered by these shells, each local application can function autonomously and yet be able to coordinate information interchange without the need for global serialization (a known limitation of existing approaches to CIM integration using distributed database management systems). The metadatabase acts as the data and knowledge server that distributes operating knowledge to the local shells at the construction time and manages them during the operation time **when** there are additions or changes to the global knowledge. In the evolution process, a requirement change is reflected as a model change that is operationalized as new rule generation or rule update to the CIM application shells. Figure 10.7 shows the architecture of the manufacturing enterprise applications using the ROPE technology.

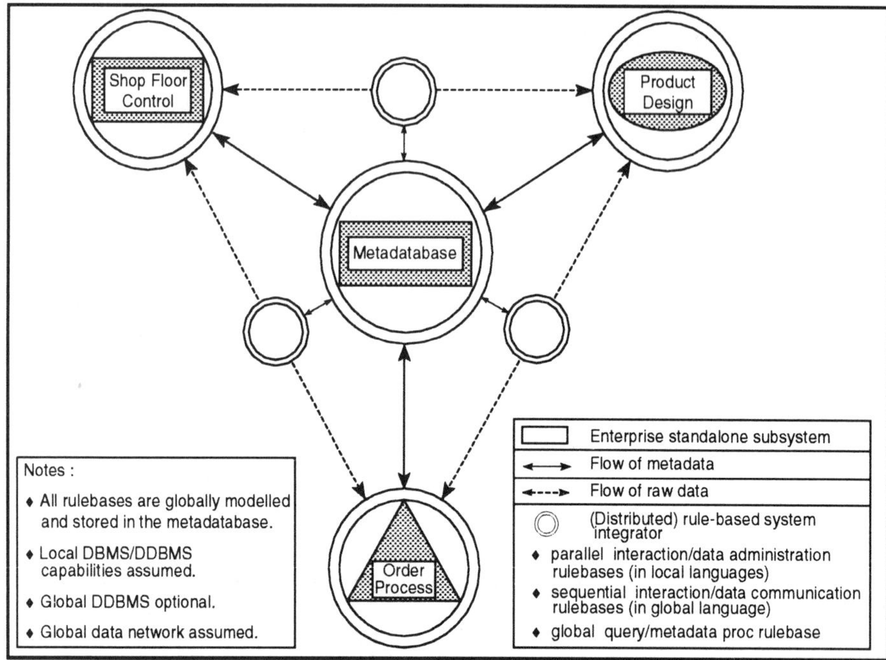

Figure 10.7. The Concurrent Architecture of Metadatabase System

10.5. CONCLUSION

Enterprise integration and re-engineering is a much-talked about but not often attempted topic in many organizations large or small, because the effort required could be prohibitive in terms of time, expertise, and all other forms of cost. This is why major players such as large consulting firms tend to use their proprietary reference models of information systems as a common starting point for systems development to many integration problems. This is also why industrial standards community has called for a variety of public reference models to facilitate integration for all companies. Yet, these efforts still tend to tilt towards comprehensiveness and hence err on the over-kill side. Why should, for example, a small or medium-sized manufacturer who just wants to have a decent CIM information system to assist with mundane factory-level tasks go overboard to adopt the CIM-OSA architecture which extends well beyond the basic scope of requirements? Furthermore, the CIM-OSA model (or other similar models for that matter) does not provide specific contents for the manufacturer's information model. A compact information model that satisfies the basic needs of integration for core manufacturing functions and the development methodology for the metadatabase model make the information integration approach feasible and practical.

To conclude, the vision of adaptive manufacturing discussed above entails enterprise information integration that supports the capability of virtual organizations. A layered architecture is clearly implied here. At the bottom, there are mundane systems whose information requirements must be satisfied; at the top, there are the enterprise views that cannot be confined to organizational boundaries.

Enterprise modeling and enterprise model-supported adaptive integration becomes the key to effecting the objective. There is a theme underlying the evolution of the systems concept from database (file integration) to enterprise information integration: a conceptual model separating end users (applications) from the physical resources. In databases, external schemata are in effect virtual organizations of data resources based on the conceptual schema; in metadatabases, it is the enterprise conceptual models that promise to support virtual organizations for the enterprise. Finally, in the same framework of enterprise integration, facility-level manufacturing information systems are sufficiently supported throughout their life cycle in terms of systems development methods, models, and techniques.

Acknowledgment

Mr. Jangha Cho created the operating rules of the core model in Section 10.3.3. Mr. Alan Rubenstein created Figures 10.1 and 10.3.

11

VISUAL INFORMATION UNIVERSE

This chapter is co-authored with **Lester Yee**, Ph.D.
Lecturer, The Hong Kong University.

Information visualization provides a new generation of user interface for integrated (extended) enterprises. Its significance has been discussed in chapter 1 and elsewhere. It is also a basis for electronic commerce and other global information enterprises. From a producer's and customer's perspective, doing business over the Internet, or in the cyberspace, requires electronic currency, marketing channels, and other electronic counterparts to the traditional market mechanism. However, from an information user's perspective, once an engagement between the customer and the producer/provider is established in the electronic marketplace, the rest of the activity is but some information jobs between them both of which are indigenous constituencies of the extended enterprise in cyberspace. Thus, information visualization applies to distributed information enterprises such as electronic commerce on the same foundations as it is applied to a traditional enterprise. A new four-dimensional method using ubiquitous enterprise metadata is presented.

11.1 THE CONCEPT OF 4-D INFORMATION VISUALIZATION

Electronic commerce holds enormous promise for tomorrow's economy - this is the observation that would not escape anyone who has been a part of the recent explosive growth of the World-Wide Web or other enterprises on the Internet. However, conducting business on the network demands novel user-interface technology which not only presents the information involved in a way natural to the user, but also assists the user immersing and commanding in the myriad universe of information with ease. Without such an user-interface, the National Information Infrastructure could collapse under its own weight. Such an interface, however, has not been availed yet - not by GUI, hypertext, nor 3-D visualization. The hyper-link system for the Web (e.g., Mosaic and Netscape) is a case in point. This phenomenal success of user-interface has ironically shown the limits of current technology. That is, due to lacking global contextual knowledge about the Web and relying on texts as opposed to visualization, the hypertext-based "first window to the cyberspace" (as hailed justifiably by some) could leave its visitors lost in the windows and thousands after thousands of home pages. We envision combining the strengths of traditional visualization technology with the emerging metadata technology (for online knowledge) to effect a next generation user-interface for electronic commerce as well as traditional enterprise information management.

Specifically, there are two stages in the information enterprise of electronic commerce. The user, whether a customer or a vendor, searches over the international-scale network for the appropriate sources at the first stage, and at the second stage engages the particular sources' own information systems to conduct business over the same network. In this manner, the second stage is no different from the mature field of enterprise information management where the user is but an integral part of the extended view of an enterprise. Therefore, the new technology must (1) enable a seamless integration of both stages; (2) support global query across sources or within a source; and (3) remove some major limitations of the traditional computer-human interface environment. A four-dimensional information visualization solution based on the Visual Information Universe (VIU) model is developed towards this end. The VIU model is characterized with a time-space metaphor design, a metadatabase for network and enterprise knowledge, a visual interpreter/language for information processing, a model-based global query method, and connections to Virtual Reality tools and network application protocols. Major foundations for the new technology are partly in place.

The key elements of the VIU system are depicted in Figure 1, the VIU architecture. The three elements in the core and their connections to virtual reality (VR) tools and the common network protocols (including Mosaic) comprise the particular technology of VIU for enterprise integration, modeling, and management.

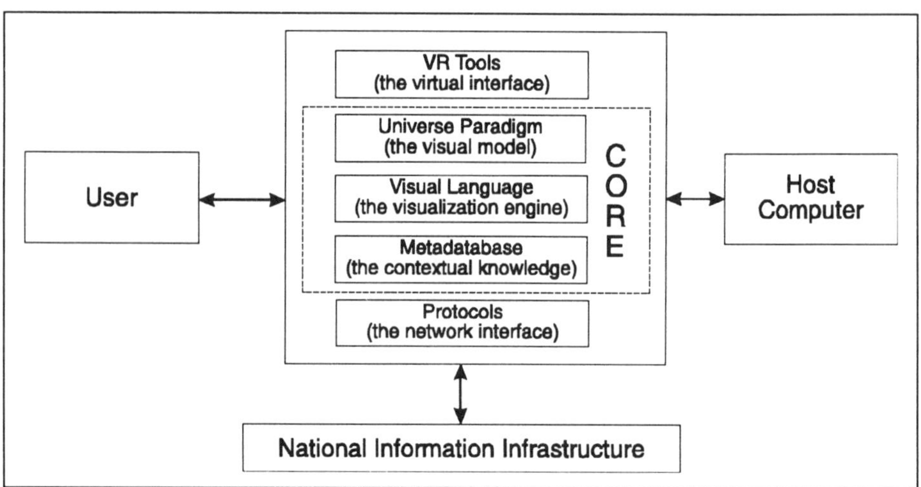

Fig. 11.1. The VIU Architecture

The first question to answer is what is the 4-D functionality? Basically, we can characterize the evolution of interface technology along with two main axises: media and knowledge. The media axis is marked clearly with the movement from linear text (one-dimensional) to graphical user-interface, or GUI (two-dimensional), and most recently to the vision-based visualization (three-dimensional). The knowledge axis shows such major efforts as natural language (artificial intelligence), ubiquitous computing, and on-line intelligence (in the form of, e.g., enterprise metadata). Clearly, a new dimensionality could be opened up should knowledge be satisfactorily incorporated into 1-D, 2-D, and 3-D interface technologies. Consider the latest generation of GUIs, hypertext, and scientific visualization. These technologies by themselves do not provide users with a global road map of the information resources (on the network), nor enterprise metadata about the underlying information systems. Users tend to get lost in windows, hypertexts, or other interfacing objects used; and would have to possess considerable technical knowledge to perform global query. On the other hand, systems with on-line knowledge tend to be narrow in design and still prone to the same problems facing the traditional 1-D, 2-D, and 3-D technologies. A full 4-D approach resolves these problems. Figures 11.2.a to 11.2.f represent snap shots of a user "flying by" an illustrative information universe visualized with the 4-D approach envisioned, where system-possessed knowledge helps illuminate complex objects and relationships for the users.

Such a new user-interface technology has been undertaken (in preliminary phase) at Rensselaer for enterprise information management. The knowledge and global query capabilities are provided by using the metadatabase technology that has been developed for enterprise information management (see the previous chapters). Extending it for network search (the first stage) aas well as for business transactions (the second stage) requires primarily the modeling effort to acquire adequate metadata about the distributed sources. Since there exists an array of cataloging and searching servers in the Web, one could reasonably expect the modeling to be focused only on these severs. This way, the metadatabase for both stages would still be tractable. As a matter of fact, the common use of the metadatabase which is established for enterprise information management virtually assures that, once applied to the first stage (network search), the results developed can be naturally integrated for electronic commerce as a whole.

Fig. 11.2a. Viewing A Universe: Each Globe Represents an Information Universe

Fig.11.2b. The Metadatabase World Emerging from the Horizon

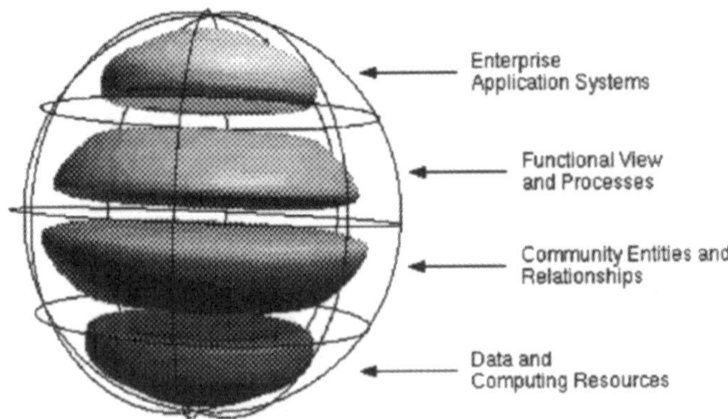

Fig. 11.2c. Visiting a Globe: The Metadatabase World

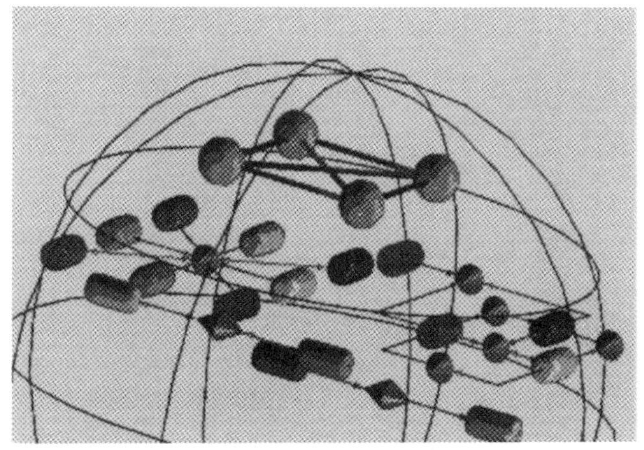

Fig. 11.2d. Closing on View of Application and Functional Model Layers

Fig.11.2e. Exploding Close-up View of ShopFloor System and Application Layer

Fig. 11.2f. Exploring Complex Relationships Between Application Models

11.2 THE CONCEPTUAL MODEL OF VIU

11.2.1 The Goals of the 4-D Information Visualization

Once the objective of electronic commerce is formulated, certain goals for the VIU technology become evident: (1) that an advanced, next generation user interface technology is required; (2) that the technology should support global query in both stages (network search and business transactions); and (3) that design methods are needed to optimize user satisfaction and computing performance for the implementation of the technology. The key question demands to be answered is, why is 4-D information visualization the required user interface technology? The conceptual model below responds to this question.

The popular hyper-link system for the World-Wide Web is a good reference point to use. The system's success stems entirely from its utilization of hypertext technology for user interface. Therefore, it demonstrates the crucial role of advanced user interface technology in the success of national-scale information enterprises. Most interesting to VIU is the fact that the power of hypertext in this case is not necessarily derived from its absolute ease of use, nor its ease of use relative to GUI or any other visual technology that is commonplace nowadays; but rather from its "hiding" technical details such as the exact syntax of network address from the user. Its very nature actually falls into the category of freeing users from such burdens by system-possessed contextual knowledge - even though hyper-link does not possess any knowledge other than the straight mapping between addresses and texts. Clearly, full-fledge on-line knowledge providing, for instance, a global road map and contents directory could invigorate the user even more since the system would become even easier to use and more powerful to utilize. Ironically, the hyper-link systems' use of text as the primary object of interfacing has made the system inherit the many problems of textual GUI well-known to novice users and experts alike; such as the loss of context (in the midst of windows) and the lost in the hypertext. Visualization with its proven power in cognition is evidently a promising alternative for better results.

Combining these observations leads to a vision of combining visualization with on-line knowledge played out over dynamically defined time intervals--as the approach to the next generation technology. We call this vision the four-dimensional (4-D) information visualization where the fourth dimension is the **dynamism** defined as **knowledge**-generated space-and-**time** segments of **visualization** for communications in the human-computer interface. Dynamism possesses four characteristics: 1) **continuity** in the logical presentation of views and information resources, 2) **synthesis** of information contents represented in terms of multi-media and multi-modal association, 3) **multiplicity** of disparate systems or regimes in the sources of information, and 4) **time-space field** of physical representation in terms of user-interface metaphors and visual language. The integration of knowledge into visualization with proper metaphor enables the first three characteristics; which, then are played out on the physical stage availed from the fourth characteristic.

Given the general definition, the specified goals that the envisioned dynamism should achieve for information visualization beyond previous results are defined below:

1. Visual Interface extending 1-D, 2-D, and 3-D concepts: Succession from the restrictions typical to text-based command languages, diagrammatic GUIs, and static 3-D visualization to take advantage of the high-bandwidth of comprehension provided through multi-modal (visual and aural) means of communication.

2. Visual language for the direct manipulation and articulation of information: assistance in the form of metadata for the user-interface is made available to facilitate direct articulation of information for enterprise information management activities.

3. Visual interpreter to take advantage of available on-line contextual knowledge: the use of intelligent "agents" empowered by contextual knowledge (information models, user models, application models, etc.) to mediate the human-computer communication in EIM applications. The interface needs to take advantage of pre-declared contextual knowledge that is available on-line to minimized the technical knowledge requirements for the user tasks.

4. Metaphors for information representation: choice of metaphors that support the unified presentation of multi-dimensional information structures and relationships in a way with which the user is familiar.

The characteristics of dynamism are determined following these goals. To illustrate this determination, we turn to an example which indicates the nature of dynamism.

11.2.2 An Illustration

The building-blocks of dynamism is the **integral**, as the lexical token of communication derived and generated by the system according to contextual knowledge and user profile. The time-dimension of the integral is the key in providing the higher bandwidths of communication of information than its predecessor methods of 2-D GUI and 3-D Visualization. With time-elapsed expressions, an integral allows continual presentation of images generated from multiple sources under dynamic interpretation to convey a single idea; yet, in the traditional technology it must be accomplished with a single frame of image.

Consider an object-oriented information model representing certain firms on an electronic commerce network. The model encompasses two orthogonal planes of inter-relationship hierarchies (decomposition and inheritance). An integral conveys this understanding to the user with two time-based colorization operators. High-level decomposing objects project a light ray to lower level objects, then coloring them with a single color; next, cycles to the next coloring scheme to project inheritance to lower level entities by using narrow laser-light beams. The user maintains a persistent image of the information model in his view throughout. A static 3-D visualization would be convoluted, if at all possible, to represent both planes and multiple associations for the same objects.

The user, in turn, requests browsing through the model. S/he points to a starting location in the space and verbally expresses "Start Here", then points to another destination and says "Pass Here", and finally to yet another location to command "End Here". The system will automatically interpret this input integral and respond back by generating an integral of a logical flyby path for the user traversing through the information space revealing information of interest as the user requested. Figures 11.3a to 11.3d exhibit similar ideas on the preliminary VIU system already developed at Rensselaer.

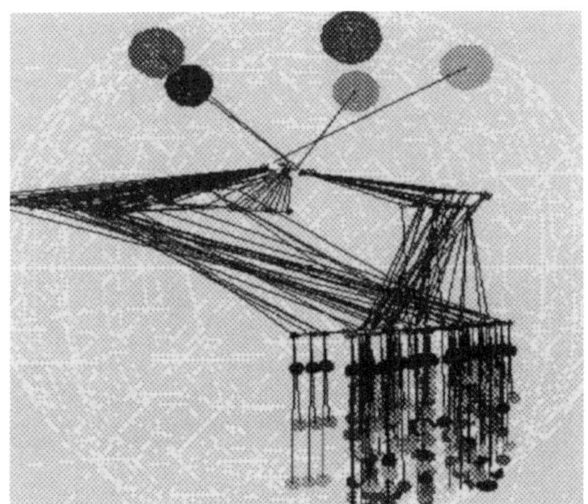

Fig. 11.3a. A Globe of the EnterpriseInformation Model Presents Itself in Rotation

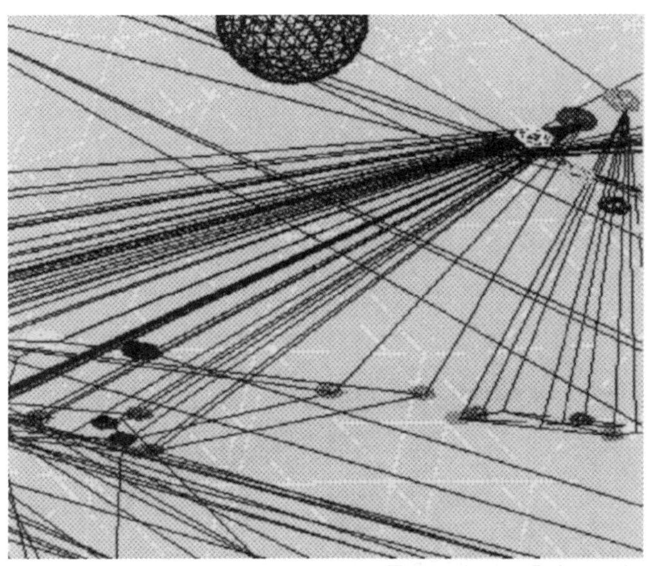

Fig.11.3b. An Integral of User Fly-by Through the Information Model in the Time-Space Field

Fig. 11.3c. User Zooms to Resolve Enterprise Object Details

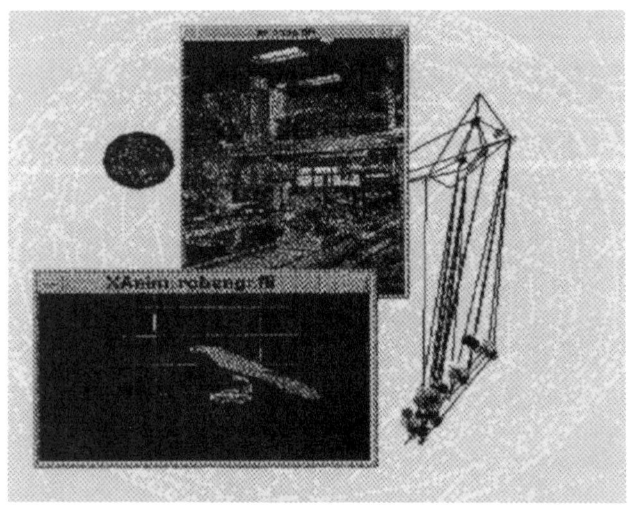

Fig. 11.3d. An Integral of Dynamism reveals an Enterprise Object Definition with an Image and a Video.

In review of the above example of integrals, the relative power of 4-D visualization for communication and expression as compared to GUI and 3-D visualization is evident. A GUI-based approach in presenting the two planes of relationships in the information model would require segmented views in multiple windows. The user may lose context as s/he views and calls up segments of the model in a 2-D static representation. This prospect becomes frightfully unmanageable when the number of objects is increased to say, more than 10. The zooming and traversing capabilities of dynamism make the increase in size a non-issue. The same observations apply to other examples.

11.2.3 The DYNAMISM: A Functional Definition

From the above analysis, a definition of dynamism is derived which specifies the (functional) characteristics, the operations, and the primitives comprising the four-dimensional visualization. The definition is presented in terms of three levels: The first level establishes its roots in the literature, where dynamism is considered as a combination of three areas. The second level articulates the functionality characteristic of dynamism. The third level, then identify the operational primitives giving rise to the above characteristics.

Level 0: Four-Dimensional Information Visualization is characterized by Dynamism.
Level 1: Dynamism is characterized by Continuity, Synthesis, Multiplicity, and Time-Space Field.
Level 2:

Continuity is characterized by the following operators that effect seamless contextual flows across multiple views (as such, they show simultaneously the global and local contexts in fluent visual flows, supporting information conveyance for cognition):

- Progressive zoom-in/zoom-out to show image details and maintain global views.
- User fly-by (zooming) for global contextual views.
- Automatic rotation of images to reveal structure, extent, definition.
- Progressive light-ray casting to illuminate inter-links and relationships.
- Colorization (phase coloring) to reveal and present multiple-simultaneous relationships.
- Color highlighting/de-highlighting to filter images.
- Progressive transparency (opacity/color) changes of images to reveal/hide inner depths.
- Morphing to convey multiple representations.
- Scaling/re-scaling of images to bring attention to details.
- Rotation of Universe/Globe interior to overcome information complexity density of views.

Synthesis is characterized by the following operators that apply knowledge to achieve the coordination for the visual communications:

· Mosaic assemblage and presentation of video, images, text, and sound icons (embedded with enterprise metadata and user knowledge) for context adjusted identification of information images.
· Light-projections from image to image to guide the user in operational tasks.
· Color cycling with aural signals to draw user-attention to areas of significance.
· Top-down progressive coloration and illumination to convey hierarchical dependencies based on enterprise metadata.
· De-highlighting (changes in color/opacity) of non-relevant information structures to visually filter out insignificant information images.
· Context-dependent voice guidance in information applications.
· Automatic scaling/re-scaling of specific images to highlight its significance to the user's task.
· Colorization (flashing) of images to show operational status.

Multiplicity is characterized by the following operators that integrate possibly heterogeneous and distributed information classes and applications (as such, they support concurrent and multiple virtual existence of systems and allow the interface and information domain to be logically independent):.

· Light-beams across globes/universes to illuminate integration among them.
· Clustering of information images by same/similar color association.
· Zooming in/out for concurrent views of activity in enterprise application.
· Morphing to show multiple definitions (e.g., equivalent information objects are melded or morphed to show this representation).
· Colorization of images and illumination of related images to distinguish sub-components from enterprise metadata.
· Fade-in/fade-out images to show multiple co-existence.

Time-Space Field is characterized by the following operators to signify the medium on which dynamism takes place:

· Representation metaphors supporting recursive and continuous operations.
· Zoom-in/out to traverse recursive field.
· Spatial communications of gesturing, pointing, and drawings.
· Navigational model of interaction.
· Lighting rays inter-associate metaphors.

The third level characteristics lead directly to the technical approach appropriate for developing certain execution methods for the VIU model. We, therefore, discuss them in the next section.

11.3 BASIC DESIGN OF VIU

From a system architecture point of view, the realization of 4-D information visualization involves three basic elements (see Figure 7): (1) a metadatabase, (2) a visual interpreter, and (3) a visualization environment. The metadatabase provides contextual knowledge of applications in the form of metadata necessary for electronic commerce activities. The visual interpreter becomes the engine to drive the human-computer communications using a dynamism-based language. The visualization environment defines the paradigm and the metaphor used, as well as the hardware and software implementation methods binding the input/output devices with the visual language and interpreter.

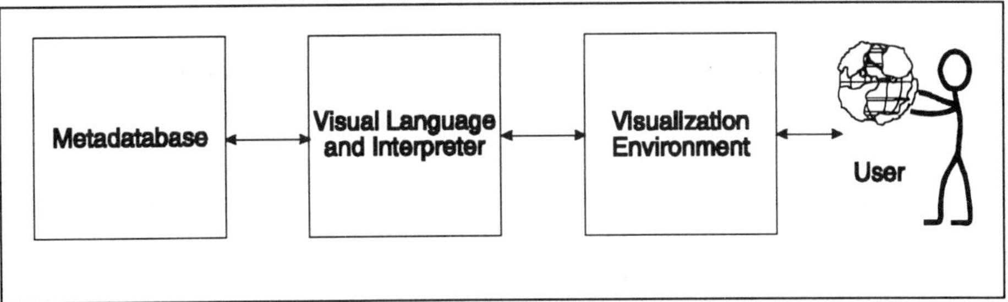

Fig. 11.4. Basic Vizualization System Elements

11.3.1 The Metadatabase: A Common Structure

VIU system taps into the metadatabase technology to effect contextual knowledge for the fourth dimension, dynamism. The metadatabase itself is detailed elsewhere in the book. For the sake of smooth reading, major points about its contents and structures are listed below.

(1) The scope of enterprise metadata includes data models, knowledge models, and implementation models in terms of both (clusters of applications and IT resources); which are structured using the GIRD model.

(2) The GIRD model can be implemented in the same manner as a regular schema using a relational DBMS, where the TSER constructs of the model provide design specifications.

(3) The model is self-descriptive and stays stable, since the structure is derived from basic modeling concepts rather than tenuous application semantics (i.e., application-domain independent).

(4) Enterprise information models (represented in the metadatabase as metadata tuples) can be added, deleted, or modified without causing the metadatabase to restructure nor recompile - referred to as metadata independence.

(5) The modeling and creation of metadatabase follow exactly the tradition of data and knowledge systems analysis and design.

(6) The metadata independence nature of the architecture supports scalability in terms of adding new systems while its implementation using a regular DBMS assures scaling up in software engineering.

11.3.2 The Visual Language Design: the Definition of Dynamism

The functional characteristics of dynamism discussed above in Section 11.2 lead to a further formalization of the definition (the third level) which provides the basis for the visual language design. Dynamism is defined as a collection of integrals which visualize (using space-based, image-generating operations) over time (using time-based and image associating operations) according to the knowledge (using metadata); i.e.,

$$D = \{ I \mid S, T, k \}$$

where

S is a set of space-based and image-generating operations

T is a set of time-based and image association operations

k is a set of system-possessed knowledge represented as metadata

I is an integral of interpreted images in space over time using S, T, and k.

Definition of S

The space-based and image generating operations consist of the primitives of image, color, and sound; which are mutually exclusive and collectively exhaustive for space. Image categorically encompasses 1-D, 2-D, and 3-D graphics. Color is defined for hues and textures. Sound encompasses speech and tones.

S - Types	Definition
Image	This represents shape geometry, 2-D icons or pictures, graphics, and text.
Color	The attributes of colors, textures, opacity.
Sound	An aural entity corresponding to speech or tone(s).

Definition of T

The time-based and image associating operators pertaining to T are zooming, rotation, colorization, illumination, morphing, scaling, and amplification.

T - Types	Definition
Zooming	Movement of images in space. Used to resolve details or to gain global context.
Rotation	Image spinning on one or more axis. Used to reveal structure and extent
Colorization	Color change for images and lights. For images, it is used for classification and association. It is also used to depict status and show distinction.
Illumination	The progressive projection of light. Used to show context of logical relationships among images. The illumination can take the form of laser (as inter-connecting lines). Illumination can be colored.
Morphing	Image geometry metamorphosis to represent transformations of information from one representation to another.
Scaling	Image sizing relative to other images. Used to show relative size or scalar values.
Amplification	The audibility of sounds and is variability of sound level. Used to draw attention, warn, and document.

Definition of k

The set of system possessed knowledge contains enterprise metadata, user profile, and application context.

k - Types	Definition
Enterprise Metadata	Logical structuring of enterprise data, relationship among data, representation of data, location of data, models of data Next layer of information: Data models, contextual knowledge, decision models, and access protocols.
User Profile	User experiences, handicaps, expertise, privileges and preferences.
Application Context	Activity of application or function. (e.g., information browsing, global query formulation, simulation, data modeling, and other EIM activities.

11.3.3 The Visualization Environment: Universe and Globes

A central element for the visual interpretation of enterprise information and its management is a visualization paradigm for information characterizing the time-space field of dynamism. We propose using the notion of the Universe in which we both physically live and logically conceptualize our existence for the paradigm. Its basic elements are stated below.

The Universe Paradigm

1) The logical world of human enterprises interpreted into an information universe(s), which, whenever necessary and appropriate, is extended to include a similar representation of the physical universe.
2) The Universe consists of worlds: the primary world (the world surrounding us, the earth), the other worlds (solar systems and planets), the sub-world or the world inside (e.g., cells and organs), and the super-world or the world containing (some of) the primary world and the other worlds (e.g., the universe as a whole); while each world may exist in multiple spaces (i.e., contexts), thereby constituting multiple virtual universes.
3) Each world is represented with a generic visual metaphor: the Globe, which further employs color, light, sound, and other human senses to allow reference to multiple virtual universes through a single visual assertion.

The Globe Metaphor

1) The Globe represents a world, has surface and interior, and spins, travels, and evolves (e.g., change color, shape, or appearance) in the Universe. Corresponding to the sub-world and super-

world, the Globe also features respectively sub-globe and super-globe (e.g., a universe may be represented by a single globe called super-globe, and part of the interior of a globe may also be recursively represented as a globe, or a sub-globe.)

2) The interior of the globe in general represents information resources, systems, and other logical contents of the enterprise; while the surface typically represents user's needs of the interface, such as applications, management, and other utilization of these information contents for the enterprise.
3) The Globe is totally integrated; i.e., the user can traverse from any part of the Globe (interior or surface) to anywhere else.
4) The logical connections of individual elements on these interior planes and surface continents of the Globe is visualized with color and light, across interior and surface; these markers also show the significance of elements and connections.
5) The connection, traversal, and indeed the Globe itself are not static, but rather visualized in a dynamic way (e.g., spinning, zooming, and illustrating) depending on the nature, the time-frame, and the results of the user applications.
6) The Globe is supplemented with texts, windows, and voice to assist the user requesting information through the interface.
7) The detailed design of the metaphor, such as the shape of the application continents on the surface and the particular symbols of the information resources in the interior of the Globe, is application domain-specific. However, the design (including also the use of contextual markers such as color and sound) is (a) be based in part on and computationally coupled with the contextual knowledge that the user interface contains, and (b) generally should allow for direct input from and output to the user (e.g., touching on the Globe surface and "virtually" traversing its interior).

11.4 COMPARISON

The proposed 4-D information visualization approach draws unique capabilities from the combination of three previously separate concepts: visualization, on-line knowledge support, and space-time field. When compared with other results in the field, it stands as a unique model in the following aspects: (1) its scope and functionality of visualization (i.e., the four dimensions), (2) a metadatabase approach to enable comprehensive knowledge support, and (3) the particular metaphor design which is amenable to the 4-D approach. This general comment applies to other ongoing efforts in the field, such as the notion of intelligent yellow pages and the hypertext-based cataloging and searching systems. We summarize the comparison into three categories below.

11.4.1 Graphical User Interfaces

The hypertext-based systems, including their multi-media advancements, all leave a burden left to the user in terms of 1) locating specific pieces of information without getting lost in hypertext, 2) paging through the numerous frames of text-supported information and thereby losing context across the many windows, and 3) comprehending large amount of data and complicated tasks which require detailed knowledge to interpret or plow through. Intelligent electronic yellow pages for the WWW do not help much since they tend to be just a listing of what information is out there. With the 4-D visualization approach, a user would fly through the dynamic information universe that reveals itself in the time-space field. The present need to continually take mental notes for associating one frame to the next and to back-track out due to static presentation of information would be gone. In the time necessary to read a frame of information in GUI, a 4-D integral can be expressed to convey the information blending multi-media information with available contextual knowledge into a "true" mosaic of information for comprehension.

Knowledge has been a dimension historically neglected in user-interfaces. The context of information user, and application tasks can all be defined and captured in rigorous models and then used to drive the interface - in as accomplished in the 4-D visualization formulation. The links to hypertext and hypermedia in existing Web sites are fixed mainly through the HTML authoring language. There is no knowledge in either the client software nor the WWW servers to interpret information particular to users or guide them in their applications. Emerging Web authoring languages do not change much of this limitation. The 4-D integrals representing expressions of visual communication are explicitly driven by the knowledge to directly support users' comprehension of information in their task domains of applications.

11.4.2 Metaphor Design

In order to sufficiently represent information in a 4-D visualization, we need to overcome the limitations of the "flat-land" desktop metaphor (of GUIs) and elevate the interface into a full-body, time-and-space dimension capable of handling both logical and physical information representations. The Visual Information Universe model employs the Universe Paradigm and Globe Metaphor is the new metaphor and medium for the time-space field of 4-D information visualization. To best compare this design model, we present the following summary table based upon a survey of the literature on 3-D metaphors for information; the 2-D desktop GUI metaphor is also provided as the baseline reference.

From this table, the limitations of the other proposed metaphor choices become quite apparent.

Table 11.1 Metaphor Comparisons

Metaphor	**Levels of Abstraction**	**Interlinking / Associating Operators**	**Recursive**
2-D GUI	3-levels - Desktop, Folder, Icon	Icon aggregation in Folders for association only.	Folders* (middle-level)
Problem: 2-D flatland and desktop boundaries. Representation of enterprise information: Static 2-D diagrams and 3-D images. * Recursive in Macintosh, X-desktop, OS/2, but not in MS-Windows.			
House[1]	3-levels - House, Room, Floor	none	no
Problem: physical phenomena, force-fit of information structures Representation of enterprise information: Information models in each room. Question of how to relate rooms, and global perspective of the house.			
Book Library[2]	5-levels - library, bookshelf, books, chapters, pages	sequential location	no
Problem: Implications of strong linguistic language-based and linear search methods Representation of enterprise information: information expected to be "flatten" to the pages.			
Information Landscape[3]	1-level - (no hierarchy)	grouping, paths	no
Problem: Surface-oriented paradigm, lacks recursive depths. Representation of enterprise information: Information is bound to the surface and/or suspended above a surface representing the landscape.			
Universe Paradigm and Globe Metaphor[4]	4-levels - Universe, Globe, Globe Surface, Globe Interior	light beams and aggregation	Universe and Globe (highest-levels)
Problem: Interpretation of Universe and Globes. Representation of enterprise information: All categories of information are bound within a globe based upon some rational arrangement.			

[1]House metaphor (a.k.a., Information Visualizer) [Card, 1991; 1993]
[2]Library metaphor (a.k.a., Book House) [Pejtersen and Goodstein, 1988]
[3]Landscape metaphor (a.k.a., SGI 3-D Fusion) [Fairchild, 1993]
[4]Universe paradigm and globe metaphor (a.k.a., VIU Model) [Hsu, 1992]

To highlight the benefits defined for the VIU model, consider for example the much heralded research of the "Information Visualizer" in the Xerox PARC labs [Card, 1991; 1993]. The design seems to be specific for a few classes of information structures such as Unix file directories, organization charts, spreadsheet data, and the like, and therefore lacks a common structure to decouple the visualization model from the underlying data, application, and user. The 4-D information visualization approach affords this common structure through the use of a metadatabase to achieve interface independence. Furthermore, the house/room metaphor provides no associating operators between, e.g., rooms (specific visualization) to show relationships and other dynamics that usually exists.

11.4.3 Knowledge Methods

A few of researchers have also accepted the thesis that knowledge should be an integral component of the interface. We will consider three high-profile knowledge-using systems and interface designs.

The CUBRICON architecture and system by Calspan - UB Research Center coordinate a number of knowledge-sources in the user-interface [Neal and Shapiro 1991]. Although attempting to address the knowledge issue, they seem to be 1) only being able to support physical classes of information (e.g., geographical-based systems) 2) still orienting towards being user-interface design only, and 3) lacking rigorous contextual knowledge of applications and data.

The Lockheed Artificial Intelligence Center's CHORIS (Computer-Human Object-oriented Reasoning Interface System) provides an implementation of a generic architecture for intelligent interfaces [Tyler, et. al. 1991]. The CHORIS system operates through its GUI with a prototype system demonstrating a geographical system. The knowledge seems to be ad hoc and lacking a general model; while the limitations of GUI are apparently inherited.

The KIM Query system is designed for global query access of distributed information [Ferrara 1994]. This system utilizes knowledge to assist the user in formulating queries using its diagrammatic Entity/Relationship interface. The interface itself and its use of knowledge fall short of significance in that it is bound to the problems of GUI (textual-orientation, planar views of hierarchical and networked information, and a high requirement of technical knowledge and database terminology for its use).

A common thread across these knowledge-using systems is their lacking a rigorous knowledge model (such as the metadatabase) to afford a full-fledge fourth dimension - i.e., *the integral of knowledge and visualization over time*. The users are still responsible for knowing and managing the exact metadata (i.e., information models and contextual knowledge) of the underlying systems.

11.5 CONCLUSION

Information superhighway has rapidly taken hold on the economy of tomorrow and prompted new waves of rethinking of Corporate America. Any serious thoughts on enterprise integration and modeling cannot afford to discount this prospect. A prime case in point is the emerging alliance or even fusion among the traditional industries of computing, publishing, entertainment, mass media, marketing, and education. Closer to boardrooms are such information-based visions as concurrent engineering, enterprise re-engineering, virtual corporations, agile manufacturing, distributed global enterprises and electronic commerce. The notion of electronic commerce lends itself naturally to extending all models of enterprises to involve everyday users everywhere, since there have existed national and international networks (such as the Internet) and the numerous information resources connected to them, such as the World-Wide Web. A consensus emerging is the observation that, in order for the new information enterprises to be accepted by lay people, user interface is crucial to any efforts; otherwise the promises of IT and all information-based enterprises would become unfulfilled.

One key area that has not received adequate attention - or more accurately, has not been sufficiently understood - is the level of novelty that the next generation user-interface must effect for the information superhighway. We submit that this next generation technology will and must go beyond the present concept of GUI (graphical user interface), 3-D visualization, hypertext, and VR (virtual reality). It should feature a new thinking of information visualization with designs suitable for cyberspace ideas and applications; should possess application knowledge of the underlying information resources to assist end users acquire and assemble any pieces of information desired from everywhere needed; and should, thereby, bring about a virtual environment for information access over networks where the user navigates freely and globally inquiries in the environment, with little or no prior technical knowledge about the system required for him/her to process. In short, it should effect a four-dimensional visualization of information for end-users, where the fourth dimension is enabled by system-possessed knowledge interpreting the information resources with dynamic presentation of images (and possibly other media). An analogy would be the medical visualization technology such as CATSCAN and MRI, where anatomical knowledge is integrated with 3-D technology to "illustrate" dynamically the biological information that may not be visible physically. The new concept is referred to as the Visual Information Universe (VIU) model which entails the new Globe design (representing information resources), some basic VR tools (for direct spatial manipulation), and a metadatabase (containing models and other application knowledge). The VIU model is envisioned to connect on the one hand with the National Information Infrastructure to allow users immerse in the network, and, on the other hand, with the particular information systems of individual enterprises to support business transactions. Both are required to conduct electronic commerce. An important note is, the VIU model does not assume a super central database or control; rather, it would be implemented at individual sites and become an indigenous user interface system to those particular enterprises.

A preliminary VIU technology has been developed at Rensselaer for certain manufacturing enterprise integration applications. This result can be the basis for an effort to develop a complete solution for the next generation user interface for not only enterprise information management but also electronic commerce and other global information enterprises. The solution will accomplish the following goals: (1) the user can conduct information search (for, e.g., an appropriate source to conduct business with) as well as business transactions in the same VIU environment; (2) pertinent information on the same search questions can be assembled from different sources, not just one source at a time; and (3) the environment possesses on-line knowledge to assist the user much in the same sense as CATSCAN and MRI assisting physicians. Since the existing VIU model has already been able to connect to individual enterprises' particular information systems, the first goal will be accomplished when the VIU model is applied to network search applications. The second goal will be achieved by, in a similar way, incorporating into the VIU model the information retrieval methods of metadatabases. The third goal is essentially an agenda for applying the generic model to particular domains for electronic commerce or other models of enterprises.

While the advantages of the VIU model are discussed above, its disadvantages would mainly be the system capabilities required. The virtual environment of users' immersing in a VIU and "flying by" needs obviously VR tools and high performance visualization machine. To mitigate against the drawback, a range of results progressing from a basic VIU for network search only (on regular workstation) to the full model with all add-on modules will be obtained. Users of different needs and infrastructures should still be able to apply select aspects of the technology

The VIU model also provides a conclusion for the metadatabase approach to enterprise integration and modeling. Its ability to support mundane information management needs (in business, design, and manufacturing functions) and to scale up to multiple systems for extended enterprises is a unique property in the field of IT for EIM.

INDEX